PULP FOOTBALL

AN AMAZING ANTHOLOGY OF REAL FOOTBALL STORIES YOU SIMPLY COULDN'T MAKE UP

NICK SZCZEPANIK

First published by Pitch Publishing, 2016

Pitch Publishing
A2 Yeoman Gate
Yeoman Way
Worthing
Sussex
BN13 3QZ
www.pitchpublishing.co.uk
info@pitchpublishing.co.uk

A CIP catalogue record is available for this book
from the British Library.

ISBN 978-1-78531-202-1

Typesetting and origination by Pitch Publishing

Printed by Bell & Bain, Glasgow, Scotland

Contents

Acknowledgements

A S a football writer for a number of national newspapers and magazines, and as a fan, I've been lucky enough to witness many of the events described in this book first-hand: the Northern Ireland arrests, David James trying out with the Miami Dolphins, five penalties in one match, the highest-scoring game in Premier League history.

But you can't be everywhere at once, and not everything makes it into the papers. So I've shamelessly picked the brains and memories of many good friends among Her Majesty's sporting press – too many to mention them all.

However, particular thanks go to Phil Shaw, the compiler of the magnificently thorough *Book of Football Quotations* and a man with a rich store of footballing memories. He can even remember when Leeds United were a force to be reckoned with. Ditto Richard Whitehead, who fell out of love with football and concentrated on supporting Aston Villa instead.

Thanks too for clarifications and information to Chris Davies, John Ley, David Anderson, Vikki Orvice, Roger Titford and James Reid. And the chapter on stadiums owes a tremendous debt to Simon Inglis' various books on football grounds and their history.

Introduction

*"Football. Fucking football.
Imagine not being into it. Those
poor, poor half-alive bastards."*

Danny Baker on Twitter

WHEN director Quentin Tarantino was looking for a title for a movie that mixed slapstick comedy, sex and drug-fuelled violence, *Pulp Fiction* was a perfect fit. The pulp magazines of the mid-20th century were so-called because of the cheap paper they were printed on, and the content was not exactly highbrow. The stories were mostly sensational, ranging from science fiction and monster yarns to tales of hard-boiled gunplay and lurid murders.

What has this got to do with football, you ask? You'll find all those elements and more in this book too. The club chairman who saw a UFO, the dinosaur that appeared at a fan's wedding, the director threatened at gunpoint, the murder discovered when Blackburn rebuilt their main stand.

Football is the most popular sport in the world. And therefore, as far as we know, in the entire universe. We love the beautiful goals, the sublime passes, the telepathic teamwork, the brave defending, the unbelievable saves. We appreciate the effort, the athleticism, the never-say-die spirit. We applaud the tactical acumen of a great manager, the vision of a far-sighted chairman, even the wisdom of a referee who applies the advantage law intelligently and allows us to enjoy a moment of magic several seconds later as a result.

None of these appear in this book. This is the pulp end of the game – the pratfalls, the bloopers, the moments of downright farce. The punch-ups between teammates and the nights out that ended in the courts.

Football is a game of eleven players, but also umpteen subs and several frustrated reserves. And they, and the managers, coaches, administrators and officials are all human. They make mistakes. Spectacular ones. And that's before you include the fans, the agents, even the mascots, the builders who erect stadiums and the visually-impaired people who design away kits.

They all contribute to the rich kaleidoscope of modern football. With so many moving parts, how can things not go spectacularly, entertainingly, wrong?

Because football is part of the entertainment industry. At its best it can rival Shakespeare in its drama, intensity and revelation of character. And it can be the base comedy of custard pies and wheels falling off. This book looks at what might be termed the farce side.

It's the mad moments you remember. You probably can't recall who scored in Sheffield Wednesday's match against Arsenal in September 1998 and neither can I without looking it up. But no one forgets Paolo Di Canio pushing the ref over, and his curious, stumbling fall to the Hillsborough turf.

I can't call to mind the season, the result of the game in question or anything else, but the picture is clear in my mind of Brighton forward Kit Napier running half the length of the field with toilet roll streaming behind him after a load of it had caught in his studs. Football is fun, or should be.

And British football is football at its distilled best. We invented it. We almost ruined it with hooliganism, 'the English disease'. But then the Premier League and Sky Sports invented it all over again. Or so they will tell you.

It is surely no accident that comedians including Norman Wisdom and Eric Morecambe have been directors of football clubs. And as many fans will tell you, there are still plenty of jokers among players, managers and referees.

If you are a billionaire who can't think of anything new to do with your money, you used to buy an expensive painting, then stick it in a bank vault and never look at it. Nowadays you buy a football club, watch it from the directors' box every week and give yourself extra pleasure by sacking a few managers and changing the kit from blue to red.

Meanwhile we, the fans – and all football writers are fans, however it may appear – either laugh or cry. With any luck, these stories will at least cause a wry smile or two.

The order of chapters was chosen in time-honoured fashion, with numbered balls being shaken up in a velvet bag then pulled at random out of a glass bowl. If nothing else, this book respects British football tradition.

1.

Ground Nuts

"Wembley is the cathedral of football."

Pelé

"Maine Road is the Theatre of Base Comedy."

Stuart Hall

THERE'S nothing like being there in person when someone scores a crazy own goal or the referee gets the ball in the nuts. And it helps if you've got a good view from a safe and comfortable seat and have been able to get to the stadium without too much trouble. A decent pie and a cup of tea too if possible.

If the game is entertaining and your team wins, you probably won't have time to consider that the stadium you're in could have been the site of a murder, cursed by a witch, that an international footballer has fallen through the roof above your head or that someone has had to paint a gaudy mural in one of the dressing rooms to improve the feng shui.

First you have to get there, and that is not always as straightforward as it could be, especially by public transport. For every Carrow Road, a pleasant stroll along the River Wensum from Norwich Station, there is an Anfield, reachable only on crowded buses or by expensive taxi. And getting back to Lime Street after the final whistle is even worse.

For years, visitors to Bolton's Reebok Stadium endured the frustration of watching trains speed along a railway line a matter of yards away, with no station in sight. But that was solved with the opening of the highly convenient Horwich Parkway, with connections to Manchester via Bolton or London via Preston.

That frustration, though, was as nothing compared to that suffered by fans of Coventry City. As part of a £13.6 million upgrade to the Coventry to Nuneaton line, £3.4 million was spent on building a station to serve The Ricoh Arena, conveniently located adjacent to the stadium. It opened in summer 2015, only for London Midland, the train operator, to announce that it could not be used by Coventry City FC or Wasps supporters on matchdays for safety reasons.

London Midland claimed it would have to close the station for an hour after games and major events as it could only provide an hourly service for 75 people due to a shortage of the right sort of trains. "The issue about the Coventry to Nuneaton corridor remains the shortage of diesel rolling stock to provide enhanced services for matchdays and events at the Ricoh Arena," a jobsworth – sorry, a spokesman – said. "We only have the one diesel train. It only has 75 seats. Until further infrastructure changes are made, we are limited. There just aren't the trains available. We're working with the arena owners to see if there are other solutions."

Get the bus, apparently.

Many fans will wonder what was wrong with the club's old ground at Highfield Road near the city centre and walkable from Coventry Station. Much better to redevelop your traditional home where possible, so that the old pre-match rituals can still be observed and local pubs visited.

That was what Blackburn Rovers did after lifelong fan Jack Walker put in the investment that transformed the club's fortunes, but a wholly unexpected result of the rebuilding of Ewood Park was the discovery and solution of a murder mystery. It was in 1994 that a row of houses in Nuttall Street was demolished to make room for the new Jack Walker Stand, and the former back garden of number 84 yielded a grisly discovery.

"For workman John Griffiths, Tuesday 19 July 1994, was just another day on site as he busied himself excavating a boundary trench with JCB operator Tony Rowe," the *Lancashire Telegraph* reported. "The work was small change compared to the giant stand going up piece by piece nearby.

"Everything was slightly behind schedule but as the clock ticked past 11am John's mind began drifting towards his lunchtime pie order. Then he saw it. An eerie crack was followed by the sight of a human head falling forward out of the banking only feet from where he stood. A flurry of blond hair covered most of the face but nothing could hide the empty stare of two, wide open eyes and the silent gasp of an open mouth."

That open mouth, improbably, revealed gleaming white teeth, which, together with the blond hair and a pierced ear, at first led detectives to believe that it was the head of a woman. But when the rest of the corpse was unearthed, it turned out to belong to a local man, Julian Brookfield, a former child actor who had been working in a local sex shop when he disappeared, aged 19, in August 1984.

Within hours, the police arrested Brian Blakemore, who had owned 84 Nuttall Street at the time and killed Brookfield, burying him in the back garden of his newly renovated house in the shadow of Ewood Park – never suspecting that when that shadow grew longer his misdeed would be discovered.

Blakemore was later sentenced to 12 years in prison for manslaughter and perverting the course of justice. The judge said there were a number of possible reasons why Blakemore had killed Julian, including that they were engaged in some sort of simulated hanging during the taking of pornographic pictures, or there was a falling out between the two men in connection with mucky photos.

Blakemore was a well-known character in the area, who had had a number of jobs but also wrote jokes and songs for performers including Keith Harris (the ventriloquist with his hand inside Orville, not the former chairman of the Football League) and penned the official Accrington Stanley centenary song. Sort of. "We heard from him out of the blue," a Stanley spokesman said. "He said he had written this song and wanted our permission to market it. Our dealings with him were really quite sketchy. He has never been a supporter or come to games regularly. After the tape I don't think we ever saw him again." Try cell block number nine, Strangeways prison?

There was no doubt that Ewood was in need of an upgrade. Before Walker began the redevelopment, two of the dwellings in Nuttall Street housed things other than corpses – including a gymnasium and the club offices, and the room where Kenny Dalglish would speak to the media. It is recalled that one reporter, a little late filing his copy, hurried across the road to collect the Scot's pearls of wisdom and knocked on the wrong door in his haste.

Invited in and offered tea and cakes by the elderly couple who lived there, he was still marvelling at Rovers' hospitality and wondering when Dalglish would show his face while his colleagues and rivals were adding the manager's quotes to the rewrites of their match reports.

All sorts of things are buried under football grounds. Arsenal's old Highbury Stadium was supposed to be the final resting place of a horse. According to club legend, while the foundations of the North Bank were being dug in 1913, local traders were invited to dump hardcore in the excavations. One coalman's horse and cart ventured too close to the edge and toppled in. The creature broke its leg, could not be saved and was destroyed, buried where it lay.

The only trouble was that no equine remains were discovered when the North Bank was redeveloped in 1992, apparently spoiling the story. But when Arsenal moved over to the Emirates Stadium, the redevelopment of the old ground as Highbury Square required further digging – and then workers with main contractor Sir Robert McAlpine discovered two horseshoes alongside the remains of some timber, believed to be the cart.

"We were digging at the north end of the site, where we are excavating for the foundations of the Highbury Square apartments and discovered what looked like two rusty old horseshoes," Pat Brennan, one of the workers, told Arsenal. com. "I took them to the site offices and one of the lads, who is an Arsenal fan, mentioned the story about the horse. It's great to think that I may have found some items which have a place in Arsenal's history."

What's that, Tottenham fans? You think they might be donkey shoes, discarded by Tony Adams? Shame on you.

Highbury had a cart, but Wembley Stadium has a train. According to a spokesman for the national stadium, a locomotive dating from the period of the original ground's construction in the 1920s is under the pitch, while some say that an old carriage filled with rubble from a previous structure on the site – an abandoned attempt at a London version of the Eiffel Tower – is also down there.

The stadium was built very quickly as part of the British Empire Exhibition of 1924/25, and a series of narrow-gauge rail tracks criss-crossed the site during construction, which was completed in time for the 1923 FA Cup final between West Ham and Bolton. According to one worker's reminiscences, a locomotive became derailed and fell into a pit and it proved easier to bury than remove it. The train's presence was confirmed when drainage work was being carried out as part of the stadium's refurbishment for the 1948 Olympic Games, but removing it was not a priority, and the rebuilding of Wembley between 2002 and 2007 did not involve excavating the old pitch.

Football grounds have been shoehorned into some inconvenient spaces – the footprint of the main stand at Everton's Goodison Park is triangular, as was the East Terrace at Brighton's Goldstone Ground and both ends at Swansea's old Vetch Field – but surely none has been as unsuited to hosting crowds as The Nest, the home of Norwich City between 1908 and 1935. Stand next to the site today, just off Rosary Road, a couple of long goal kicks north of Carrow Road, and it is almost impossible to believe that league football was once played there.

The Nest was a disused chalk pit owned by the club's chairman, and it was a hazardous environment for both players and spectators, with a sheer cliff face at one end and a drop at the other. According to Bernard Robinson, a former City player, in a feature in the *Eastern Daily Press*, "it should never have been a football ground and I was glad to get away from the place – it was a wicked ground. At one end of the ground it just went straight up and to stop all the earth coming down onto the pitch they had a huge cement wall. It was five or six feet from the touchline so wingers had to be careful. Behind the other goal were the dressing rooms and a small stand and apart from that there was just a row of houses and the gardens were 15 to 20 feet below the level of the pitch. There was a big wire netting fence to stop the ball going in there. It was very dangerous."

The luckiest fans crammed into a wooden stand along one side, but others took their chances on a series of terraces and earth banks wedged in above the concrete retaining wall, some risking life and limb by sitting on top of the wall, their legs dangling 20 feet and more above pitch level – enough to give a modern safety officer heart failure, had any local authority been unwise enough to grant a licence.

Amazingly, there was only ever one serious accident there, when barriers gave way above the cliff in 1922 and dozens of spectators fell to the ground, although only one was badly injured. Somehow Norwich were allowed to keep on playing there until 1935, when a 25,000 crowd for a Cup tie against

Sheffield Wednesday finally convinced the FA that the Canaries needed a bigger and more practical home.

Plenty of other grounds have been constrained by their geographical locations. The Manor Ground, for instance, was perfectly adequate for non-league Headington United for most of its history, but when the club became Oxford United and entered the Football League, it had to cope with the demands of larger crowds, especially when the team somehow made it to the old first division in 1985 under the ownership of Robert Maxwell.

With The Manor hemmed in by suburban semis, a hospital and even a bowls club, development was never a long-term prospect and a move to a more suitable location with more room was the logical answer. But in the meantime, extra seating was forced in wherever possible, and the result was one of the strangest collections of constructions ever assembled around a football pitch. By the time it staged its final match on 1 May 2001, the 9,500-capacity Manor boasted seven different stands, but only 2,803 seats, with half the fans still standing in the open.

The London Road end was fully covered, but the main stand went only halfway along one touchline. Next to it, in the north-west corner, were two tiny stands holding no more than 150 seats each, mainly occupied by club staff and players' friends and families. The Cuckoo Lane End was exposed and open terrace for away fans, and the Osler Road side housed the other three stands, the longest and lowest looking like a bike shed. To add to the sense of a village team playing in the big leagues, the pitch sloped from end to end and corner to corner.

It was the cramped nature of the Manor that led to one of the strangest episodes to occur there on one of its biggest days. It was at Oxford on 8 November 1986 that Alex Ferguson took charge of his first game as manager of Manchester United. Photographs recorded his disbelief as his new charges lost 2-0 while he fidgeted in the dugout alongside physio Jim McGregor, substitute Jesper Olsen, reserve manager Brian Whitehouse, kit-man Norman Davies and Derek Sutton. Derek who? Exactly.

Sutton was not even a United employee, but worked for Manchester coach company Finglands, and drove City and United to away games. Nicknamed 'Sooty' and apparently described as a 'larger than life character' – surely a warning there – Sutton had become friendly with Ron Atkinson, Ferguson's predecessor in the Old Trafford hot seat, who sometimes allowed him to sit in the dugout. On this autumn Saturday, Sutton had not been included in the visitors' seating allocation at the space-challenged Manor, so naturally made his way down to the touchline and sat down on one end of the visitors' bench.

Fergie, though, was unaware of this custom, and when he came down the tunnel to take his place in the dugout, he greeted Sutton with a distinctly chilly "Who the f*** are you?" The result hardly improved his mood and it meant the end for courtesy spots for coach drivers.

"Sir Alex wasn't happy to see Derek in the dugout at Oxford and made it clear that it wasn't going to happen again," Chris Turner, the United goalkeeper, recalled. "Derek was also Manchester City's coach driver and when Sir Alex found out he was a City fan, too, he blew his top. He used to make the half-time cuppas but Alex didn't want poor Derek anywhere near the dressing room either."

The Dell, Southampton, was another ground built on a site that nowadays seems ridiculous, a parallelogram with two triangular ends caused by the angles of Milton Road and Archers Road. Many options were tried in an attempt to squeeze as many spectators as possible into the Milton Road End, including the so-called 'chocolate boxes', three sections of open terraces on stilts above another terrace below, a unique arrangement at any English league ground.

They were later replaced by a new triangle of open terracing that leaned out backwards over Milton Road and eventually, after Hillsborough, a new stand that was 30 metres deep at one end and had room for only a couple of seats per row at the other.

Wacky but impractical, The Dell's days were numbered and the Saints moved across town to St Mary's in 2000 but the new ground failed to inspire them. In fact they failed to record a victory in any of their first five matches at St Mary's. Were they missing the homely surroundings of The Dell? Were they unused to all that extra space around the pitch? Were they simply not very good? Or was there a more sinister explanation?

Just to be on the safe side, the club decided to take no chances and invited an expert on pagan rituals to cast out any evil spirits on the eve of their home match against Charlton Athletic. Cerridwen Dragonoak Connelly, a pagan witch and archaeologist, sprinkled water from a wooden chalice and urged any bad influences to depart. Lo and behold, Saints beat Charlton 1-0, Marians Pahars scoring in front of a club record crowd of 31,198.

"I performed a ritual there and, because of my upbringings, I did it in Welsh," she said. "I performed a cleansing of the ground in Celtic tradition but athletes are a very superstitious bunch and I did a blessing for some positive energy and it has obviously worked."

Whether the absence of evil spirits was responsible for Charlton's Steve Brown hitting the post rather than the back of the net in injury time is not recorded. But Gordon Strachan, the manager, was impressed with the witch's work. "If she's that good she can take training for the next two weeks and I can get on with my golf while she gets rid of the ghosts," he said. "Maybe she can play up front."

In fact the stadium had been built on the site of an ancient burial ground, and archaeological finds during excavations included a gold ring, swords and hairbrushes, now visible in glass cases in the corridor leading from the upper seating areas in the main stand to the lounge and media areas (and the press toilets).

But some believe that any jinx was caused not by the spirits of disturbed pagans but a much more recent intervention. Modern legend has it that some of the contractors who worked on the construction were supporters of Saints' deadly rivals Portsmouth who buried a shirt and other Pompey memorabilia in the foundations and spelled out PFC in the brickwork under the metal cladding at the Northam End.

The rivalry between the two clubs made it all the more inexplicable that, for ten years between 2003 and 2013, Portsmouth used as their training ground a former school playing field in Eastleigh – very much Southampton territory and close to a site where Saints had considered building their new stadium before settling on St Mary's.

If Pompey had ever wondered why nothing that went on there ever seemed to be a secret from the press, they need have looked no further than some of the local security staff they employed, who were almost all Saints supporters. One even ran a Saints fan shop in Northam Road, just round the corner from St Mary's.

As to why the club chose to train 22 miles away from the city whose name it bears, one possible answer is that Eastleigh is 22 miles closer than Portsmouth to then-manager Harry Redknapp's home in Poole. It was certainly not the quality of the facilities, which included cold showers, a rock-strewn patch of waste ground used as a car park for the millionaire players to park their Lamborghinis and Mercs in, Portakabins as offices and pitches that were regularly unplayable.

Pompey's own ground at Fratton Park is regarded as one of Britain's most atmospheric football stages, especially by correspondents who visit it once in a blue moon and then only for big games. For reporters on a hot day, the position of the cramped press box, vertically above the gents' toilets, makes it the sort of atmosphere you can do without. Arsène Wenger's first visit to Fratton is well remembered by writers. Used to conducting post-match press conferences in the marble-clad precincts of Highbury at the time, he was bemused to be surrounded by a gaggle of reporters in a gloomy concourse under the wooden main stand. Eventually he backed against a wall that turned out to be that of the aforementioned gents. The urbane Frenchman's nose visibly wrinkled as the questioning went on!

Wenger, of course, is notorious for claiming that he has not seen incidents involving his players committing acts of violence on opponents, but if he had been reporting at Fratton rather than managing, he might have had a point. Several press seats in the otherwise admirable Archibald Leitch Stand have pillars in the way of BOTH goals. At least the press seats at Goodison Park (and, formerly, Highbury) afford a decent view of one goal.

Spectators are not as lucky as the press, of course. At some of the older grounds you can find views severely restricted, and some clubs will even own up to that fact when selling tickets, But few are as honest as QPR, who describe some seats at the School End of Loftus Road as having a 'diabolical view'.

Back to curses, though. Legendary Leeds United manager Don Revie was a superstitious man, so of course he could not ignore a message about the ground being cursed. "Gypsies used to live on Elland Road before it was a football ground," he told the documentary *Leeds, Leeds, Leeds*. "I got this letter saying that it had been cursed when they were moved off and the only way to get the curse lifted was to get a practising gypsy to come and do it. I sent a car to Blackpool to bring a certain Gypsy Rose Lee over and she shooed everyone out of the ground except the office staff and the cleaning lady. Then she went out and stood in the middle of the pitch, scratched the grass, threw some seeds down, went to each corner flag and did the same. She came off the pitch and into my office for a cup of tea, and she said: 'Now you'll start winning things.' And we did, from that year on."

Perhaps Birmingham City should have brought in the same woman. Blues followers have no trouble believing that their entire club is under a hex, let alone their unlovely St Andrew's ground. The club, then known as Small Heath, played at Muntz Street in their early days but eventually began looking for a bigger ground. In 1905, they identified wasteland occupied by Romany folk, at the present St Andrew's, as the ideal site. Like those at Elland Road, the gypsies had to be evicted and they are said to have put a 100-year curse on their former home.

It seems to have begun to take effect almost immediately, as the opening game, against Middlesbrough on Boxing Day 1906, was almost snowed off and was delayed for an hour while the pitch was cleared. After all that, the game ended 0-0 and the disappointment did not end there. The club, renamed Birmingham City, were relegated from the First Division at the end of their first full season in their new home. They continued to defy logic, their lack of success improbable for a club of their size in the nation's second city, with an FA Cup final defeat by Manchester City their closest brush with glory until they won the new-fangled League Cup in 1963.

That might sound grand, but in those days the competition did not merit a Wembley final, there was no European place for the winners, many of the top clubs did not bother to enter, and even though Blues faced local rivals Aston Villa in a two-legged final, they struggled to fill either ground. So that was not taken as evidence that the curse had lifted.

As the club's trudge through football history continued, manager Ron Saunders came up with the idea of hanging crucifixes from the floodlight pylons to dispel the evil spirits, but to no avail. Then Barry Fry tried urinating in all four corners of the pitch. Novel, but ineffective. "We went three months without winning," Fry said later. "We were desperate, so I pissed in all four corners, holding it in while I waddled round the pitch. Did it work? Well, we started to win and I thought it had, then they fucking sacked me, so probably not."

There was nothing for it but to wait for the curse to run out in 2006. And, only five years later, Blues duly won their first major honour, beating Arsenal 2-1 in the League Cup final. Even then, the brief taste of glory was tainted by relegation, and the following season the Europa League slot that now came with the Wembley win proved too heavy a burden along with 46 Championship fixtures, and the team had run out of steam, losing in the play-off semi-finals.

Derby County had a similar problem with gypsies, who had cursed the Baseball Ground after being forced off the site in 1895. Their curse was more specific, decreeing that The Rams would never win the FA Cup. It did not prevent them from reaching finals, as they played in three in six seasons between 1898 and 1903 but lost them all, the third by 6-0 to Bury, the biggest margin of defeat in a final. When they reached a fourth, against Charlton in the first post-war season of 1945/46, Jack Nicholson, the club captain, is said to have paid the descendants of the original Romanies to lift the curse. With the score at 1-1, the match ball burst and with it, apparently, went the curse as Derby scored three more goals without reply.

Some Burnley fans also believed that their club had been cursed, although they did not know by whom or why. The curse manifested itself in the form of identical cruciate ligament injuries to the knees of Lucas Jutkiewicz, Sam Vokes, Kevin Long, Dean Marney and Ashley Barnes within 18 months of each other. They turned to a gentleman named Kevin Carlyon, whose website describes him as a 'witch, paranormal researcher and tarot consultant'.

"The situation goes beyond any coincidence," he told the *Daily Telegraph*. "With all the injuries being the exact same, it seems as if evil has been to work. The spell was most likely cast upon Burnley around 20 years ago. It will escalate and start affecting other areas of the club. Financial backing could be lost, or maybe maintenance issues could occur within the ground."

He performed a ritual incantation calling on 'elements of nature' to send 'these malicious and demonic energies' back where they came from, and requesting 'that a psychic wall be placed across the goalmouth of Burnley FC each time they play'. However, the fans would have been well-advised not to hope for instant results. Kev also used his powers when Liverpool were losing the 2005 Champions League final to AC Milan and, sure enough, they eventually won on penalties after a 3-3 draw. But Kev worked his magic when they were only 2-0 down and they went 3-0 behind before launching their second-half comeback.

Half of Cardiff's Millennium Stadium was also believed to be cursed when the first 12 soccer teams to use the south dressing room in Cup and play-off finals all lost before Stoke City became the first team to win after changing there, in the 2002 Division Two play-off final.

Although the stadium management had denied there was any kind of hoodoo, in March 2002 they brought in a feng shui expert named Paul Darby, who carried out a blessing using bells, incense sticks and sea salt in a bid to counter-balance the 'bad spirits' at the south end of the giant stadium ahead of the LDV Vans Trophy final. He also led a horse around the pitch to try to remove the 'negative energy' he allegedly discovered.

That failed to do the trick as Cambridge United promptly lost the LDV Vans Trophy final 4-1 to Blackpool after using the unlucky end. So instead it was decided that the bare walls of the dressing room needed a mural to try to defeat the 'bad spirits' and an artist was found to paint one.

After Stoke's triumph, journalists, including the writer of this august volume, were taken down to see for themselves and were astonished to learn that what they had taken to be children's paintings done by one of the manager's offspring were in fact painted by a Welsh artist named Andrew Vicari who claimed to be a multi-millionaire, to live in Picasso's old house in the south of France, and to have sold many paintings to wealthy Saudi Arabians – proof positive that money can't buy good taste.

This one was apparently done for free – and even then this writer thinks he overcharged – in just over an hour, featuring a fiery sun, a galloping animal supposed to be a horse and a phoenix rising from the ashes. "They [Stoke] were the better team but I think I can claim some credit for banishing this losing streak once and for all," Vicari said. "I've never painted on breeze block before but it was well worth it to lift the curse that has blighted this beautiful stadium."

Tottenham Hotspur's White Hart Lane was also once a beautiful stadium, and its pride was the enormous wedding cake of an East Stand, with a press box situated on its roof. Unfortunately it was allowed to decline, the press box was condemned, and the members of the fourth estate moved elsewhere. The stand was due to be re-roofed in 1988, but the work was delayed and a certain Paul Gascoigne spotted the old press facility as an excellent vantage point for a spot of pigeon shooting.

Roy Reyland, the Spurs kit man and one-time fishing partner to the England midfield player, recalled an occasion when a knock came at the dressing-room door as he was laying out kit for the next day's training. It turned out to be Gascoigne, with his old friend Jimmy Five Bellies, who explained that a pigeon-shooting mission had gone wrong and that Gascoigne had fallen through the rotting floorboards of the old press box and onto the seats below.

"There sat the most influential midfielder of his generation, on my dressing-room table, bleeding and bruised," Reyland said. Gascoigne himself later estimated that he had fallen 30 feet onto the seats below and sustained bruising down his side and arm. "Gaffer, I don't think I can train today," he claims he said to manager Terry Venables. "A pigeon did it."

Swansea's Vetch Field also had a rooftop press box as did Rangers' Ibrox Park – a grand castellated affair – but this type of eccentric flourish has disappeared from the British football landscape as identikit new stadiums become the norm. Only the colour scheme distinguishes St Mary's from Leicester City's King Power Stadium, Derby from Middlesbrough's Riverside Stadium.

Nowhere these days will you find county cricket sharing with football as happened at the three-sided grounds at Northampton's County Ground – shared with Northants – or Bramall Lane, Sheffield, occasional home of Yorkshire and, on one occasion in July 1902, a home of Test cricket, making it one of only two grounds (The Oval is the other) to stage a Test and an England football international.

Former United winger Colin Grainger recalls that in one half, he would play on the wing with the crowd on top of him, kicking and screaming, and the pitch full of mud. In the other half, he would be at the cricket side of the football pitch, where there was no crowd, and a deathly silence when he had the ball. But the grass on that wing was like a bowling green.

Although league football and cricket no longer co-exist, you can still find an elegant cricket pavilion gazing across the cricket square to a distant football pitch at War Memorial Athletic Ground, the home of both Stourbridge FC and Stourbridge cricket club. Worcestershire CCC have played there and it has also hosted international cricket. Bermuda played Papua New Guinea in 1979 and Argentina faced East Africa in 1986, both in the ICC Trophy, and an England XI played Ireland in the 1997 Triple Crown Championship.

And while corporate naming rights have deprived us of stadiums called Pride Park, Dean Court and Valley Parade, non-league football still boasts colourful monikers such as the Dripping Pan (Lewes), the Giant Axe Stadium (Lancaster City), Five Heads Park (Horndean) and the Old Spotted Dog Ground (Clapton).

The Old Spotted Dog, in fact, has European pedigree – Dutch giants Ajax once played at the splendidly named east London ground. Clapton have an extensive history of European fixtures and are recognised by the FA as the first English club to play abroad, beating a Belgium XI 8-1 in Antwerp in 1890. They also played in Germany, Holland and the former Austro-Hungarian Empire. Never easy to get a result against an Empire.

Football grounds are the new cathedrals, the pride of their communities – but often they are quiet places on non-match days, as cathedrals are except on Sundays. A great example was given the night that Gianluca Vialli was sacked as Chelsea manager. A number of sports editors had clearly had the same idea of sending a reporter down to Stamford Bridge to see what the fans were saying, because around half a dozen football writers and a Sky Sports crew converged on the Fulham Road – which shows you what sports editors know about the world outside their offices.

Instead of the throngs of supporters baying for the blood of chairman Ken Bates, they found a predictably deserted street. Rather than interview each other – which would not have been much use, because not many football writers are Chelsea fans – the reporters headed for the bars in the hotel behind the Shed End in search of some supporters, and, to their delight and relief, finally found two. Sadly they turned out to be Arsenal fans who had dropped in to watch the Champions League live on the televisions.

I know, for I was one of those reporters.

2.

Back of the Net

"It amazes me when people say:
'All he can do is score goals.'"

Sir Alex Ferguson on Andrew Cole

GOALS are what the game is all about. Beautiful goals, ugly goals, 30-yard thunderbolts and nudges from an inch out that barely reach the back of the net. And they all count the same.

Unless they are away goals, of course.

The first goal in the history of the Football League was scored by Kenny Davenport of Bolton Wanderers – a local lad who played for the Trotters for a decade – after two minutes of their game against Derby County on the opening Saturday of league action, 8 September 1888.

For those who believe that football began in 1992, the first Premier League goal was scored, not by a big name such as Alan Shearer or Matt Le Tissier, but by Brian Deane of Sheffield United in their 2-1 victory over Manchester United at Bramall Lane on Saturday 15 August 1992.

Deane is not remembered as one of the stars of the early days of the new 'Greed-Is-Good-League', as the great football writer Brian Glanville called it, which is unfair on Deane. He had been signed by manager Dave 'Harry' Bassett for £40,000 from Doncaster Rovers four years earlier and his pace and strength helped the Blades win promotion to the old Second and then First Division in successive seasons, between 1988 and 1990. The latter elevation tasted even sweeter for fans in the red half of the Steel City with Sheffield Wednesday relegated on the same day, 5 May 1990.

Unfortunately, life back at the top for Bassett and company began badly and they picked up only four points from their first 16 matches, the worst start ever made to a top-flight season. But things improved around Christmas and a sequence of seven wins in the new year took them to safety. The following season, 1991/92, followed the same pattern – only one win in the first 12 games, a precarious position a point outside the relegation zone at Yuletide, but a rally to finish ninth.

In both seasons, United's second-half form was good enough to challenge for a European place if they had kept it up all season. So the wily Bassett hit upon an idea – move Christmas forward to summer. That way, the players could get into the winning mood at the start of the season that they had only begun to show around the festive period in the previous two campaigns.

He ordered the squad to attend a pre-season Christmas dinner in August. A suite at Bramall Lane was decorated in appropriate seasonal style, turkey was served with all the trimmings and there was a visit from Father Christmas. The cover of the match programme for the visit of Alex Ferguson's men continued the theme, featuring Bassett in Santa gear, Deane draped in tinsel and captain Brian Gayle wearing a hat from a Christmas cracker – all bathed in bright summer sunshine.

It worked. The Sheffield United team cost a fraction of the money their visitors had spent – Dion Dublin made his debut for Manchester United as a second-half substitute after his million-pound move from Cambridge United, which made him worth about the same as the Blades' starting line-up, in which the costliest player was Glyn Hodges, a £400,000 signing from Crystal Palace in 1991 – but they made a winning start.

Impossible as it seems nowadays, there was no early kick-off shown live, so all the Saturday games began at the traditional time of three o'clock. And, five minutes into the Brave New World of satellite TV-funded riches that would make players such as Leon Best, Roque Junior and Fraizer Campbell wealthy beyond the dreams of the average fan who watched them, Carl Bradshaw aimed a long throw-in on the right towards Alan Cork at the near post, Clayton Blackmore back-headed the ball across his own goal and Deane nipped in front of Gary Pallister to head past Peter Schmeichel.

"Whatever happens, wherever I am, that will be the one moment fans all over the world will remember me for," Deane told the Premier League website. "It was a fantastic feeling and even to this day people remind me of it – and it's now a classic quiz question too.

"I got word that David Hirst had scored for Sheffield Wednesday early on, but then the news filtered through that I had scored before him. I knew I was going to be close because of the time I scored the goal but to realise I was the first ever to score in the new Premier League, well, it took a while to sink in."

Deane added a second from a penalty after Pallister brought down old Bassett favourite Cork before Mark Hughes pulled one back, and the tone was set for a successful season that included an FA Cup semi-final appearance at Wembley, even if defeat by Sheffield Wednesday beneath the twin towers spoiled the day.

Deane scored 71 Premier League goals, which would make him a valuable commodity these days. Goalscorers will always command top dollar in wages and transfer fees, because scoring is deceptively difficult.

People who have never played the game – which, managers would have you believe, includes all football writers and referees – cannot see why this should be so. After all, they reason, a goal is eight yards wide and eight feet high, which works out as a target of 192 square feet. How demanding can it be to put a ball that is only 9 inches across into that big gap between the posts and under the crossbar?

After all, even inanimate objects can score. And no, we're not talking about that lumbering forward who once wore the number nine shirt for your team. In October 2009, Sunderland's only goal of a 1-0 victory over Liverpool was scored by a beach ball. After five minutes of the game at the Stadium of Light, Darren Bent hit a shot that was going straight at Reds goalkeeper Pepe Reina until it struck a bright red ball that had been thrown onto the pitch – ironically by a Liverpool fan as the club crest on the ball showed. The match ball was deflected to Reina's left, the beach ball to his right, and his eyes followed the larger object while the ball he should have been trying to save spun over his left shoulder into the net.

It was the only goal of the game and apart from it being a self-inflicted wound by a Liverpool fan, it was made worse for the Reds by the fact that the goal should not have stood. The laws of the game clearly state that if the ball hits an 'outside agent' the game should restart with a drop ball. Referee Mike Jones was cast into the outer darkness of Peterborough v Scunthorpe the following weekend.

Sometimes players can score without even knowing about it. In December 2014, Liverpool's Adam Lallana was chasing down a back-pass in a match against Swansea City at Anfield when Swans' goalkeeper Łukasz Fabiański's clearance hit him on the shoulder and looped into the empty net at the Kop end to put the home side 2-0 up.

Sweden forward Tomas Brolin never really showed the skills in British football that had impressed viewers of Channel 4's *Football Italia* coverage when he starred for Parma, and his first goal for Leeds United, in a Yorkshire derby away to Sheffield

Wednesday, demonstrated anything but Italian stylishness. Brolin did well to outjump Wednesday defender Peter Atherton to reach Gary Kelly's cross, but things got messy after that.

Kevin Pressman, the goalkeeper, rushed out and his attempt to block hit the ball off Brolin's knee and towards the vacant goal. Brolin tripped head first over Pressman and Ian Nolan's attempted clearance hit Brolin full in the face and bounced in.

Brolin had the brass neck to run away in celebration as if he had known anything about it, not that there was much to celebrate beyond the fact that it was the Swede's first in English football. It barely helped to save face for Leeds, cutting the home team's lead to 3-1 and failing to inspire a fightback from the visitors, who went on to lose 6-2.

Pressman, by the way, saved and scored in FA Cup penalty shoot-outs against Wolves in 1995 and Watford – including netting the decisive final kick – in 1998. He also holds the record for the earliest red card in a season, sent off for handling outside his area after 13 seconds at Molineux in Wednesday's opening match of the 2000/01 campaign.

Goalkeepers, of course, are supposed to stop the ball going in, but sometimes they get it wrong and end up helping the forwards out.

Heurelho Gomes, for example, did Manchester United a favour in a match at Old Trafford in 2011. United midfielder Luís Nani fell in the penalty area under a challenge from Younès Kaboul, appearing to handle the ball. Tottenham goalkeeper Gomes gathered the ball and rolled it a few yards forward – actually quite a distance away from where the supposed offence had taken place – and prepared to take the free kick.

However, referee Mark Clattenburg had either not seen the handling incident, or had decided to give Spurs the advantage. What he had not done was blow his whistle. Nani seemed dimly aware of this as he tentatively trotted towards the ball and even took a couple of glances at Clattenburg before, visibly unable to believe his luck, knocking the ball into the net. Gomes, who had earlier looked over his shoulder to see where Nani was in case he could take a short free kick to a defender, had walked back for a run-up to a long free kick, and realised only too late that the ball was still live.

Many in the Old Trafford crowd may have thought they were witnessing something unique. But incidents such as this have been going on whenever players fail to play to the whistle. Or the one outside their heads, anyway.

In the 1971/72 season, Chesterfield goalkeeper Alan Stevenson collected the ball amid a scramble in the south goalmouth at Brighton's old Goldstone Ground, put it down and stepped back to prepare to take the inevitable free kick. Brighton's Kit Napier ran up and smashed the ball into the empty net before rushing back upfield pumping the air with his fists.

The crowd reacted with bemusement, wondering whether Napier had completely lost his mind and waiting for the referee to call him over for an equally inevitable booking for wasting time. Except that the man in black signalled a goal, Stevenson having only assumed – incorrectly – that a foul had been awarded.

There was obviously some malign force at work on goalkeepers in that goalmouth as Andy Collett of Bristol Rovers found out in October 1995. After fielding a shot, he looked upfield before putting the ball down in preparation for a kick upfield. But in contrast to the Chesterfield incident, the danger was not from a Brighton player in front of him but one behind him. Midfield player George Parris was lurking by a post, and when Collett let go of the ball, he charged forward, dispossessed the surprised goalkeeper, turned and rolled the ball into the unguarded goal.

"Goalkeepers usually look behind them but he didn't and I'm glad he didn't," Parris said after the match. "I stood by the post and waited for him to turn round and see me and then I would have run back to the halfway line. But he didn't turn around and as soon as he threw the ball, I was in there." The goal might have been disallowed for a foul by Parris, who seemed to knock Collett over as he ran past him, but referee Paul Rejer saw nothing wrong – a bit like Collett.

Dion Dublin scored a similar goal in a Premier League match for Coventry City against Newcastle United at Highfield Road in November 1997, but had no thoughts of surprising Shay Given when the goalkeeper intercepted a cross aimed towards him. He was more concerned with avoiding a painful spill into the stands as his momentum took him off the pitch behind the Irish goalkeeper, who put the ball down and looked upfield for a target, not noticing that Dublin was still behind him. The forward was trotting back onto the field and saw his chance, nipping in front of Given and rolling the ball into goal. Given was the only Irishman in the world who didn't know where Dublin was.

Both Given and Collett could be excused for not having eyes in the back of their heads, but it was Kevin Dearden's ears that were playing tricks on him when Bristol Rovers' luck evened itself out almost exactly one year after the Parris incident. Dearden, the Brentford goalkeeper, handed the Pirates' Marcus Browning his first goal of the season on a plate in the Bees' 2-1 defeat at the Memorial Ground.

Dearden fielded a through ball then put it down at his feet. Browning, who had begun trotting back, instantly turned and tapped the ball in to give Rovers a 2-0 lead, while Dearden stood and watched, thinking he had heard the referee blow for offside against Browning. But any whistle must have been in the crowd as the referee, who was standing ten yards away, never lifted his Acme Thunderer to his lips at all, and Browning certainly had not heard anything. "I just thought, 'He's rolled this out a bit too far,' and it was a tap-in," Browning said afterwards.

Andy Dibble, the Manchester City goalkeeper, must have thought there was no danger of conceding with the ball still in his hands after catching a cross from Nottingham Forest's Garry Parker in a match at The City Ground (in 1989/90). He even had a look behind him and noticed Forest's Gary Crosby before preparing to throw the ball upfield with his right hand.

But as Crosby ran back past Dibble, he nodded the ball out of the goalkeeper's hand and ran it into goal, as Dibble objected to the referee, Roger Gifford, that he had had the ball in his hands. Well, not hands but one hand.

The goal was allowed, but the arguments went on. "I can't believe it," City manager Howard Kendall said. "Is it only hand-ball if you touch the ball with two hands? There's no way that is a goal." George Courtney, a World Cup referee, agreed. "The letter of the laws doesn't accommodate a goal being scored in that way, but in the spirit of the laws, I wouldn't have allowed it."

FIFA took note and by 2012, had ruled that in such situations the ball is deemed to be in the goalkeeper's control. So when Liverpool defender Daniel Agger 'did a Gary Crosby' to Anzhi Makhachkala keeper Vladimir Gabulov in a Europa League group match at Anfield, he was shown a yellow card.

* * * * *

By the way, remember that first-ever league goal, scored by Bolton's Kenny Davenport? The second was an own goal.

As long as there has been league football, hapless defenders have been kicking, heading and chesting the ball into their own nets, to the delight of opposition fans and, it must be said, neutrals. Well, almost as long. But it only took 30 minutes of league play back in 1888 before Aston Villa fullback Gershom Cox scored against his own team for Wolves in a match that eventually finished 1-1.

But if the league could not claim an own goal as its first score, Wycombe Wanderers could. The opening goal of their debut in the league on Saturday 14 August 1993, a 2-2 draw away to Carlisle United, was scored by the Cumbrians' Chris Curran. In his own net.

Any own goal is a disaster to the scorer, but in a derby the embarrassment is magnified. To a generation of fans, 'doing a Sandy Brown' was another way of talking about an own goal in recognition of an extraordinary moment in the first Merseyside derby of the 1969/70 season.

Liverpool were already 1-0 up at Goodison Park when the Reds' winger Peter Thompson took on Everton sweeper John Hurst and crossed into the Park End goalmouth. It looked like a wasted ball as Bobby Graham, the sole Liverpool player in the penalty area, was outnumbered by defenders and struggling to catch up with play. But Gordon West, the goalkeeper, missed the cross and left-back Brown, covering behind him, inexplicably launched himself into a diving header and nodded the ball firmly into his own net from a horizontal position.

The game was on *Match of the Day* in the days when only two matches were shown, and a nation saw the luckless Brown end up face down inside the goal before picking himself up off the turf and booting the ball back upfield. Everton went on to lose 3-0, but they had the last laugh as they not only won the return match at Anfield 2-0 but went on to collect the league title.

A Second City derby at St Andrew's was the setting for Aston Villa goalkeeper Peter Enckelman's moment of horror on Monday 16 September 2002. His teammate Olof Mellberg took a throw-in and sent it to the Finnish keeper, who seemed to take his eye off the ball as it rolled towards him. Had he missed it completely, it would have trundled into the net for a corner-kick – a goal cannot be scored directly from a throw-in, of course. But poor Enckelman was ruled to have got the slightest touch of the ball, making it an own goal. So distraught was he that he was almost oblivious to the Blues fan who danced in front of him while making what might be termed an obscene gesture.

Sometimes a player is credited with an own goal when the blame clearly lies elsewhere. Gary Neville, for example, who caressed a pass back towards goalkeeper Paul Robinson in the 69th minute of England's 2-0 defeat in Croatia in a Euro 2008 qualifier on Wednesday 11 October 2006. The ball hit a divot just as Robinson was swinging his boot in his attempt to clear, and bounced up, leaving Robinson kicking empty air, the ball progressing gently onward into the net and England in a hole that they were unable to climb out of. Rather like the one Robinson must have wished he could climb into.

Some own goals are classics. Tony Popovic scored what would have been a goal of the season contender for Portsmouth against Crystal Palace at Fratton Park on Saturday 11 September 2004, if he had not been playing for Palace at the time. Steve Stone crossed from the right, about waist high. The ball had almost sped past Popovic before he could react, so in desperation to make some sort of contact he flung his right leg out behind him – and, with a backheeled flick, volleyed the ball in an unstoppable loop over the head of goalkeeper Julián Speroni and in.

But perhaps the 'best' own goal was scored by Jamie Pollock of Manchester City against – sorry, for – QPR at Maine Road on 25 April 1998. It was a goal worthy of a Paul Gascoigne or a Matthew Le Tissier if it had been scored at the right end.

Pollock, a solid defensive midfield player, had joined City in March to help with their battle to avoid a first-ever drop to the third tier of English football, but the club were still in mortal danger, in 22nd place, when they faced the Londoners, who were one position better off, in the penultimate game of the season.

As QPR right-back David Bardsley crossed the ball towards the dangerous Kevin Gallen after 21 minutes with the score 1-1, Pollock, chasing back diligently, anticipated the danger and hooked it away from Gallen and over the forward's head. So far, so good. But then, as the ball dropped, he attempted to cushion a header back to Martyn Margetson, his goalkeeper. Sadly, he put a little more pace on it than he had intended and nodded it over him and into the net.

To make matters much worse, although Lee Bradbury levelled soon after half-time, City could not find a third goal, even after QPR's Nigel Quashie had been sent off, and the game ended 2-2. That meant that QPR were safe, while City had to hope that results went their way in the final matches of the season eight days later. Pollock and company did their part, winning 5-2 away to Stoke, but unlikely away wins for Portsmouth and Port Vale sent City down.

Without Pollock's own goal, it would have been QPR who went down and City who stayed up. According to the Loft For Words website, "Pollock was subsequently named the most influential human being of the millennium, beating Jesus Christ and Karl Marx into second and third places, in an American university poll hijacked by QPR supporters."

Pollock's nightmare was unusual in that most own goals are the result of a single touch of the ball – a misdirected header, a sliced attempt at a clearance. Nobody dribbles the ball past their own goalkeeper. But Chris Brass of Bury managed two touches when he scored for Darlington on 22 April 2006. As a hopeful ball was lobbed forward from midfield after only eight minutes of the match, defender Brass, eight yards out, attempted to hook the ball away over his shoulder. Unfortunately his aim was off and the ball hit him full in the face and rebounded past the flat-footed goalkeeper, Kasper Schmeichel, who was enjoying an early taste of league football on loan from Manchester City. It was the only goal Brass scored in 28 matches in a Bury shirt and a painful one, but there was no lasting damage as Bury went on to win 3-2.

"I think the thankful thing is we actually got the result," Brass later told *Sky Sports News*. "I can laugh about it but I had an untold weekend of ribbing about it, including 'Kammy' [*Sky Sports* pundit Chris Kamara], who started it on Sunday morning.

"When it happened, I truly didn't know whether to laugh or cry. Some of our players have said they were laughing. I can't explain it, I really can't. I couldn't have hit it any sweeter and the unfortunate issue is it broke my nose again to boot!" In 2008, Brass became Bury's caretaker manager for half a dozen games. Presumably he did not demonstrate his unique skill in training.

Own goals are usually accidental, but Mick Harford later admitted that his headed own goal in a vital match between Luton Town and Derby County on the final day of the 1990/91 season was deliberate. To stay up, Luton needed to beat Derby, who were already down. Harford, a Luton legend who had played for the Hatters for five seasons, had joined Derby halfway through the previous season, but did not forget his old Luton loyalties. Four minutes before half-time, he met a free kick with a glancing near-post header past Peter Shilton and Town were on their way to a 2-0 win and safety. Down instead went Sunderland, whom Harford was to join in March 1993.

In September 2010, former Liverpool legend Jamie Carragher intentionally blasted the ball past a Liverpool goalkeeper in his own testimonial match against Everton at Anfield – from the penalty spot.

Like a number of other Reds favourites including Ian Rush, Robbie Fowler, Steve McManaman and Michael Owen, Carragher had been a Toffees fan as a boy, and it had been his lifelong ambition to score a goal for them, and on that day his chance arrived. Everton were awarded a penalty at the Anfield Road End and as Yakubu Aiyegbeni stepped up to take it, Carragher rushed past him and slid the ball past Liverpool keeper Brad Jones. "As an Everton fan as a kid I've always dreamed about scoring against Liverpool so that is why I did that," he explained.

Carragher, in fact, once described himself as "The biggest Blue in Bootle" and applauded fans who wrote 'Thank You Arsenal' on the wall of a local pub when the Gunners' 2-0 win at Anfield denied the Reds the title in 1989.

"I was a total Everton fanatic right through my childhood and teens," he said in 2008. "Everton controlled my life and dominated my thoughts 24/7. I went to the away games, followed them across Europe and in the mid-80s went to Wembley so often it began to feel like Alton Towers. When I talk about that Everton team I still say 'we'. Even when I was playing for Liverpool reserves I'd want Everton's first team to win the derby every time."

That explains the penalty own goal, but not all the others he scored – more than he managed at the correct end, including two in Manchester United's 3-2 win at Anfield in the Premier League in 1999/2000 and one in the 3-3 draw with West Ham United in the 2006 FA Cup Final.

Three players, though, went one better by scoring for both sides in an FA Cup final: Bert Turner of Charlton Athletic against Derby County in 1946, Manchester City's Tommy Hutchison against Tottenham Hotspur in 1981 and Spurs' Gary Mabbutt against Coventry City in 1987. All three finished up with runners-up medals.

Teams are sometimes the victims of a collective own-goal madness. Sheffield Wednesday were obviously in a generous festive mood when they gifted West Bromwich Albion a hat-trick of own goals through Vince Kenny, Norman Curtis and Eddie Gannon in a 5-4 home defeat on Boxing Day 1952. On Christmas Day two years later, Danny Murphy, Kenny Boyle and George Underwood of Rochdale all helped Carlisle to a 7-2 home win.

The Premier League is held up by some as the pinnacle of footballing excellence, which makes it hard to explain how Sunderland scored three own goals in just seven minutes in their home defeat by Charlton Athletic on 1 February 2003. Jody Craddock had already deflected a Mark Fish shot before Steven Wright got the final touch to put the Addicks ahead, a rebound off goalkeeper Thomas Sorensen went in off Michael Proctor, and Proctor scored a second when he turned his back on an incoming corner and turned the ball past Sorensen again.

Portsmouth decided on Saturday 6 February 2010 that anything Sunderland could do they could equal, so Anthony Vanden Borre, Richard Hughes and Marc Wilson each scored own goals in their 5-0 defeat by Manchester United at Old Trafford.

Frank Sinclair of Leicester City scored own goals in the last minute of matches on successive weekends at the beginning of the 1999/2000 season. On the opening day, he beat his own goalkeeper in the 90th minute of the Foxes' game at Highbury to give Arsenal a 2-1 victory. He stayed off the scoresheet as Coventry were beaten at Filbert Street on the Wednesday, but was deadly again as the referee was looking at his watch in the home game against his former club, Chelsea, the next Saturday, a minute after Muzzy Izzet thought he had won all three points for Leicester with a penalty.

The quickest own goal in Football League history was recorded on Monday 3 January 1977. Visiting Cambridge United kicked off at Torquay United in a Fourth Division fixture, Ian Seddon hit a high ball into the Torquay penalty area which was headed past his own keeper by Gulls defender Pat Kruse. The goal was timed at six seconds, and Torquay had not finished, scoring another own goal later in the match, a 2-2 draw.

Most own goals tend to be scored from close range, as defenders crack under extreme pressure. But two famous full-backs have beaten their goalkeepers from distance. Arsenal's Lee Dixon collected a Coventry City goal kick in a match at Highbury in September 1991 and looked upfield for options. When none was immediately obvious, he decided to give his goalkeeper David Seaman an early touch of the ball instead. Without looking, he turned and lobbed the ball gently back towards his own goal. Unfortunately Seaman was eight yards off his line and the ball looped high over his head and in. Peter Ndlovu added a second and Arsenal lost 2-1.

Alex Elder of Burnley managed to score from long range and an acute angle to boot in a crucial match against Leeds United at Turf Moor late in the 1965/66 season. An hour had passed in a tense and bad-tempered clash between second-placed Burnley and Leeds, a point behind them in third, when Leeds forward Jim Storrie chased Elder down near the corner flag. Instead of putting the ball out for a throw-in or trying to win a goal kick by playing the ball off Storrie, the experienced Northern Ireland defender tried to loft a pass back to goalkeeper Adam Blacklaw. Unfortunately for Elder, Blacklaw was also off his line and the ball sailed past him from the narrowest of angles.

Turf Moor must bring the worst out of defenders, for it was there in January 2005 that Djimi Traoré of Liverpool double-backheeled the ball into his own net in an FA Cup tie. As a low cross from Richard Chaplow came in from the left after 51 minutes, Traoré attempted to control the ball with his left heel and turn simultaneously, Zinedine Zidane-style. But his first touch was too heavy and as he tried to locate the ball, it hit his heel again and went in. It was the only goal of the game, but Traoré had a consolation prize at the end of the season in the form of a Champions League winners' medal.

So when goalkeepers are happy to drop the ball at forwards' feet and defenders are willing to score goals for you, how can it sometimes be so hard for even top professionals to score? Ask Roger Davies, Ronny Rosenthal or Ryan Giggs. Or, on second thoughts, probably best not to.

Davies was signed for Derby County from Worcester City by Brian Clough's assistant and ace talent-spotter Peter Taylor. He finally made the first team in 1972, and his finest moment was a hat-trick in a 5-3 victory after extra time in an FA Cup replay against Tottenham Hotspur at White Hart Lane in February 1973. He collected a League Championship medal under Clough's successor Dave Mackay in 1975.

But it is safe to say that the moment he would most like to forget in a Derby career of more than 150 games came against Chelsea at Stamford Bridge when he rounded goalkeeper Peter Bonetti but, with the whole goal to aim at, managed to get his standing foot in the way of his shooting boot and prodded the ball harmlessly wide of the near post.

Rosenthal was another player who scored a memorable hat-trick in a cup replay, for Tottenham Hotspur away to Southampton in a 6-2 victory in the FA Cup fifth round in 1995. Three years earlier, like Davies, he had also done all the difficult bit involved in scoring in a match for Liverpool away to Aston Villa, running onto a clearance from David James and going round Villa keeper Nigel Spink. He even took an extra touch, but with the whole Holte End goal to aim at and defenders nowhere, he chipped the ball against the bar and out. There was no score at the time and things might have turned out differently if the Israeli had scored. Although he did find the net late in the game, Liverpool were 4-1 down by then.

Giggs scored one of the greatest FA Cup goals of all time in the 1999 semi-final against Arsenal in Manchester United's treble-winning season. But against the same opponents in a fifth-round tie at Old Trafford in 2003 he missed the ultimate sitter. Running onto a hoof forward from David Beckham, he went past Martin Keown, goalkeeper David Seaman and covering defender Sol Campbell. That gave him a shot at an empty Stretford End net from 18 yards, but he swung his right foot and the ball drifted harmlessly over the top. Again, the match was goalless at the time and Arsenal went on to win the game 2-0 with goals by Edu and Sylvain Wiltord. And the Cup itself.

* * * * *

But if scoring a goal is not as easy as it sounds, then deciding when a goal has been scored must be, mustn't it? The whole ball simply has to cross the whole goal line, between the posts and below the crossbar.

Except that sometimes it has been so difficult to prove that it has happened – or not happened – that goal-line technology had to be introduced. That tech has allowed officials to determine whether a ball has crossed the goal line, but in the past they have had trouble deciding whether the ball had even gone between the posts.

Nothing improves a goal like a billowing net, but the way that net is supported has led to confusion and drama over the years. We speak, of course, of the stanchions, the metal tubes that used to do dual service holding the posts up and supporting the net. These structures are no longer seen in senior matches, and part of the reason is the difficulty caused when a ball hit them and bounced back onto the field of play – too fast for the ref.

The earliest incident that really hit the headlines happened at Stamford Bridge on 26 September 1970 when Chelsea played Ipswich Town. In the 63rd minute Chelsea's Alan Hudson, in what used to be called the inside-left position, ran onto Peter Houseman's pass from the left wing and smacked a first-time shot at goal from around 22 yards. The shot was well hit but the ball went narrowly wide of the near post, hitting the stanchion. It rebounded onto the pitch, so far outside the post that it crossed the angle of the six-yard box.

Town goalkeeper David Best went to take the goal kick but was horrified to see Roy Capey, the referee, pointing back upfield to signal a goal. How the geometrically challenged ref thought the ball could have ended up where it did if it had gone in, and why Houseman had made an obvious gesture of frustration, is anyone's guess. Capey was persuaded to speak to one of his linesman – on the far side of the goal, so who must have had a worse view than he had – but refused to change his mind.

"I was amazed when the players queried it," he told the next day's *Sunday Express*. "We all agreed it was a goal." Best was still arguing at the final whistle. "There were only three people in the ground who didn't see what happened," he said. "The referee and his linesmen." Town manager Bobby Robson announced he would complain to the League and ask for a replay. He was supported by Sam Bartram in *The People*, who called it "the daftest decision I have seen in 36 years of football". But that was never going to happen.

The stanchion giveth, the stanchion taketh away. During Dundee United's 4-0 victory over Partick Thistle on 13 February 1993, Paddy Connolly of United was perfectly positioned by the far post when Michael O'Neill's corner was headed on by John Clark to crack the ball home from close range. It hit the stanchion and rocketed back across the goal line, where Thistle defender Martin Clark picked it up.

But instead of signalling the goal, World Cup referee Les Mottram had turned away, presumably under the impression that Connolly's shot had hit the post. And somehow neither Mottram nor his assistant had spotted what was therefore, if the ball was still in play as they believed, the clearest possible case of handball by Clark.

One of the most famous incidents of this type happened on 6 September 1980 when Crystal Palace visited Coventry City. Mick Coop, the Coventry right-back, fouled Palace's Jerry Murphy just outside the penalty area and Gerry Francis tapped the free kick to Clive Allen. His rocket shot, slightly deflected by a player in the defensive wall, soared past goalkeeper Jim Blyth into the top corner of the goal, rebounding from the stanchion.

The speed of the strike also beat BBC match commentator John Motson – "Oh, what a tremendous shot by Allen, and the ball came back off the woodwork" – so perhaps it was not surprising that it also fooled Derek Webb, the referee, even though he was at pitch level, 20 yards out and looking directly at the goal.

"The referee didn't give the goal," Allen said. "We all crowded round him and got him to go to the linesman." After much theatrical finger-waving from the ref as he attempted to motion the players away, he decided to trot across the pitch to consult the other linesman. But the verdict was the same: no goal. It would have levelled the scores at 2-2 but Palace eventually lost 3-1, their fourth defeat in their opening five matches, and the side hyped as 'the team of the eighties' ended up relegated at the end of the first full season of the decade.

Palace have suffered from having legitimate goals ruled out more than most. Manager Trevor Francis was furious with referee Dermot Gallagher and his assistant for not allowing a perfectly legitimate goal in Palace's 2-1 defeat to Leeds United at Selhurst Park in the FA Cup fifth round in February 2003.

With the score at 1-1 late in the first half, Tommy Black's shot from close range was first handled by Leeds defender Michael Duberry and then cleared from well behind the goal line by Danny Mills. Neither Gallagher nor his assistant gave a goal or a penalty for the handball, and Leeds went on to win the game with a goal by Harry Kewell.

"I saw it very clearly and actually got it wrong," Francis said, somewhat confusingly. "I thought it was six inches over the line but it was nearer two foot. The referee should have seen it quite clearly but he also has to rely on his assistants. It was a handball but it was over the line in any case and still he didn't give it."

On 15 August 2009, Palace were hard done-by again. Freddie Sears, on loan from West Ham, knocked the ball home to open the scoring for the Eagles against Bristol City at Ashton Gate – or so he thought until referee Rob Shoebridge, after consulting his assistant, awarded a goal kick, somehow imagining that Sears had wheeled away celebrating missing from six yards out. True, the ball had bounced out of the net, but there was no stanchion for it to have hit, so Shoebridge can only have assumed that the ball had rebounded from the advertising hoardings behind the goal.

"I feel sorry for the players, I feel sorry for the fans," then Palace manager Neil Warnock said afterwards, his mood not helped by a late City winner. "If it had happened at the other end there would have been an absolute riot. The fourth official told me the linesman on the other side was trying to invent a free kick. I thought [City manager] Gary Johnson and his players could have shown more sportsmanship because they knew it was a goal, like everyone else. But I'm 60 years old and maybe I expect too much."

Warnock had refused to shake the hand of Johnson, who was sympathetic. "In Neil's position, I would feel the same as he does," he said. "Sometimes as the away manager a big decision goes against you, the crowd get on your back and it's very hard to keep things under control. It was a goal, of course, but I don't see what I could have done about it at the time."

He could have followed the example of Steve Kember, the Palace captain during their home match with Nottingham Forest on 28 August 1971. Palace's Terry Wharton hit a shot that clearly deflected off the chest of a defender on its way into the side netting and when referee Ronald Judson gave a goal kick, the home players were furious. They persuaded the ref to consult his linesman, which he did, and then astounded everyone in the ground by signalling a goal. Now it was Forest's turn to go nuts.

Eventually referee Judson, not knowing what was going on, appealed to Kember for help. Kember owned up that it hadn't been a goal, and Palace didn't even get their corner as the game restarted with the decision that had caused all the fuss in the first place – a goal kick.

Words were exchanged between the club and Kember afterwards, but they could not, of course, publicly criticise him, especially when he won the *Evening Standard* player of the month award for August. "I am sure his sporting attitude in the game against Nottingham Forest when he gave an honest opinion about the disputed goal must have stood him in good favour," Palace manager Bert Head wrote in his programme notes for the next home match, no doubt with gritted teeth.

"There was some talk in the newspapers that our chairman Mr Arthur Wait was going to have a quiet word with Steve and remonstrate with him about his action. Let us get this matter straight once and for all. Mr Wait, the rest of the board and all of us at Crystal Palace back our captain all the way. We know that the goal could have meant a lot to us as a club and to the players as individuals but Steve saw it clearly and reacted as we knew he would. There is always plenty of room in this game for honesty and I am certain that his action will not be forgotten."

Kember, though, was never quite the fans' favourite after that that he had been before, which made it easier for Head to sell him to Chelsea and Alan Birchenall to Leicester later that autumn, using the money to rebuild the side, which stayed up by the skin of its teeth. Forest, although a point better off than they might have been, went down.

Many years later, another goal was mistakenly awarded after another miss, and not even a near one – and this time it stood. It happened at Vicarage Road in September 2008 in a match between Watford and Reading, when a Reading corner from the right taken by Stephen Hunt sailed into the Watford six-yard box. The ball hit Watford midfield player John Eustace in the midriff and went wide to the right. Reading's Noel Hunt, Stephen's brother, trying to keep the ball in play, scooped it back across goal, where it was headed against the crossbar and a follow-up shot was blocked by a defender.

At that point referee Stuart Attwell blew his whistle, and Watford keeper Scott Loach – who had come on after only four minutes for injured starter Mart Poom – placed the ball on the six-yard line expecting to take a free kick, or a goal kick – neither of which would have been the correct decision. "When the whistle went I wondered what it was for as I could not see a foul," Reading manager Steve Coppell said.

But the officials' error was on an entirely different scale. Attwell had blown for a goal, signalled by Nigel Bannister, his assistant. Bannister had seen the ball come off Eustace and cross the goal line before Noel Hunt touched it, unaware that it had done so outside the net, and signalled a goal. Why he thought that a Reading forward would have been trying to hook the ball back into play in the circumstances is a mystery.

Attwell, more centrally positioned, must have seen that the ball had not gone between the posts at any point, but awarded the goal anyway, and confirmed his decision after consulting Bannister. "I've never seen anything like it," Watford manager Aidy Boothroyd said. "It's like a UFO had landed." Which, when you think about it, is a reaction almost as inexplicable as Attwell's decision.

The unlucky Eustace went into the record books as the scorer of an own goal that never was. "Everyone could see what happened," he said. "It's a bit embarrassing. We thought he'd given a goal kick and then it was a goal. It's ridiculous. Everyone was amazed by the decision."

Stephen Hunt described it as "probably the worst decision I've ever witnessed in football", but neither he nor any other Reading player saw fit to correct the officials. "It wasn't our mistake," he said. "You can't say, 'Hold on, ref, don't give us a goal.'" Really? Why not?

Coppell, to his credit, admitted that the decision strengthened the case for allowing referees access to video replays, as did an incident on Humberside later that season. Clubs are not allowed to replay contentious incidents on big screens at grounds for fear of undermining the authority of referees and their assistants by proving them wrong, although they are permitted to show replays of goals and near misses. But the two got tangled up, to the embarrassment of referee Peter Walton, in an FA Cup replay between Hull City and Sheffield United at the KC Stadium on 25 February 2009.

After 24 minutes, United right-back Kyle Naughton, attempting to intercept a cross from the right, powered a header against the underside of the crossbar and down onto the goal line. The referee's assistant signalled a goal and Walton gave it. The video technicians immediately showed a replay on the stadium screens, not realising that there was any controversy involved.

But the footage instantly proved that the ball had not crossed the line and the 'goal' should not have been awarded. Of course at the time there was no mechanism for referring decisions to replays so the hapless Walton had no option but to restart the game with a kick-off while the United fans seethed in frustration. Hull went on to win 2-1.

It at once confirmed that replaying controversial incidents for fans to see is a bad idea and that referees could have access to replays without slowing the game down too much, as some objectors claimed. After all, the KC Stadium techies had done it before the teams had kicked off again!

And video replays would compensate for the physical impossibility of being in two places at once, which undid linesman Rob Lewis in a notorious incident in the dying moments of a game between Manchester United and Tottenham on 4 January 2005. Pedro Mendes attempted to lob United goalkeeper Roy Carroll from near the halfway line and the ball, fumbled over his shoulder by Carroll, dropped a yard or more over the goal line before he clawed it back into play. Neither referee Mark Clattenburg nor Lewis, his assistant, were close enough to award the goal, and you cannot give what you cannot see.

"The linesman has kept his flag down," roared outraged commentator Alan Parry, but linesman Lewis had been correctly positioned, level with the last United defender, 40 yards upfield, when Mendes hit the ball. Barely four seconds passed before Carroll dragged the ball back across the goal line. To put that into perspective, prospective NFL players run a 40-yard dash as part of pre-draft tests and the fastest time ever recorded is 4.24 seconds. Needless to say, Lewis was barely level with the penalty area when Carroll clawed the ball back into play.

Parry continued: "That is a travesty. It certainly is a decision that Mark Clattenburg, the referee and in particular Rob Lewis, his linesman, will want to forget." Perhaps so, but not because they could have done any better without video assistance.

* * * * *

However they go in, fans love goals, and it is generally accepted that the more are scored, the happier everyone will be – except, of course, for managers and goalkeepers.

Bigger goals have been suggested as a way to increase scoring and make the game more attractive, and we almost had a chance to see what that might be like on 31 August 1996, when Bristol Rovers hosted Stockport County in their first match at the Memorial Ground.

The Gas had moved back to their home city after a ten-year exile at Bath City to share with Bristol Rugby Club, who had fallen on hard times which would later mean Rovers, the tenants, becoming the joint-owners and eventually the landlords.

But the groundstaff were obviously still coming to grips with hosting two codes of football on that opening day, because shortly before kick-off, an eagle-eyed official spotted that the crossbar at one end was six inches higher than the other. The match was delayed while red-faced staff hurriedly made alterations.

Another way to guarantee goals is to decide drawn games with penalty shoot-outs. Five each, and then sudden death after that. But sometimes it can be a very long drawn-out business, with nothing sudden about it.

Liverpool and Middlesbrough scored 27 times between them in a Capital One Cup tie at Anfield in September 2014 before Liverpool won 14-13, thanks to Albert Adomah's miss, one of only three unsuccessful attempts in the 30 shots fired at the Kop end goal.

That equalled the British record in a match between professional clubs, set by Leyton Orient and Dagenham & Redbridge in the Johnstone's Paint Trophy in September 2011. But non-league Tunbridge Wells and Littlehampton Town hold the overall English record, taking 40 kicks in an FA Cup preliminary round replay on 31 August 2005 before Tunbridge Wells won 16-15 after a 2-2 draw.

Brockenhurst and Andover Town only took 30 before Brockenhurst won 15-14 win in the Hampshire Senior Cup in October 2013, but before Andover's Claudio Herbert, who had already converted one kick, had his second effort saved, the previous 29 in a row had all been converted, which is believed to be a world record. The match itself, by the way, had finished goalless.

The world record for the largest aggregate score was set when Argentinos Juniors beat Racing Club 20-19 in November 1988, in the days when all drawn Argentine League games went to penalties, from 44 attempts overall. On 3 June 2015, it was equalled when Sundsøre IF beat Nykøbing Mors 20-19 in a penalty shoot-out in a preliminary round of the Danish FA Cup. They were tops in sheer number of penalties converted, but according to the Guinness Book of Records, the shoot-out after the 2005 Namibian Cup final was of longer duration. Although

KK Palace beat Civics by a relatively modest 17-16, 15 kicks were missed.

Penalties are usually straightforward shots, bar the occasional Antonín Panenka-style chip – more often missed than any other sort, we'd guess. But there have been novelty attempts such as the one taken by Plymouth Argyle in a match against Manchester City in 1964. John Newman put the ball on the spot, but instead of shooting, nudged the ball forward for Mike Trebilcock to run in and score. "Big Malcolm Allison was the manager," Trebilcock recalled later. "It was one of his mad ideas."

Barcelona tried something similar against Celta Vigo in February 2016, with Lionel Messi passing for Neymar to score, but it almost went wrong when Luis Suarez nipped in first to poke the ball home. Replays showed that the penalty should have been retaken, as Suarez, who was not in on the plan, encroached before the ball was touched by Messi, while Neymar, who knew what was coming, was careful not to enter the area prematurely.

Arsenal also attempted the same trick in a match against Manchester City in October 2005 in their final season at Highbury, but bungled it spectacularly. Robert Pirès had already successfully converted a penalty just past the hour to give Arsenal a 1-0 lead with Arsenal's 500th goal at their old stadium when Stephen Jordan fouled Dennis Bergkamp to give Pirès a second go.

But he only brushed the ball with his studs as he attempted to pass to Thierry Henry and the ball barely moved on the spot. Henry had run past the ball expecting a pass into his path, and with Pirès unable to touch it again, City defender Sylvain Distin nipped in to clear.

Puzzlingly, Mike Riley, the referee, awarded City an indirect free kick, which was only the correct decision if Pirès had touched the ball twice. But Pirès touched it once, and then only just – unless each stud counts separately. In fact, as Law 14 says that the ball must move forward from a penalty kick, which it did not in any meaningful sense, Riley should have ordered the kick to be retaken.

City defenders remonstrated with Pirès and Henry for what they considered a lack of respect. "I take all the blame, it was my idea," Henry said later. "If it had worked it would have been a brilliant idea, but it did not work." Fortunately for him and Pirès, Arsenal hung on to win 1-0.

Where had Allison got his original 'mad idea'? In 1957 Rik Coppens and André Piters of Belgium had worked a more complex version in a match against Iceland. Coppens nudged the ball into the path of Piters, who drew Iceland goalkeeper Björgvin Hermannsson and rolled the ball back for Coppens to tap in.

Johann Cruyff and Jesper Olsen repeated that for Ajax against Helmond Sport in December 1982. Cruyff lined up the kick but instead of shooting, passed it diagonally forward to his left where Olsen, who had run forward as soon as the ball was played, collected the ball and crossed it back for Cruyff to tap in.

They all count. Except when the ref gets it wrong.

3.

The Beautiful Games

*"There's no rule to say a game
can't finish 9-9."*

Watford manager Graham Taylor after a
7-3 defeat at Nottingham Forest

I N the end, it all comes down to the 90 minutes on the pitch,
plus injury time. Then extra time and penalties.

The players, the managers and even the owners may
be fascinating individuals. The stadiums may be architectural
gems. The fans and their devotion may make for revealing social
studies. But in the end, it's what goes on in those 90, or 120
minutes, that matters.

Anything can happen between the first and last blasts of
the referee's whistle, and it usually doesn't. Even the best games
contain uneventful and predictable passages of play, and some
never rise above that. But every now and then, the unusual
will occur. Some matches live in the memory for great football
or amazing skills. But just as many will stick for more banal

reasons: a player kicking a ball boy or a referee going penalty crazy.

When a single sporting contest has a name of its own you know that it is something special.

When Muhammad Ali met George Foreman in Zaire in October 1974 it was a fight for the undisputed World Heavyweight Championship and the WBC/WBA Heavyweight Championship. But this epic punch-up has gone down in the annals of boxing as the Rumble in the Jungle.

The 1967 Dallas Cowboys versus Green Bay Packers game that decided the NFL Championship and was played in the NFL's lowest temperature ever will always be known as The Ice Bowl.

And Sheffield United's home game against West Bromwich Albion on 13 March 2002 will forever be The Battle of Bramall Lane.

The match itself never finished. It was abandoned by referee Eddie Wolstenholme after 82 minutes, with the visitors 3-0 up, because United were down to six players. The International Football Association Board states that "a match should not continue if there are fewer than seven players in either team". It was the first time an English professional match had been called off for that reason.

The fixture had history, with a red card in four of the previous meetings between the clubs, and the two managers coming from opposite sides of the Sheffield footballing divide. Gary Megson, the Albion manager, was a former Sheffield Wednesday player, and United manager Neil Warnock a lifelong Blades fan, who later admitted that Megson was one of two managers he disliked (the other being Stan Ternent – the number who admit to disliking Warnock is rather larger).

This time the drama began after nine minutes when the Blades' keeper Simon Tracy was sent off for handling Scott Dobie's shot outside the penalty area. Warnock brought off Peter Ndlovu and sent on reserve goalkeeper Wilko de Vogt, who conceded the game's first goal ten minutes later, a header by Dobie from Andy Johnson's cross.

Albion added a second goal just after the hour, and it was a superb strike, captain Derek McInnes meeting a short corner-kick from Igor Bališ with a first-time shot from outside the penalty area that flew into the top far corner of the net.

Warnock responded by sending on Georges Santos and Patrick Suffo for Gus Uhlenbeek and Michael Tonge in the 64th minute, and neither substitute had touched the ball when Santos launched himself into a horrendous two-footed, over-the-ball challenge on Johnson. Once again, there was history; Santos had suffered a broken cheekbone in a collision with Johnson in their previous meeting while Johnson was with Nottingham Forest.

The decision to show Santos a red card was one of the easiest of referee Wolstenholme's career. Players on both sides began squaring up, and another red card was shown, to Suffo for butting Albion's Darren Moore. Play resumed with United down to eight men, but it would be exaggerating to suggest that calm had been restored. For a while it seemed that Blades' captain Keith Curle was trying to join his three teammates in taking an early bath with lunges at McInnes.

West Brom scored a third in the 77th minute when Dobie knocked the ball into the net from close range after Moore's header across goal somehow got past goalkeeper de Vogt and several defenders. Then United's Michael Brown limped off, leaving the Blades, who had used all three substitutes – and lost two of them – down to seven men, the minimum for the match to continue.

Robert Ullathorne, who had been sent off in the match against Albion at The Hawthorns the previous season, was then judged unable to continue by the United medical staff with muscle spasms and the match was abandoned.

A furious Megson thought that Warnock had deliberately sought an abandonment. "The authorities have to do the right thing otherwise they reward cheating, and that was cheating," he said after the game. "Sheffield United didn't cause that, one person did. The things going on both on the pitch and on the line were disgraceful and have no place in football. They should be severely punished by the FA.

"People were being told to go down, to come off, and the ref was being asked to send people off in the knowledge that it would mean the game couldn't continue. I've never witnessed things on the sidelines like that before. It was very difficult to keep your temper because it was lunacy from the other team."

Warnock admitted that he "wouldn't imagine Gary will be having a drink with me tonight," but denied the allegations. "I can say that 100% I did not tell my players to come off," he said. "I was not trying to get the game called off. I accepted we had lost that game and my only thought was that we have a tough game against Millwall on Tuesday night and I didn't want anyone aggravating their injury.

"I have no complaints about the sendings-off and we are going to have to deal with that as strongly as we can. I don't think Georges will ever play for us again and Patrick Suffo will be transfer-listed." He was as good as his word. Neither player made another appearance for the club.

A Football League spokesman said that options included a replay or awarding the points to Albion, but Megson made his feelings clear. "There will be no replay," he said. "If we are called back to Bramall Lane we shall kick off and then walk off the pitch. I've been in professional football since 16 and I'm 42 now. I've never ever witnessed anything as disgraceful as that. There is no place for that in any game of football, let alone professional football." Five days later, the League announced that Albion's 3-0 win would stand.

Of course, it is a football commonplace to say that it can be harder to play against a team reduced to ten men than against eleven – usually said by a manager whose team has just failed to beat an undermanned opponent, or done so only narrowly. If it is true, it is because teams who lose players tend to go into a defensive shell, sacrifice a forward player, and aim only to avoid defeat or minimise damage. And most coaches practise playing a man short as referees have tended to become more card-happy.

But a two- or three-player disadvantage is too much to overcome. That was proved on May Day 1999, when Leeds United visited West Ham. It was a good time for goal-happy neutrals to be watching the Hammers. In their previous home game they had beaten Derby County 5-1, and in their next outing they lost 6-0 away to Everton before ending their season by beating Middlesbrough 4-0 at the Boleyn.

On this occasion, Leeds won 5-1 and booked their place in Europe. West Ham just got players booked – and sent off. Ian Wright, Shaka Hislop and Steve Lomas were shown red cards by referee Rob Harris, and Wright, who went in the first half, kicked down the door of the referee's dressing room and trashed it.

We did not know that at the time, of course. Those of us in the press box were just trying to keep up with the goals and cards – eleven in total. Jimmy Floyd Hasselbaink gave Leeds the lead after just 20 seconds, running at West Ham central defender Neil Ruddock before placing a low shot in the corner from 18 yards. Wright was shown a yellow card for an elbow on Alf-Inge Haaland and then a second yellow, and a red, for a wild challenge on Ian Harte.

Now West Ham, already weakened by defensive injuries that meant midfield players Lomas and Marc-Vivien Foé playing in the back four, were up against it. However, they still looked the more dangerous side until Harry Kewell set up Alan Smith to make it 0-2 from close range late in the first half.

Paolo Di Canio and Eyal Berkovic seemed to be inspired by adversity, and combined for Di Canio to halve the deficit. Almost unplayable, the pair seemed to be indulging in a private game of their own, but as the Hammers pushed forward for an equaliser, Leeds took advantage. Hasselbaink went through and was felled for a penalty by Hislop, who was dismissed.

West Ham manager Harry Redknapp decided with regret that the tiring Berkovic was the player who had to be sacrificed to put on reserve keeper Craig Forrest, whose first act was to pick Harte's successful spot-kick out of the net. Two goals within two minutes from Lee Bowyer and Haaland actually distorted the score before Lomas was dismissed for a bad challenge.

Leeds extended an unbeaten run to 11 games, while Wright was fined £17,500 and suspended for the first three matches of the following season.

The FA said that Wright "offered a full and frank admission for his conduct and apologised unreservedly for the distress he caused." He wrote in his *Sun* column: "I was so upset I behaved in an unacceptable manner. I don't even remember properly what I did."

Robbie Savage remembers what he did when he burst into the referee's room before a match between Leicester City and Aston Villa at Filbert Street in April 2002 and told referee Graham Poll that he had to answer an urgent call of nature.

Savage later claimed that he had been suffering from a case of diarrhoea so severe that most people in his position would not have played in the match. Nevertheless he somehow completed the full 90 minutes and also bravely managed to attend a supporters' function afterwards.

But then reality and Robbie Savage have not always been close companions. He justified a move from Birmingham City to Blackburn Rovers on the grounds that it would mean he was closer to his family in Wrexham. According to the AA website, the distances are more or less identical.

The astonished Poll later told the full story of the restroom incident to the *Daily Mail*. If you do not wish to know the results, look away now.

"With the door wide open, he gave a running commentary as he defecated," Poll wrote. "We could not believe what was happening. I saw his teammate Matt Elliott in the corridor and asked if the toilets were working OK in the Leicester dressing room. He confirmed this to be the case.

"While Robbie was in the cubicle, Dennis Hedges, the match observer, entered the dressing room. According to Robbie's version of events I said: 'You'll never guess who is in our loo?' as if it was all a hoot.

"If I did say that, it was in appalled astonishment and, when Robbie was finished, I told him that his behaviour was unacceptable. 'I'll leave it floating and you can see for yourself,' he said. And he did, laughing as he left the room. Now I was almost lost for words, but remarked that he should consider washing his hands. 'No need,' he replied. Then he promptly wiped his hands down the lapels of Dennis's jacket."

Savage was fined two weeks' wages by Leicester, and then £10,000 by the FA for improper conduct.

The referee's dressing room should be sacrosanct, of course, if not actually a sanctuary – Jimmy Case, then Brighton manager, locked the referee in his room for his own protection after a pitch invasion had caused a match against York City at the Goldstone Ground in 1996 to be abandoned.

If officials can be intimidated, then the game is in trouble. Which is why some felt that Paul Ince was let off lightly with only a five-match stadium ban when, as manager of Blackpool, he pushed Mark Pottage, the fourth official in a match away to Bournemouth, against the wall of the players' tunnel and threatened to knock him out.

Nathan Delfouneso missing a scoring chance had frustrated Ince into throwing a plastic bottle to the ground, where it bounced and struck a female steward. Pottage told the referee, Oliver Langford, who sent Ince to the stand. Afterwards, Ince – his eyes "bulging", according to referee Langford – confronted the officials in the tunnel.

Giving evidence to an FA tribunal, Pottage said: "Mr Ince asked why he had been sent to the stand. He then said: 'And where's your busy fucker of a fourth [official]?'

"I was immediately behind him and said: 'I'm here.' Mr Ince turned round, looked me in the eyes and violently shoved me by pushing me with two hands on my chest, making me slightly lose my balance and banging my back into the wall. The stewards quickly stepped in and tried to usher Mr Ince towards his team's dressing room. As they were doing this, he shouted to me, saying: 'I'll knock you fucking out, you c***' repeatedly in an aggressive manner."

When giving evidence, Ince claimed somewhat improbably that he had been "intimidated" by Pottage. This, remember, is a man who insisted on being called 'The Guv'nor' in his playing days. He denied using "the c word" but accepted that he "could have referred to the fourth official using an f-word." In addition to his stadium ban, Ince was fined £4,000 and told to pay £500 costs.

* * * * *

Stewards, ball boys – all these extra people around these days that always seem to cause trouble. Take the case of Charlie Morgan, a 17-year-old ball 'boy' at Swansea City's Liberty Stadium, who also happened to be the son of the club's largest shareholder, Martin Morgan. He decided that part of his brief was to help the Swans out, tweeting before a Capital One Cup semi-final second-leg match at home to Chelsea in January 2013: 'The king of all ball boys is back making his final appearance #needed #for #timewasting.' And, as a ball ran out of play with Chelsea trying to overturn a 2-0 aggregate deficit, he was as good as his promise, trying to pick the ball up rather than allowing Hazard to kick it quickly back to the Swansea goalkeeper, then falling on the ball and lying on top of it.

The frustrated Chelsea winger tried to kick the ball out from under the teenager, which footage later showed he had succeeded in doing. But Morgan had obviously used his position close to the action to study top-level feigning of injury, rolling around in a fashion worthy of Jürgen Klinsmann in his pomp, and having to be helped away by colleagues as if he was an injured player. Hazard, though, was shown a red card by referee Chris Foy for violent conduct.

Revealingly, instead of the sort of outrage at Hazard's action that might have been expected from the authorities, the FA decided against extending the three-match ban for the red card, and football people generally sympathised with the player. Reading's Noel Hunt tweeted: "I kick the ball from under my niece like that and she starts laughing and she's only 2!" Stoke's Robert Huth added: "Ball boys staying down injured ... they'll be elbowing players off the ball next."

"Why is the kid lying on the ball in the first place?" Harry Redknapp, then QPR manager, mused. "You can imagine the frustration – you're a player trying to reach a cup final but there's this kid behaving like an idiot who won't give you the ball back.

"Hazard didn't kick the kid, he kicked the ball underneath him, but the whole thing got blown out of all proportion. I can think of a lot of players who would have kicked a bit harder than he did. He just toe-poked the ball away. The boy was tweeting before the game that he's a super time-waster. The way he behaved was disgusting."

Ball boys were an important part of match days at the Britannia Stadium when Rory Delap's long throw-ins were part of Stoke City's attacking arsenal. On damp days they were provided with towels so that Delap could dry the ball and get a good grip before flinging it towards the heart of the visitors' penalty areas.

It was not until 29 November 2008, a 1-1 draw with Hull City, that a visiting team came up with a workable plan to counter Delap's prodigious throws. Hull manager Phil Brown told substitute Dean Windass to warm up on the touchline near Stoke's right wing, effectively obstructing Delap's run-up. Unfortunately, referee Keith Stroud eventually took exception to Windass's antics and booked him for obstruction.

But Hull had a late, last laugh. With time running out and the scores level, they were awarded a throw-in deep in their own half and Paul McShane did not exactly hurry over to take it, to the frustration of the home crowd. He picked the ball up, and then had the bright idea of asking the nearest ball boy for a towel.

The bemused lad looked over to the bench, knowing that he was supposed to give Delap a towel, but flummoxed by a request from an opponent. Referee Stroud, though, ruled that if Stoke were entitled to a dry ball then so were Hull and McShane painstakingly towelled it off and eventually took the throw. The final whistle blew almost immediately.

A referee's whistling was very much the topic of conversation after a derby encounter between rivals Crystal Palace and Brighton at Easter 1989. Managers complaining against the award of a soft penalty against their team often say that if referees pointed to the spot for every foul then there would be five penalties in every match. And that is more or less exactly what happened that day at Selhurst Park. Referee Kelvin Morton awarded five spot kicks – a League record – but only two were successfully converted.

The Suffolk official refereed between 1982 and 1995 but surely never experienced another afternoon like this. Palace were leading 1-0 after a stunning strike that Ian Wright rated his best in his time at the club, and Brighton were down to ten men after the dismissal of midfield enforcer Mike Trusson for a high challenge on Eddie McGoldrick, when Morton launched his assault on the record books. Mark Bright appeared to back into Brighton defender Larry May as they jumped for a free kick, but Morton saw it the other way and Bright knocked home the first penalty of the game.

Next Dean Wilkins tripped McGoldrick but Bright put his second kick in exactly the same place as his first and Brighton goalkeeper John Keeley guessed where it was going and saved. But Brighton never really cleared the resulting corner and when Paul Wood brought down Bright, Wright was chosen to take the next penalty, only to crash it against the post. And that all happened before half-time.

Perhaps to even things up, referee Morton gave Brighton a penalty when Jeff Hopkins pulled back Kevin Bremner, such a soft award that the visitors had not even appealed for it. Alan Curbishley, Brighton's regular penalty-taker – who surprisingly said later that he felt all the penalty awards were correct – scored with no bother to make the score 2-1.

By now, both sets of fans were yelling 'penalty!' at every challenge, but there was only one more, when Mr Morton judged that Brighton left-back Ian Chapman had deliberately handled after Keith Dublin missed a cross by Phil Barber. This time Palace right-back John Pemberton stepped up. The ball was last seen in orbit over Beckenham.

Palace were also involved in another record-setting match on 12 September 1989, but they were on the wrong end this time. When they lost 9-0 at Anfield in the old First Division, their conquerors, Liverpool, had eight different scorers, the most by a team in a competitive match between English professional clubs.

Strangely, the man who scored twice was not Ian Rush, John Aldridge or John Barnes but Steve Nicol.

Palace got their own back later that season in the 1990 FA Cup semi-finals, which also set a record for different goalscorers. 16 separate players hit the back of the net – seven in Palace's 4-3 defeat of Liverpool at Villa Park, six more in Manchester United's 3-3 draw with Oldham Athletic at Maine Road, and another three in United's 2-1 win in the replay at the same ground.

The significant fact about West Ham's 8-1 home victory over Newcastle United on Monday 21 April 1986 was not the number of scorers. Or even that it was their biggest win in their best league season, when they finished third, and their biggest league victory for 18 years. It was the number of goalkeepers, three in all. And one player, central defender Alvin Martin, scored a hat-trick – the only one of his career – with each goal going past a different keeper.

Martin Thomas started the match between the posts for the visitors, responding to a goalkeeper crisis at the club despite a shoulder injury.

But he could not continue after the interval, so Chris Hedworth, a utility player making only his fourth appearance for the Magpies, took over. Sadly he broke a collarbone in a collision with Tony Cottee and England forward Peter Beardsley volunteered to take over.

Martin put the ball past Thomas to open the scoring after only three minutes, a close-range volley after he had strolled unmarked onto a free kick from Alan Devonshire near the left-wing corner flag. He struck again against Hedworth after 64 minutes, a six-yard header to make it 5-0 after Tony Gale had nodded on Mark Ward's right-wing corner. When Newcastle central defender and future West Ham manager Glenn Roeder, who had earlier scored a surreal backheeled own goal, handled in the area, Martin completed his treble and the scoring with a penalty against Beardsley.

"It's something I get asked about a lot and I do quite a bit of after-dinner speaking and that story can go on for 15 minutes," Martin told the *Sex & Drugs & Carlton Cole* Facebook Page. "I didn't know I had scored against three different goalkeepers. With five games to go we still had a chance of the title and the pressure was on. So this was a night when the cigars could come out and we could relax and enjoy the game for what it was – something you can lose sight of as a pro.

"I knew they'd had problems in goal and the first goalkeeper, Martin Thomas, had been injured previously and shouldn't have played. It was one of the lowest-quality hat-tricks you've ever seen. Fortunately I don't think there's too much footage of it about so I can tell people it was better than what it was [oh yes there is].

"It was Trevor Smith, a local reporter with the *Recorder* who was very close to the club, a lovely man, who came up to me and told me. 'Did you know that every goal was against a different goalkeeper?' I'd never thought about it, I just wanted to get the match ball for the hat-trick. The number of people who have told me they were there, there must have been 500,000 in the ground!

"But I do remember the third was a penalty, against Peter Beardsley, and Ray Stewart was our penalty taker, a great penalty taker, so he obviously picked the ball up. I wasn't thinking about taking it, I was standing on the half-way line. But then a chant went around the ground wanting me to take it. The West Ham fans knew what the score was, they were aware of the significance of it even though I wasn't, I was wrapped up in the game. I'm looking round and thought: 'Why not? We're 7-1 up, Peter Beardsley in goal – shouldn't present too much of a problem, should it?'

"So I went up to Ray and said: 'Look Ray, I think I should take this.' I don't think Ray was [keen] but in the end I did take the ball, put it down and put it in. But when I was coming off the pitch, John [Lyall, the manager] wasn't happy. John had a bit of a go, because I was captain at the time. 'What if you'd missed? The title could be decided on goal difference.' But that's the way John was, every minor detail he was aware of. So I said: 'If it happens again, John, I won't do it!'"

Speaking of goalscoring centre-halves, Aston Villa's Chris Nicholl went one better than Martin with all four goals in a match against Leicester City at Filbert Street in March 1976. Sounds like a thumping Villa win? It was actually a 2-2 draw, two of the strikes going past his own goalkeeper.

He put Leicester in front twice – ending the season as the Foxes' fifth-highest scorer – and on each occasion levelled for Villa.

Nicholl later said that his third goal, an unsaveable diving header, was the best he had ever scored, and this was a man who had netted from 30 yards in the 1977 League Cup final replay victory over Everton, picking up a clearance, charging forward and striking a left-foot rocket that dipped late on its way past Toffees keeper David Lawson.

His regret was that the referee refused to give him the match ball after the match, even though, in one sense, he had scored a hat-trick and more. Nicholl was tired of teammate Ray Graydon showing him match balls that commemorated hat-tricks – five in all. "After I scored those four goals in that 2-2 draw, I asked the referee if I could have the ball," he told the *Birmingham Post* in 2006. 'No,' the ref said. 'This is my last match and I am keeping the ball.' Just my luck, I suppose. My first hat-trick in a Villa shirt and I don't even get the ball!"

Former Chelsea and Leeds United defender Michael Duberry fell one goal short of emulating Nicholl's feat in January 2012 when playing for Oxford United against visitors Hereford United. After 32 minutes, with Oxford 1-0 up, Duberry slid in at the near post to guide a low cross from Hereford's Joe Colbeck past his own goalkeeper, Ryan Clarke.

Four minutes from time, another delivery from Colbeck proved too inviting to turn down, this time a high cross that Duberry, rushing in towards his own net, met with a glancing header from four yards out. But he made amends, partially at least, with a last-minute equaliser, prodding Tom Craddock's pass home from six yards.

"Wow, didn't expect an afternoon like that," he tweeted. "Scored the imperfect hat-trick, left foot (OG), header (OG) and right foot (OG)." The third was not, of course, an own goal as he later corrected himself, blaming a 'stressful afternoon' for his earlier error of attribution.

Stress can do funny things, and foreign managers and players who come to Britain are often taken aback to realise that our leagues do not have a mid-season mental health break. And they are even more surprised to learn that we play on Boxing Day and New Year's Day.

It could be worse. Matches used to be played on Christmas Day itself, most recently in 1959 in England. In Scotland the practice continued until 1976, although bad weather and fixture rearrangements meant that only two of the games originally scheduled went ahead on the day. The last time a full set of Christmas Day fixtures was played in Scotland was in 1971.

Boxing Day matches have a different feel about them, no doubt partly a consequence of the amount of food and drink consumed the previous day by the spectators. Crowds are usually higher than normal, and teams are usually spared a long journey – the Boxing Day fixtures are the only ones that are hand-picked rather than spat out of a computer – so there is often an element of local rivalry. Actual derbies are rare, though. Clubs know they can expect a decent crowd on 26 December anyway so prefer to keep their highest gate of the season for another day.

A while ago, however, it was traditional that clubs would play home and away against the same teams over the festive period, with the players even travelling on the same trains for the reverse fixtures. And some of the scores suggested that the visiting teams were none too pleased to be spending the holiday on the road.

For example, on Boxing Day 1963, Burnley beat Manchester United 6-1 at Turf Moor and Fulham beat Ipswich Town 10-1 at Craven Cottage. Blackburn Rovers bucked the trend of heavy away defeats, beating West Ham 8-2 at Upton Park.

But two days later, all those results were reversed. West Ham won 3-1 at Ewood Park, Manchester United beat Burnley 5-1 at Old Trafford, and Ipswich beat Fulham 4-2 at Portman Road.

"There always used to be strange results at Christmas," Alan Mullery, a Fulham player that year, later recalled. "It was something you just couldn't get the gist of. You could win heavily and lose heavily." He is not kidding. Five teams have conceded ten or more on Boxing Day, and Wolves lost 10-3 away to Hull City on 27 December 1919, so their Christmas must have been especially merry.

* * * * *

The explanation for the goal avalanches in matches at other times of the year is less obvious. The Premier League record high score was Portsmouth's 7-4 victory over Reading on 29 September 2007, which must have been a major, and pleasant, surprise to the home fans. Portsmouth failed to score in ten of their home games that season, and both their previous and their next home games were goalless draws.

Reading were a slightly different case. They drew a blank seven times on their travels that season, their second in the Premier League, but also scored four on three occasions – at Portsmouth, a 6-4 loss at Tottenham in another goalfest, and a 4-0 win at Derby on the final day of the season. They had to win that game to have a chance of staying up, but went down when relegation rivals Fulham won 1-0 – at Portsmouth.

That afternoon, though, was one of collective madness. Chris Kamara, who was at Fratton Park for Sky Sports' *Soccer Saturday*, was not the only witness who lost count. International defenders lost their heads, with Ívar Ingimarsson of Iceland and England's Sol Campbell scoring own goals, Portsmouth centre-half Sylvain Distin popping up on the left wing to cross for left-back Hermann Hreidarsson to score from a central striker's position, and goalkeeper David James nearer the corner flag than the posts when he lost the ball for Reading forward Dave Kitson to score from the tightest of angles. Zimbabwe striker Benjani scored a hat-trick and it would have been 7-5 if James had not saved a penalty by Nicky Shorey.

Managers hate the randomness of high-scoring games, and Harry Redknapp of Portsmouth delivered his verdict – that he'd rather watch such a match than a 1-0 – through gritted teeth. Reading boss Steve Coppell said: "It's difficult to analyse a match like that and if you try you will be there a very long time. Both sets of strikers looked irresistible at times going forward but both sets of defenders will be unhappy at that scoreline."

'Embarrassing' was the word Shorey chose. "We've let everyone down, mainly ourselves," he said. "The fans who came to support us today will go away thinking the worst, and you wouldn't blame them. I wouldn't like to single out the defence. Everyone makes out that it's just the back four and the goalkeeper but it's a team thing, defending, we've got to take it as a collective."

Nice try, son. Kitson, watching his defence's antics with obvious disbelief, described the match as "ludicrous" and "insane". His remark to BBC Radio Berkshire that "You can't be everywhere at once and I get paid to score the goals" hinted that he felt that the forwards had done their jobs rather better than the rearguards, but he added: "You just have to say it's a freak game. Two teams clash every now and again with contrasting styles and the outcome is fireworks, and that's what happened today."

Reading, though, would also play a part in another high-scoring match, a League Cup tie that featured one of the greatest comebacks in recent football history. Not that they would necessarily want to be reminded of their collapse in Arsenal's 7-5 victory at the Madejski Stadium on 30 October 2012.

The Royals cannot have felt too optimistic before kick-off. They had faced the Gunners nine times and lost on each occasion. But Jason Roberts, an own goal by Laurent Koscielny, Mikele Leigertwood (with help from a dreadful error by Arsenal goalkeeper Damian Martinez) and Noel Hunt put Reading 4-0 up after only 37 minutes.

Theo Walcott pulled one back in first-half injury time, and Johan Djourou made it 4-2 just past the hour, but it still looked as though the home side had done enough as the score remained unchanged as the game entered the 89th minute.

But then Koscielny made amends for his earlier aberration with a header and, after the fourth official had held up a board indicating that there would be four minutes of added time, the clock showed 95 minutes as Shorey blocked Walcott's shot on the goal line with his arm and Carl Jenkinson knocked in the rebound.

It seemed that momentum was now with Arsenal in extra time and Marouane Chamakh put them ahead for the first time, but Reading's Pavel Pogrebnyak headed in with five minutes left to make it 5-5. Sadly for Reading, they could not turn the match back their way and with penalties looming, Walcott restored Arsenal's lead after Shorey had cleared off the line again –

legitimately this time – from Andrey Arshavin. Incredibly, there was still time for Chamakh to break away and lob a seventh.

"It was that goal just before half-time," was the somewhat baffling explanation of Reading manager and former Arsenal player Brian McDermott. "I wasn't comfortable at 4-1, I don't know why. What happened tonight was extraordinary. I've never seen anything like it from the team at Reading. I'm absolutely gutted, I can't say I'm not."

Arsenal manager Arsène Wenger must have sympathised because he and his team had let a four-goal lead slip in a Premier League match against Newcastle United the previous season. Arsenal led 4-0 after 26 minutes but Abou Diaby was sent off after becoming irritated by Twitter's philosopher prince Joey Barton and Newcastle believed again. Barton converted two penalties either side of a goal by Leon Best and Cheick Tioté's stunning late volley from 25 yards completed the Toon revival.

If it is any consolation to Reading, Huddersfield Town once scored six and still lost. On 21 December 1957, they were 5-1 up in the second half of their match away to Charlton Athletic, who had only ten players after their captain, England centre-half Derek Ufton, had broken his collarbone early in the game. But Charlton's Johnny Summers turned the game on its head.

The match was a last chance for Summers, who had been struggling so badly for form that Charlton manager Jimmy Trotter had contemplated dropping him. On his first-half performance his days at The Valley might still have been numbered, but now, with Charlton 2-0 down at half-time, Trotter moved him from inside-left to centre-forward. Although Summers scored, with his less-favoured right foot, it seemed destined to be nothing more than a consolation as the visitors knocked in three more.

But Summers scored a second, laid on another for John Ryan, then scored another three himself to put the Addicks 6-5 ahead. Perhaps exhausted by their efforts, Charlton allowed

Huddersfield an equaliser, but Summers was plainly not going to settle for a point and set up Ryan to score his second and the winner with the last kick of the match.

Summers, a former Fulham, Norwich City and Millwall winger, who worked part time as a compositor in Fleet Street to supplement his maximum-wage income, changed into new boots at half-time and said: "I have never scored a goal with my right foot before. Today I got all five with my right."

Huddersfield's collapse was especially unexpected because they were managed by a certain Bill Shankly, and included Ray Wilson at left-back, one of the greats in his position, who went on to win the World Cup with England in 1966 – although 17-year-old prospect Denis Law was rested. "It was pure madness, and few people in the crowd could keep up with the score," Wilson recalled. "Even we players were asking each other 'What's the score?'"

Our old friends Ian Wright and West Ham were on the wrong end of a slightly less dramatic comeback at that home of strange games, the Boleyn, on 9 September 1998. It was actually Wright's first appearance there in claret and blue after moving across London from Arsenal and looked like being a dream debut when he scored his first and second goals for his new club to add to John Hartson's opener and open up a 3-0 lead after only 27 minutes.

Even when Marcus Gayle pulled one back in the 30th minute, there seemed no danger. Then in the 64th minute, a defensive error by Chile defender Javier Margas allowed Jason Euell to reduce the arrears to 3-2, Gayle levelled in the 77th minute and four minutes later substitute Efan Ekoku won it for the visitors. "You wouldn't have thought it was possible," said Hammers manager Harry Redknapp. Joe Kinnear of Wimbledon claimed he had never doubted it.

Rivalling Upton Park as the home of the lost lead is White Hart Lane. Tottenham managed to squander a three-goal and one-man advantage there against Manchester City in the FA Cup fourth round on 4 February 2004. Spurs led 3-0 at the break and City's Joey Barton – another name that just keeps cropping up – was sent off. But Tottenham still allowed City back into the game and Jon Macken scored a dramatic late goal to give them a 4-3 victory.

It was only fair that Spurs gifted City a win, though, having done the same for their rivals Manchester United on 29 September 2001. Again Spurs went in at half-time 3-0 to the good, and so dominant had they been that an internet gambler based in Blackpool put £10,000 on them at odds of 1/16, in order to net £625 – not bad for 45 minutes' work. But any Tottenham fan would have warned him what to expect, and, sure enough, they allowed United back into the game with a vengeance. It finished Spurs 3 United 5.

Of course it is one thing to blow a lead in a league game and another to do it on British football's biggest club stage of all. That was what Bolton Wanderers did at Wembley on 2 May 1953 in the FA Cup Final, although the occasion is better remembered for the exploits of their opponents, Blackpool, especially Stanley Matthews, who, at 38, was playing in his third cup final after two previous defeats.

It was a classic game that featured some of the game's biggest names – Nat Lofthouse, who had already scored in every round, put Bolton ahead and fellow England striker Stan Mortensen equalised. Bolton left-half Eric Bell tore his hamstring and was a virtual passenger with no substitutes allowed but the Trotters still took a 3-1 lead, captain Willie Moir distracting Blackpool goalkeeper George Farm to allow Bobby Langton's cross to drift in and Bell, despite his injury, limping into the right place to head the third from Douglas Holden's cross.

Bolton had done well considering that, according to David Tossell's book *The Great English Final*, the Duke of Edinburgh had remarked that their shiny rayon shirts made them 'look like a bunch of pansies'. But the momentum shifted when Bolton keeper Stan Hanson flapped at a centre from Matthews and Mortensen was there to knock it in. Mortensen levelled three minutes from time with a thunderous 20-yard free kick.

"Here's a man who's really fighting for his cup medal," said commentator Kenneth Wolstenholme as Matthews led a last charge. "Could he score the winning goal now, himself?" No, but the wing wizard crossed for Bill Perry to smash home the winner. "It's there!" yelled Wolstenholme, before adding, almost as an aside: "Perry ... Perry" in the relieved tones of a man who had kept completely quiet about Langton's goal, probably, in the days before replays, having no idea where the ball had come from. The game, the subject of one of the first mass-audience sporting TV broadcasts with many televisions having been bought or rented by many households for the forthcoming Coronation, has gone down in legend as The Matthews Final, which – and Matthews himself agreed – is harsh on Mortensen, the only man to score a hat-trick in an FA Cup final. Indeed, when Mortensen died in 1991, Matthew Engel of the *Guardian* remarked: "They'll probably call it The Matthews Funeral."

* * * * *

Bolton and Blackpool belong to a bygone age when town teams battled for the game's major honours. Nowadays money talks and the big city clubs tend to monopolise the trophies. That being the case, and even more so in Scotland, you would think that the same pairs of teams would contest the League and FA Cup finals most years.

But in England it has happened only once, in 1993, and it was not the pairing you would expect – Arsenal beat not Manchester United or Chelsea, but Sheffield Wednesday in both finals. And in Scotland, where you might expect Celtic and Rangers to have contested every major final for long periods, it has occurred only three times. As in England, the last time the same clubs met in both matches was in 1992/93, when Rangers beat Aberdeen 2-1 in both finals. The previous two occasions were both Old Firm Cup Final doubles, in 1965/66 and 1970/71, and in both seasons each club took one trophy.

The Arsenal-Wednesday League Cup final was notable for being the first in which squad numbers were used, as a trial for the following season, when they were introduced in the Premier League. It also boasted the first goal scored in a major Wembley final by an American, John Harkes giving Wednesday the lead after only eight minutes.

But Arsenal hit back through Paul Merson and Steve Morrow, who suffered one of the most bizarre of injuries during the post-match celebrations. Arsenal captain Tony Adams attempted to hoist Morrow on his shoulders but dropped him, breaking the unfortunate Morrow's arm. While his teammates went up to lift the trophy and receive their medals, Morrow was being taken to hospital and receiving only oxygen. He was eventually presented with his medal before the FA Cup final.

That, of course, was not the first time a celebration by a Gunners defender had attracted the wrong sort of headlines. Irish left-back Sammy Nelson was fined and suspended in 1979 after dropping his shorts in front of the North Bank at Highbury and showing the fans, er, his Arsenal after equalising at home to Coventry City. The story goes that he had been barracked after scoring an own goal to put the Sky Blues ahead and this was what you might call a cheeky riposte.

The authorities were more relaxed in 2007, when Stephen Ireland of Manchester City celebrated his winning goal in a match against Sunderland by revealing a pair of blue underpants bearing a (very small) Superman logo. The FA settled for 'reminding him of his responsibilities to the game'. And perhaps pointing out that Superman wears red underpants.

But back to 1993, and Arsenal became the first English club to win a domestic cup double when they also beat Wednesday in the FA Cup final, 2-1 in a replay after a 1-1 draw – the last time the FA Cup final would go to a replay, penalties being decreed after extra time to decide the winners on the day from 1999 onwards.

Ian Wright gave Arsenal the lead in both games. David Hirst equalised in the first match, Chris Waddle in the second.

And with the replay one minute away from being decided on penalties, central defender Andy Linighan headed Arsenal's winner. Okay, as goals from centre halves go, it was not exactly up there with Alvin Martin's hat-trick, or Chris Nicholl's unique foursome, but it gave him and his teammates unique pairs of cup-winners' medals.

Finally, a word about Bournemouth's 10-0 victory over Northampton Town in Division Three (South) on 3 September 1939, the Cherries' record league victory. Well, it would have been if not for a slice of bad luck. The Second World War broke out the next day and all results for the 1939/40 season were declared void.

4.

Gentlemen and Players

"If there wasn't such a thing as football, we'd all be frustrated footballers."

former Everton and Sheffield Wednesday
captain Mick Lyons

THE ability to kick or head a football in vaguely the right direction has made stars out of people who would otherwise struggle to become household names in their own households. But other players are the sort of characters who, you suspect, might have made a bit of a name for themselves in other fields.

Players are sometimes referred to in terms of other professions. They pass the ball with surgical precision, or they are ball artists or midfield generals. Everton was the School of Science. There is a danger of getting carried away. Bill Shankly once said of Dixie Dean, the former Everton forward, "He belongs in the company of the supremely great, like Shakespeare, Rembrandt and Beethoven." Who knows what superlatives Shanks would have reached for if Dean had played for his beloved Liverpool?

And some players get a little carried away with themselves. Paul Ince insisted on being called 'The Guv'nor,' and David Seaman used to add the words 'Safe Hands' when he signed autographs (the same safe hands that Ronaldinho's free kick drifted over in the 2002 World Cup quarter-final between England and Brazil).

Emmanuel Adebayor said of his many moves that "I know that everywhere I go I have the door open because I'm a great footballer and a great person." In 2008 Nicolas Anelka compared himself to "Zinedine Zidane – a humble guy who just happens to be the best."

In 2012 Mario Balotelli confided: "When I decide to score, I score. I think I'm a genius. The talent God gave me is beautiful, magnificent. I also believe I'm more intelligent than the average person." Would that be the average person who lets off fireworks in his bathroom, or the one who was caught on camera struggling to find the arm holes in a training bib?

Perhaps the most ambitious boast was Paolo Di Canio's claimed that he was "so exciting – each time I play the fans want to have sex with me." But life with Di Canio was just a bit too exciting for some managers, which could be why he never played for any one of the leading clubs in the Premier League. Both Chelsea and Manchester United contemplated bids for the Italian, but in the end his career in Britain was a grand tour of Celtic, Sheffield Wednesday, West Ham United and Charlton Athletic.

Wednesday paid Celtic £3 million for Di Canio in the summer of 1997 but only 18 months later let West Ham have him for around half that amount. Not bad for a player of undoubted skill and charisma with an unparalleled work ethic – who would have commanded a fee ten times as large if he had not also been one of the most volatile and unpredictable of men.

It was typical that Di Canio grew up in the working-class Quarticciolo area of Rome where supporting AS Roma was the norm among the left-leaning locals but chose instead to follow Lazio, whose fans are traditionally more right-wing. He played for his boyhood heroes, then Juventus, Napoli and Milan, falling out with pretty well every coach he played for, including Giovanni Trapattoni and Fabio Capello.

He moved to Celtic in July 1996 and won the Scottish Player of the Year award but was also sent off in the dressing room after an altercation during an Old Firm derby and fell out with chairman Fergus McCann. After demanding a large pay rise, he was sold to Sheffield Wednesday for £4.2 million and became a fans' favourite, but at various times fell out with David Pleat, Ron Atkinson and most of his teammates. Then, after being sent off in a match against Arsenal in September 1998, he pushed referee Paul Alcock to the ground and was suspended for 11 matches.

Enter West Ham and manager Harry Redknapp, who saw an opportunity to acquire talent on the cheap. But it still came at the cost of shredded nerves, as when the Italian asked to be substituted in a home game against Bradford City because the referee refused to award a penalty for persistent fouls on him. Then rushed back to wrestle the ball from Frank Lampard when the official finally pointed to the spot.

Yet there were great moments such as his goal-of-the-season volley against Wimbledon and his winning goal at Old Trafford against Manchester United in the FA Cup. Redknapp described in his autobiography how Di Canio was the most diligent of trainers and would complain if a player took three touches in a game of two-touch. It may not be widely known, but one of Di Canio's skills is mimicry. He does a very good Fabio Capello and a surprisingly excellent Redknapp.

When Di Canio's time was up at West Ham, he had a number of suitors, but Alan Curbishley of Charlton Athletic secured his signature by playing on the Italian's emotions. He sat him down and played him a DVD of the club's struggles to rebuild The Valley and its eventual homecoming. "When I saw the first tear trickle down his face I knew I had him," Curbishley said.

In 2001 he received the FIFA Fair Play Award for his actions in catching the ball rather than attempting a shot on goal as Everton goalkeeper Paul Gerrard lay on the ground in a match at Goodison. What a shame that such a great character was also a fascist.

He eventually went back to Lazio, where a trio of Axis-style straight-armed salutes got the avowed fan of Benito Mussolini into trouble with FIFA. The Italian FA banned him for one match and fined him £7,000 but Sepp Blatter, that paragon of the football virtues, thought that a life ban would be more appropriate. However, Il Duce's granddaughter Alessandra Mussolini thought his 'Roman' salute 'delightful'.

Of course, had Di Canio been a journeyman left-back, none of this would ever have troubled the headline-writers. But skill with a football elevates a very naughty boy to the level of a messiah and makes a bit of a joker into a maverick comedy genius. Take that other former Lazio player, Paul Gascoigne.

The Geordie genius's tears in the 1990 World Cup semi-final enchanted a nation and led to some behaviour being pardoned and indulged as Gazza being funny when the warning signs of some seriously self-destructive tendencies and actual psychological disorders could have been picked up. If the hyped-up Gascoigne had been booked for a barmy high challenge in the early moments of the 1991 FA Cup final between Tottenham Hotspur and Nottingham Forest, he might not have launched into the rash, mistimed tackle on Gary Charles that ruptured his own knee ligaments and meant that he collected his winner's medal in hospital.

But it was not just himself that Gazza was a danger to. He became good friends with Vinnie Jones, the Wimbledon hard case whose most memorable encounter with Gascoigne was in an FA Cup tie against Newcastle United immortalised in the famous photo of Jones grabbing Gazza's groin. "Talk about nearly losing your family allowance," Gascoigne later said on *Good Morning Britain*, before revealing that he had nearly gained an inadvertent revenge on the Wales midfielder in a scene that would have given a knew meaning to the title of Jones' film *Lock, Stock and Two Smoking Barrels*.

The two went clay pigeon shooting and Gascoigne, thinking that his shotgun was fully discharged, nearly shot Jones in the stomach. "If he'd have been that much closer he would have been gone," Gascoigne said. "Imagine that, 'Gazza gets his own back!' Knowing Vinnie he would have just got up and just [shaken] himself off, honestly he froze and I froze. I dropped the gun and he just stood there for a bit and said: 'It'd be a good idea if I take that off you.'"

* * * * *

The friendship between Jones and Gascoigne was an attraction of opposites. Gazza's story was of talent unfulfilled, Jones's of a medium amount of skill going a long way. The skill, of course, was heavily disguised. He was forever characterised as a 'former hod-carrier' and famed for the quickest booking in league history, after three seconds for a foul on Dane Whitehouse when playing for Chelsea against Sheffield United in an FA Cup tie at Stamford Bridge on 2 March 1992. Jones argued in his autobiography that it could not have been a late tackle. "I must have been too high, too wild, too strong or too early, because, after three seconds, I could hardly have been too bloody late!"

Close scrutiny of video of the Blades' visit to Manchester City in a league game on 19 January 1991 suggests that not much more time had elapsed when Jones, then with the Sheffield club, ploughed into an opponent, although the time of the booking from referee David Elleray was timed at five seconds. He was sent off 12 times in his career.

Mind you, even Jones could not match the feats of Walter Boyd of Swansea or Keith Gillespie of Sheffield United – yes, them again – in being sent off in zero seconds. In 1997 Boyd came on as a substitute after a free kick was awarded to Swansea in a match against Darlington, got into an altercation with opponent Martin Gray, and was sent off before the kick could be taken. In 2007, Gillespie came on as a sub for the Blades at Reading and gave Stephen Hunt a forearm smash before play could resume.

Anyway, there was more to Vinnie than violence. Opponents and rival fans might not like him, but Jones was not an outright villain. He was a favourite with teammates and supporters wherever he played: Wimbledon, Leeds United, Sheffield United, Chelsea, Wimbledon again and finally QPR. He also played nine times for Wales. He won the FA Cup with Wimbledon in 1988 and helped Leeds win promotion back to the old First Division in 1990. He topped a *Yorkshire Evening Post* poll as Leeds' all-time cult hero.

Jones's part in that Cup Final victory has gone down in legend for helping to intimidate opponents Liverpool in the players' tunnel before the game and on the pitch once it had started. But a Liverpool player laughs at the first suggestion.

"History is written by the winners," Liverpool's John Barnes told the *Daily Telegraph* in 2015 before the two clubs met again in another FA Cup tie. "That Liverpool side was vastly experienced, many had played in European finals, the idea that we would have been upset by a bit of verbals is absurd.

"Yes, Fash and Jones and a couple of others were noisy in the tunnel. They always were. But they were not the only team who were loud and aggressive in that era. We knew they were like that, we had heard them in dressing room when we had played them previously, we were used to it. It did not intimidate us one iota. There was no way with the experience we had in that team we would have been scared. Actually, I remember smiling at them in the tunnel, thinking at the time it was water off a duck's back. We lost because we did not play well."

It is also widely remembered that Jones won the game's first tackle against Steve McMahon in the opening seconds and that the midfield was Wimbledon's after that. "At 3.01pm

Vinnie went in for a tackle with Steve McMahon and that was the key moment," John Fashanu said later. "The tackle started at his throat and ended at his ankle. That was the game won; psychologically we had made our mark."

The facts are somewhat different. The first bad foul of the match was actually committed by McMahon on Dennis Wise after six minutes. Eight minutes had elapsed when Jones slid in on McMahon after the Liverpool man had played the ball past him. But Liverpool did not look particularly daunted. Jones had to clear off the line after Dave Beasant had half-saved a shot by John Aldridge and Peter Beardsley had a goal controversially ruled out when the referee decided against playing an obvious advantage. If that had stood, then who would have been writing the history?

But Wimbledon won, and Leeds paid £600,000 to take Jones to Elland Road where Gordon Strachan told him to cut out the rough stuff and prove that he could play. Which he did, collecting only three bookings all season, and becoming the Leeds squad's social organiser, dictating where post-match dinners would be held.

Every generation, though, has its comedians and hard men. A 19th-century version of Gazza was Charlie Athersmith, although with more medals and fewer off-field problems. He was one of the fastest wingers of his day and a serial winner. He scored a hat-trick on his debut for Aston Villa against Wolves and in ten years at Villa Park he won the League title five times, the FA Cup twice, the double in 1887, and 12 England caps at a time when the national team never played more than three matches a year.

His partnership on the right with John Devey, the captain, was legendary and would often result in Athersmith crossing accurately for a teammate to score. It was while stationed on the wing during a match against Sheffield United played in driving sleet that induced mild frostbite in some players that he accepted the offer of an umbrella from a member of the crowd and played the rest of the match holding it, even scoring a goal.

In a book titled *Pinnacle of the Perry Barr Pets,* author Simon Page wrote: "Such an incident would perfectly fit Charlie's personality. There was a cheeky humour about the man and he could actually have crucified any defence while wearing a three-piece suit, bowler hat and carrying a briefcase to match his umbrella."

The Villa website told Marc Albrighton, who was then the successor to Athersmith's right-wing berth. "To be fair, that's an amazing story," he said. "I'd love to see Gabby Agbonlahor's face if he looked up to check out one of my crosses and saw me getting ready to curl one in under a brolly!"

In the 1940s and '50s there was Len Shackleton, whose autobiography, *The Clown Prince of Soccer*, included a chapter entitled 'The average director's knowledge of football'. The heading appeared above a blank page. Like Gascoigne, Shackleton did not accumulate nearly as many honours as he should have.

The Sunderland team he played in for over ten years entertained but won nothing, and his approach to the game meant that he was never picked to play in a World Cup, although a goal in a 3-1 friendly victory over reigning champions West Germany in 1954, an exquisite chip over the goalkeeper, showed that he had the talent. One England selector, asked why Shackleton had not won more caps, answered: "because we play at Wembley stadium, not the London Palladium." Manager Walter Winterbottom said: "If only Len would come halfway to meet the needs of the team there wouldn't be many to touch him."

He would beat defenders by playing a one-two off the corner flag, sit or stand on the ball, feign boredom by pretending to comb his hair or look at his watch, and put so much spin on the ball that his passes would come back to him like a yo-yo.

When he was finished humiliating defenders, he might do the same to teammates. In his obituary of Shackleton in the *Guardian*, Brian Glanville wrote: "Shackleton took a malign delight in giving [Wales international forward Trevor] Ford what appeared to be perfect passes, which, in fact, had such a fiendish bias on them that the ball was impossible to control; back-spun chips which defied mastery."

An early 20th-century template for Vinnie Jones was Frank Barson. But while Jones played gangsters in his post-football movie career, Barson was not only a true hard man but the gangsters in his life were also real ones. He is said to have taken a gun into negotiations over his contract later in his career, and counted convicted murderers Lawrence and William Fowler, the leaders of a Sheffield razor gang, among his circle. "These are the sort of friends you need," he is reported to have boasted to a teammate before one match, producing a good-luck telegram sent from the Fowler brothers' condemned cell.

Barson's name is not widely remembered these days but the centre-half commanded a British record fee of £2,850 when Aston Villa signed him from Barnsley in the autumn of 1919, and they got their money's worth. Villa were bottom of the First Division at the time but finished the season in mid-table and won the FA Cup for a record sixth time, beating Huddersfield Town 1-0 at Stamford Bridge.

The Sheffield-born former apprentice blacksmith's debut for Barnsley had been delayed for several weeks after he was suspended for brawling with Birmingham City players in a pre-season friendly. And his tackling in a cup tie away to Everton resulted in him having to be smuggled out of Goodison Park to avoid a crowd of Toffees fans waiting to remonstrate with him. His reputation was such that 1920 Cup final referee Jack Howcroft warned him about his behaviour in the dressing room *before* the match.

He also had problems with authority off the field. His move to Villa came after he fell out with the Barnsley board over travelling expenses. He insisted on living near Sheffield while playing for Villa, even after he missed a rail connection and had to walk seven miles to a game at Old Trafford, and the club suspended him for a fortnight for missing a match against Bolton following more trouble on the trains. When a director objected to him inviting a friend into the dressing room, he was suspended for a week and put in a transfer request.

But he was a top-class player, especially strong in the air – as a goal headed in from 30 yards would suggest – despite suffering a broken nose on five occasions. He was also a fierce tackler and ruthless exponent of the shoulder charge. "I'd been brought up to play hard and saw nothing wrong with an honest-to-goodness shoulder charge," he said of what became known as his 'Barson bruisers'.

He was a natural choice as captain, although it was suggested that nobody fancied arguing with him when he decided he wanted the job. Yet he won only one England cap, and the suspicion was that the FA did not want a man of his reputation in the team.

He moved on to Manchester United in 1922 for £5,000, a record for a defender, and became known for his leadership despite a series of injuries, helping the club to promotion from the Second Division in 1925.

He was given ownership of a pub as a reward but did not like the publicity it attracted on opening night and gave it to his head waiter instead.

Nor did opponents like him, and after Chelsea lost to United on New Year's Day 1925, an unsigned statement was released to the press, believed to be from the London club, that read: "A certain footballer has long been under almost constant suspicion. There cannot remain any doubt that he should be. Opponents who have played against him have tired of his never-ceasing wrongdoing and there is a movement afoot to send a petition to the authorities in order to prevent the player from crocking others."

Perhaps this influenced the authorities to take what is believed to be the first retrospective action against a player after Barson clashed with Manchester City's Sam Cowan in an FA Cup semi-final at Bramall Lane. Cowan was left unconscious by what was variously described as a barge and a punch and although the referee booked him, FA Councillors watching the match decided that further action was required and Barson was later suspended for two months.

He joined Watford in May 1928, and his reputation preceded him. A teammate was sent off in his first game by a referee who mistook him for Barson. In September Barson himself was sent off for a foul on Jimmy Temple in a match against Fulham and the FA decided to make an example of him, suspending him for seven months – effectively the rest of the season – even though players on both sides spoke up for him and John Kilby, the Watford chairman, made the point that a player had recently hit a referee and only drawn a three-month ban. "I asked to be given a hearing but this was refused," complained Barson. "The most I had ever dreamed of was a month's suspension and the FA's decision is a terrible blow."

But the FA were adamant despite a 4,850-strong petition sent in by Watford fans and personally delivered by the mayor of the town, Alderman T Rushton. When the alderman was presented with evidence of Barson's disciplinary record, of which he admitted he had previously known nothing, he told the FA to destroy the petition, which was burned in his presence. The fans tried again, collecting 15,000 signatures this time, but to no avail.

Watford released Barson from his contract, and he became player-coach at Hartlepool before ending his playing career at Wigan Borough. His final act as a league footballer was to take an early bath, sent off in his final match. It's what he would have wanted.

* * * * *

You might assume that a player with Barson's qualities would have had to tone down the aggression to make any sort of career in modern football, with its far stricter disciplinary standards. But Roy Keane managed quite well.

Keane had many footballing qualities, and he won seven League titles, four FA Cups and three doubles with Manchester

United and a Scottish League title and League Cup with Celtic at the end of his career, as well as the double of Footballer of the Year and PFA Player of the Year in 2000.

But the Nottingham Forest, Manchester United, Celtic and Ireland midfield player will be chiefly remembered for his rage – icy at times, and completely uncontrolled at others. According to teammate Ryan Giggs, his nickname at United was Damien, after the character in *The Omen*. He even managed to make walking the dog into an act of aggression.

His faithful Golden Labrador retriever, Triggs, was the safety valve when the pressure built up, especially after he had walked out of the Ireland World Cup camp in Saipan in 2002, striding through a crowd of photographers outside his home in Hale with Triggs at his side to pound the local countryside. Woe betide any landowner who had chosen to block a path chosen by Keane and companion.

Triggs, whose death was wrongly announced in 2010, published an autobiography in 2012, with the help of Irish writer Paul Howard, shortly before departing for that big kennel in the sky for real.

It revealed that the four-footed member of the team was a hypochondriac and a fan of TV military history programmes who also gave Keane tactical advice on their long strolls around Cheshire.

"They've got him wrong, after all. I'm talking about the caricature with which you're no doubt familiar. The monster. The permanently angry man. The brooding depressive with no friends. He's none of those things. Take it from me – the dog who's been at his side for thirteen years, the dog I once saw described as 'the most terrified-looking pet in England' – that they are wrong, wrong, wrong.

"Wrong about Roy Keane. Wrong about me. You'd think that on the day the national press decided to try to kill and bury me, they could have got right the one fact that should have been obvious to the human eye and is not exactly irrelevant in the context of an obituary. I'm a girl."

Manchester United fans who watched every minute that Keane played may remember him differently, and even fully paid-up members of the Anyone-But-United club will recall his performance in dragging the team into the 1999 Champions League final from 2-0 down against Juventus in the semi-final even though he knew he would miss the match himself through suspension. "It was the most emphatic display of selflessness I have seen on a football field," manager Sir Alex Ferguson said. "Pounding over every blade of grass, competing as if he would rather die of exhaustion than lose, he inspired all around him."

But for most, the enduring images of Keane will be of him walking off after any one of 11 red cards for violent challenges such as a knee-high, studs-up revenge attack on Alf-Inge Haaland, made somehow more brutal in retrospect by the description of it in his book (toned down in the later paperback editions): "I'd waited long enough. I fucking hit him hard. The ball was there (I think). Take that you c***. And don't ever stand over me sneering about fake injuries."

That sort of bluntness – without the asterisks – has made Keane a popular TV pundit (except with Manchester United's in-house channel, MUTV, who pulled an interview on Ferguson's orders after Keane criticised teammates, including Rio Ferdinand, saying: "Just because you are paid £120,000 a week and play well for 20 minutes against Tottenham, you think you are a superstar.") Yet even the Anglo-Saxon expletives (perhaps selected by ghost-writer Eamonn Dunphy) cannot disguise Keane's undoubted way with words. Would even fellow Irishmen James Joyce or Oscar Wilde have come up with the anatomically-challenging invitation to "stick it up your bollocks" delivered to Ireland manager Mick McCarthy?

And it was Keane who found the two words that became the most memorable description of fans in executive boxes when he said: "They have a few drinks and probably the prawn sandwiches, and they don't realise what's going on out on the pitch. I don't think some of the people who come to Old Trafford can spell 'football', never mind understand it."

A feeling and respect for language prevented Keane from signing Robbie Savage when he was Sunderland manager. "I got Robbie's mobile number and rang him," Keane wrote in his second autobiography, *Roy Keane: The Second Half*. "It went to his voicemail: 'Hi, it's Robbie – whazzup!' – like the Budweiser ad. I never called him back. I thought 'I can't be fucking signing that.'"

Keane's books sold well, but were not popular with everyone. An FA disciplinary tribunal decided that his description of the tackle on Haaland in the first showed that he was 'improperly motivated by an element of revenge' and handed him a five-match suspension and a record £150,000 fine.

The ruling made no judgement on the book's literary merits. That was left to Sunderland midfield player and Keane's former Ireland teammate Jason McAteer, who said: "I'd rather buy a Bob the Builder CD for my two-year-old son." Ouch – everyone's a critic, eh? But not every author gets to meet the critics on a football pitch. A few days later, United visited Sunderland and Keane was sent off for elbowing McAteer in the face.

Man of words, man of action – but perhaps, when he looks back on his life, Keane will consider that his greatest feat was making his beloved Triggs arguably the most famous dog in football. Previously that had been Pickles, the collie that found the Jules Rimet Trophy after it had been stolen before the 1966 World Cup.

The trophy had been on show at an exhibition of rare stamps in Westminster Central Hall in March, and police later received a ransom demand for £15,000 – less than the value of some of the stamps the criminals could have stolen instead. Pickles was being taken for a walk by her owner David Corbett in South Norwood when she sniffed out a package wrapped in newspaper that contained the World Cup. That was the closest any major trophy has ever been to Selhurst Park.

That story had a happy ending, but Brentford goalkeeper Chic Brodie had his career finished in October 1970 by a dog that had run onto the pitch in a match against Colchester United at Layer Road. The dog chased a backpass and collided with Brodie's left leg, damaging knee ligaments. It was clearly a late challenge as Brodie had already picked up the ball, as goalkeepers were then allowed to do.

Although Brodie was able to make five more league appearances, the injury eventually caused him to retire from league football at the end of the 1970/71 season. "The dog might have been a small one, but it just happened to be a solid one," he said. He tried to carry on with Southern League Margate and was between the sticks when Bournemouth beat them 11-0 in the FA Cup a year after the canine assault.

Taking Triggs out for a walk was Keane's way of quietening his inner demons, and other players have filled the long hours after training with a variety of activities. Nolberto Solano of Peru, Newcastle United and Hartlepool played the trumpet. Arsenal goalkeeper Manuel Almunia visited World War II battlefields, while his teammate Andrey Arshavin, a graduate of St Petersburg State University of Technology and Design, went into Victoria Beckham territory by designing his own line of women's fashions.

Paul Scharner of Wigan and West Brom listed parachuting, bungee jumping and skydiving among his interests, and Moritz Volz of Arsenal and Fulham baked cakes, sometimes themed around upcoming opponents. When West Ham's Marco Boogers wanted to get away from it all, he headed home to his caravan. Or did he?

Boogers arrived at Upton Park in July 1995 after scoring 103 goals in 238 league matches in Holland for FC Dordrecht, FC Utrecht, RKC Waalwijk, Fortuna Sittard and Sparta Rotterdam. Harry Redknapp saw a tape of his performances and decided that £800,000 was a good price for a proven goalscorer – and one who had come third in the voting for the Eredivisie player of the season for 1994/1995, in competition against some big names.

Boogers was pencilled in to compete with Iain Dowie for the target man role alongside Tony Cottee, but when he arrived he looked nowhere near robust enough, and an apparent distaste for the rigours of pre-season training hardly helped toughen him up.

Despite a warm welcome from the Boleyn Ground fans, Boogers made little impression on his debut as a substitute at home to Leeds. But the same cannot be said for his second appearance, also as a sub. Soon after coming on against Manchester United at Old Trafford, Boogers competed with Gary Neville for a bouncing ball and his studs made contact with the England defender's ribs in what a certain tabloid newspaper referred to as a 'horror tackle'. Roy Keane and Julian Dicks piled in and Boogers was sent off by Dermot Gallagher, the referee, serenaded off by the West Ham fans, and given a four-match suspension.

Boogers took the opportunity to head back with his homesick and pregnant wife to the Netherlands for a bit, and Hammers fans were shocked to learn that he had not returned to the usual footballer-style mansion when the *Sun* led their back page with the headline: 'Barmy Boogers Gone to Live in a Caravan'.

Sadly, this football legend is actually a myth. Bill Prosser, West Ham's PA announcer, who also handled their travel arrangements, took a call from the Hammers' *Clubcall* reporter, who wanted to interview Boogers and hoped that Prosser would know his whereabouts as the man who booked flights for the club. In this case Prosser had made no such arrangements and said: "If he has gone back to Holland, he's probably gone by car again." The reporter misheard and said on *Clubcall* that Prosser had said: "If he's gone back to Holland, he's probably gone to his caravan."

If the caravan part of *The Sun*'s headline was definitely fiction, 'barmy' could have referred to the fact that Boogers produced a doctor's note that said he had been 'psychologically unfit to play football'. But he failed to win a first-team place from Dowie, and damaged his knee in training. After an operation, Boogers went back to Holland, where his son was born, and was then loaned to Groningen. His contract was cancelled in summer 1996, and he later became technical director at Dordrecht. Presumably his motto is: never sign a player on the strength of a video tape alone.

* * * * *

At least Boogers was who he said he was, unlike Ali Dia.

Graeme Souness was manager of Southampton at the time of Dia's 15 (actually 53) minutes of fame, and brought some good players to the club – for example Egil Østenstad, Eyal Berkovic and Claus Lundekvam. But his radar failed him when he took a call, apparently from George Weah, the AC Milan and Liberia forward and winner of the Ballon d'Or and FIFA Player of the Year. 'Weah' told Souness about his cousin, Ali Dia, a Senegalese international forward, who wanted to play in England.

Dia did enough in one brief cameo for Saints to prove that he was not an international, not related to the real George Weah, and barely qualified to call himself a player. True, he wanted to play in England, but that was about it.

Once a semi-pro and youth team coach with AL Châteaubriant of France's National League Three, Dia – if that was really his name – had ambitions to play at a higher level. He joined FinnPa of Helsinki, in Finland's top division, also semi-professional but paying their top earners a decent whack – and, as Weah's supposed cousin, Dia arranged a decent deal for himself, including a flat paid for by the club. No one ever seems to have asked why Weah's cousin was Senegalese if Weah is Liberian.

After a couple of appearances as a substitute, Dia made his first start in April 1995, which was noteworthy mainly for the number of times he was flagged offside. FinnPa lost 3-1 but Dia somehow kept his place, lasting 46 anonymous minutes before he was substituted. One more sub appearance and he was gone.

"When Ali arrived, he had something," former FinnPa teammate Simo Valakari told *Bleacher Report*. "With the outside of his right foot, he could go round a defender, but that was all he had. After the first two weeks, bam, it was gone. Maybe it was the parties or something, but then he looked like he had never played football at all."

He resurfaced at VfB Lübeck in Germany's Bundesliga II, also taken in by the fictional Weah connection and five goals scored in a trial game, in autumn 1995. Two substitute appearances and no impression later, he was off again, this time to England.

He talked his way into a game for Rotherham reserves against Stockport, but was taken off, and tried his luck with Blyth Spartans of the Northern Premier League. After one sub appearance on 9 November 1996, he pulled another vanishing trick and on 22 November, after someone – perhaps Dia himself, perhaps an agent named Sidiba Alassana – had spoken to Souness, was given international clearance to join Southampton on a one-month contract. The following day he was playing in the Premier League against Leeds United at The Dell.

The local paper had not even mentioned him as a possible to make the squad, but Souness, perhaps desperate after a 7-1 pummelling away to Everton the week before, put him on the bench, and sent him on when Matt Le Tissier pulled a muscle after 32 minutes. He brought him off again after 85. "He joined in the five-a-side on the Friday morning, and was introduced to us as a triallist," Le Tissier told the *Guardian* in 2008. "I remember at the time thinking: 'He's not very good. He's probably not going to make it.'

"Then when we turned up for the game against Leeds the following day, I was amazed to hear that he'd been named on the subs' bench. I think the picture of the faces of the boys must have been remarkable. Our jaws all dropped to the floor.

"His performance was almost comical. He kind of took my place, but he didn't really have a position. He was just wandering everywhere. I don't think he realised what position he was supposed to be in. I don't even know if he spoke English – I don't think I ever said a word to him. In the end he got himself subbed because he was that bad.

"Then it came out that he'd been recommended by someone pretending to be George Weah. It was all a bit embarrassing, and it became a taboo subject with the manager. He had been made to look very, very silly.

"Overall I'd say he's probably the worst player I played with. There are several other candidates, but I don't want to name names."

Saints terminated his contract after only 14 days, which still seems around 12 days too long, and sent him on his way £2,000 richer.

Dia appeared in Port Vale reserves, then for Gateshead, who were happy to have a supposed African international striker and even paid him a £1,500 signing-on fee. "I knew Ali's agent Peter Harrison, a Geordie who had once played central defence alongside Philippe Albert in Belgium," John Gibson, then the Gateshead chairman, said. "Peter was taking Dia over to Carlisle United for a trial but popped in to see me with Souness's tormentor in tow. Ali was quick – lightning quick – and we needed a striker.

"I spoke with my manager and a couple of other directors, then – deciding no one could take Dia at his word – I phoned the police on the south coast and the hotel where our intrepid international footballer had hung his hat. There had been a whisper Ali had made a quick getaway in his car and that his hotel bill had remained unpaid. Anyway, we got all that sorted and decided that on a match-to-match basis we couldn't lose in signing Mr Dia."

Dia scored and created a goal on his debut as Gateshead beat Bath City 5-0. The following day, the *Sunday Mirror* exposed Dia's attempt to pass himself off as a member of the Weah family, but Dia dismissed it to the local paper and claimed that he had recently scored for Senegal against Guinea. Except that no such match had taken place. And if he hoped to keep his place at Gateshead on his own playing merits, he and they were disappointed as he never hit the same heights again. If you can call them heights.

* * * * *

If Southampton can boast one of the worst players ever, they can also claim the scorer of the fastest top-flight hat-trick, Senegal forward Sadio Mané. He hit his treble for Southampton against Aston Villa on 16 May 2015. It took him two minutes and 56 seconds between the 13th and 16th minutes of the 6-1 win, and was also the earliest hat-trick scored in the top division. Mané's treble beat by four seconds the previous record, set by Graham Leggat for Fulham in a club record 10-1 win over Ipswich Town on Boxing Day 1963.

But the fastest hat-trick in all English professional football was scored a few miles along the south coast, by James Hayter of AFC Bournemouth against Wrexham at Dean Court on Tuesday 24 February 2004. It took only two minutes and 20 seconds, which was quite a significant chunk of his time on the field. He had come on as a substitute six minutes from time with the Cherries 3-0 up, but that was too late for his mum and dad, who lived on the Isle of Wight and had already left to get the ferry – and not even the last ferry, as was erroneously reported by many sources at the time.

"My parents, Mary and Richard, still shake their heads about it," Hayter told bbc.co.uk on the tenth anniversary of his feat. "They came to the game, but because I was sub and hadn't got on they left early. They thought they'd get an earlier ferry. I think I came on just after they left, and they were listening in the car to BBC Radio Solent as the goals went in. I spoke to them afterwards and they were pleased, but also very disappointed.

"I was sub on the day because I'd missed the game on the Saturday for the birth [of his son Harris]. I scored with my first touch and two-and-a-half minutes later I had a hat-trick – it was a bit surreal. I didn't realise quite how big it would be until after the game."

Records are made to be broken, they say, but with the lengthy celebrations that follow goals these days, it is hard to see how Hayter's can be. Ditto Steve Finnan's amazing full house of competitions. The Ireland full-back began his career with Welling United, and moved on to Birmingham City and Notts County before signing for Fulham, who were on their way up through the divisions under Kevin Keegan, and then Liverpool. In the process he played in all four English divisions, the Conference, the World Cup, the Champions League Final, the UEFA Cup Final, the FA Cup Final, the League Cup Final, the Club World Cup Final, the Super Cup and the Intertoto Cup.

Equally hard to better must be Fernando Torres' 2012/13 season. The Chelsea striker scored in seven different competitions: the Premier League, Champions League, Europa League, FIFA Club World Cup, FA Community Shield, FA Cup and League Cup.

But some players hold records that they might prefer to have avoided. Clive Allen became the first million-pound teenager when he joined Arsenal from QPR in June 1980, but he never played a minute of competitive football for the Gunners. Manager Terry Neill swapped him for Crystal Palace left-back Kenny Sansom before the beginning of the 1980-81 season.

Allen, though, was by no means the only big-money signing who failed to wear a first-team shirt in anger. Everton defender David Unsworth joined West Ham in summer 1997 and had a successful season in East London, but neither he nor his wife Jayne had wanted to move south in the first place, and he was pleased to hear that Everton were interested in buying him back the following summer. However, when the interest seemed to cool, he agreed to return halfway home, to Aston Villa for £3m, and the family moved into a new house on Merseyside. But the 200-mile return trip from Formby to training proved too much, delays on the M6 causing Mrs Unsworth to throw his dinner in the bin on one occasion.

So when Everton's interest was revived, he told Villa manager John Gregory that he wanted to go. Fortunately the Toffees were willing to match the £3m that Villa had paid, and he left Villa Park with only one pre-season friendly appearance under his belt. Gregory, though, was not too happy, suggesting that Unsworth had failed to look at a map properly before signing and telling reporters: "We all know who wears the trousers in that house."

Iceland defender Hermann Hreidarsson represented seven British clubs and played in 322 Premier League games, but he holds a unique distinction. He played for five different Premier League clubs and was relegated with all of them. Wales striker Nathan Blake is sometimes mentioned in the same breath but while he also dropped out of the top flight five times, he did it with only four different clubs.

First stop, and first drop, for Hreidarsson was Crystal Palace in 1997/98, which was perhaps only to be expected. In the first decade of the Premier League Palace never managed to stay up for more than one season at a time, so anyone who lasted an entire campaign with them would be sure to go down with their sinking ship.

In September 1998 he followed his chairman (and former landlord when he had first come to Britain) Ron Noades to Brentford, who actually won promotion from League Two to League One. In October 1999 he was sold for £2.5 million to Wimbledon, managed by Egil Olsen, who was in the process of losing the dressing room and sending the previously competitive club into freefall, ending their 14-year stay in the top flight.

After that, in summer 2002 it was a £4 million move to Ipswich Town, newly promoted under George Burley, who carried their success into European qualification, with Hreidarsson runner-up in the club's Player of the Year voting to striker Marcus Stewart. Surely there was no chance of another relegation at Portman Road? Actually there was, as poor summer buys and the extra strain of a European campaign on an inadequate squad caused a bad case of second-season syndrome.

By now, the Hreidarsson effect on Premier League clubs was beginning to be noticed, and chairman David Sheepshanks and manager George Burley were forced to defend the indefensible defender. "If Hermann is a jinx then he's the sort of jinx I like to have," Sheepshanks said. "He's been an inspired and super signing for us, not only as a player but as a character at the club."

Burley agreed. "This jinx business wasn't being said last season when we finished fifth in the Premiership and qualified for Europe after promotion. Hermann has done tremendously well for us since he came to the club and has never given less than 100 per cent. His attitude has always been first class and he will play his usual leading role in our battle for survival."

But that battle was lost and the Tractor Boys went down after only two seasons back among the elite. Hreidarsson stayed in Suffolk for a while but moved back to the Premier League with Charlton Athletic for only £900,000 in March 2003. But now things took a turn for the better. The Addicks were surely a fixture in the top flight after years of careful husbandry by Alan Curbishley, and for three seasons the big Icelander seemed to have found a stable and secure home. "Curbishley had done a great job," Hreidarsson said. "We were a stubborn team who could give anyone a game and I always enjoyed that."

But then, in 2006, Curbishley called it a day and, the following season, a combination of Iain Dowie, Les Reed and Alan Pardew landed Charlton in the Championship.

But not Hreidarsson, who escaped in time for the beginning of the 2007/08 season to Portsmouth, where Harry Redknapp was spending Israel-based owner Arkady Gaydamak's shekels putting together a team that would win the FA Cup at the end of the campaign. David James, Sol Campbell, Lassana Diarra, Sulley Muntari – here was one team that surely even Hreidarsson couldn't jinx. And yet it all began to fall apart the following season as warnings that the club could not possibly afford the wages and transfer fees they were splashing out were proved true. The money ran out, the team fell apart, the club went broke – and yes, Portsmouth were relegated, in 2010. Hermann went down for the fifth time.

"With all the clubs I joined they had maybe just come up and I knew there was a challenge ahead. You can only look at yourself and make sure you do your bit. Of course it's a horrible feeling to go down, something you don't want to experience."

* * * * *

Players never used to move around as much. Back around 1969, it was so uncommon that the *Football League Review* ran a cover feature on Frank Large because he moved 11 times and played for eight different clubs (he signed for Northampton Town three times, in case you were wondering).

But nowadays, as players chase one last contract in order to keep themselves in the lifestyle they have become accustomed to, they move on while they can still put one sponsored boot in front of another. Goalkeepers tend to move around the most, as we shall learn in a later chapter, but outfield players are not immune from wanderlust. Marcus Bent, Hreidarsson's teammate at both Ipswich and Charlton, played for 15 different clubs between 1995 and 2011. Other lengthy CVs employer-wise include those of Andy Cole (13), Nicolas Anelka (11) and Robbie Keane and Craig Bellamy (both 10).

The one-club man is increasingly rare, and usually revered. Of all the great players to have represented Chelsea – and in recent years the parade of international footballing talent that has passed through Stamford Bridge has included Ruud Gullit, Gianfranco Zola, Gianluca Vialli, Marcel Desailly and plenty of others – the most-loved performer among the fans is John Terry, the central defender and, for most of his career, captain.

One of the very few to come through to the first team through the Chelsea youth system – perhaps the most pointless organisation since the Swiss navy – Terry has won the Premier League title five times, the FA Cup five times, the League Cup three times and won 78 England caps. The banner the fans display at the Bridge says it all: 'Captain, Leader, Legend.'

Is there space at the end, though, to add 'laughing stock'? Because that was what Terry became immediately after the 2012 Champions League final. Terry did not play in the match, suspended for an inexplicable off-the-ball foul on Alexis Sanchez in the semi-final second leg away to Barcelona which drew a red card and had left the team a man short at the Nou Camp.

Jeopardising a club's place in the biggest club match in world football was not really the action expected of a legend, and you could have excused Terry for wanting to hide away and not attract attention to himself at the final in Munich. Photographs taken before the game show him among the other non-playing squad members, soberly attired in shirt, tie and charcoal trousers.

But after Didier Drogba's penalty in the shoot-out had given Chelsea the trophy for the first time in their history, suddenly there was Terry in full kit, including boots (somehow he had forgotten to don his shin pads), going up to receive a medal and helping captain on the night Frank Lampard to hoist the trophy.

Players wanting to get a share of other people's glory is nothing new. Gary Neville was always mocked for the way he showed a turn of speed that he never equalled when toiling in the wake of a winger when there was a goal celebration to get into, speeding the length of the field in double-quick time to join in a bundle in front of the photographers. But at least he was playing in the same match. Terry had pulled off a transformation worthy of Clark Kent nipping into a phone booth and emerging seconds later as Superman.

Photoshoppers went mad on social media, producing images showing Terry celebrating at Wimbledon, the Last Supper, the first moon landing and the wedding of the Duke and Duchess of Cambridge, and even riding piggyback on Sir Bradley Wiggins as he won his Olympic gold medal in London. Plenty of tweets used the term 'full kit wanker', usually deployed to describe members of the public who go beyond the wearing of a replica shirt and sport the shorts and socks in public too.

Terry later explained his thinking to Jason Burt of the *Daily Telegraph*. "The biggest night ever for the club and I didn't play in it. But I played in one [final in 2008], and I felt a massive part of it [in 2012], and the players made me feel a huge part of it. Along the way you look back at games, like the Napoli game [in the last 16] and other games along the way where you played a big part as well.

"Because it's me, people look and say 'he's not won it', people like to have their digs and their pops, but I know I played a huge part along the way, in the dressing room and on the field as well, so I count myself to have won it. No one speaks about the other ten players who weren't on the pitch that night as well. Maybe that's me and that's where I am at as a player." Maybe that's them staying soberly dressed in their suits.

After all that, Terry had learned his lesson. Oh wait, no he hadn't. Just a year later Chelsea reached the Europa League final, and Terry, injured this time, missed out again. Pre-match he was dressed like a snooker player in waistcoat and shirt, but shortly after the final whistle blew on Chelsea's 2-1 win over Benfica in Amsterdam, there he was once more, in full kit, lifting the trophy.

Some pointed out that, when Manchester United completed their 1999 treble by beating Bayern in Barcelona, suspended players Paul Scholes and Roy Keane remained in their suits; #dignity was the hashtag on some tweets. Which was somewhat undermined when Wayne Rooney, omitted for United's final home game of the 2012/13 season against Swansea City, watched from an Old Trafford executive box in a tracksuit before emerging on the pitch after the final whistle in playing kit to celebrate their title win and collect his medal. He was jeered by sections of the crowd, and not for being a full kit wanker. Just days earlier he had asked for a transfer.

#dignity

5.

Keepy Uppy

"It's not nice going into the supermarket and the woman at the till is thinking: 'Dodgy keeper.'"

David James

THE veteran football writer Brian Glanville said it all in the title of his 1971 children's book: *Goalkeepers Are Different*. Like drummers in bands, they are a vital part of the whole, but do something distinct from what everyone else is doing.

They are also supposed to be crazy. After all, throwing yourself at the feet of charging forwards, sticking your hands in among the flying studs trying to grab a slippery plastic-coated sphere while other people are trying to kick it past you – these are not the actions of a sane person. Thick-skinned too. When almost every mistake you make ends up with the ball in the back of your net, you'd have to have the memory of a goldfish not to let every error prey on your mind – not that the crowd behind the goal will ever give you the chance to forget it.

A goalkeeper can be perfect for 89 minutes and 59 seconds and still cost his team the game, so it is vital that he concentrates even if play is mostly at the other end, because he never knows when he will have to deal with a quick breakaway. Just ask Jens Lehmann, the former Arsenal shot-stopper, who thought he would be safe to take a quick toilet break behind some advertising hoardings during a Champions League tie for Stuttgart against Unirea Urziceni, only having to cut it short when the Romanians launched a rare attack.

Ex-Manchester United keeper Fabien Barthez was less subtle in a UEFA Cup tie between Marseille and Inter Milan in 2007, remaining in his penalty area and, er, irrigating the penalty spot. Willy-nilly, you might say.

Goalkeepers, of course, can be a long way from the action, but outfield players cannot simply leave the field and let their team be caught short, as it were. Eddie Newton, then a Chelsea midfield player, revealed that a teammate had simply let it go in his shorts during a rainy evening game, certain that nobody would notice.

But although they all got away with it, Mansfield Town's Adi Yussuf was banned for five games and fined £700 for relieving himself against a wall at the back of the disused main stand at Plymouth Argyle's Home Park in February 2016. A substitute for the League Two game between the clubs, he suddenly felt the urge while warming up on the touchline and, he said, was guided to this secluded spot by a steward and Plymouth's own subs.

* * * * *

David Icke was a goalkeeper, which may explain a lot. Perhaps it was a bang on the head while diving at a forward's feet that eventually led to the conspiracy theories about a race of lizards disguised as people directing all human operations from the moon.

He grew up in Leicester and idolised Peter Shilton. He had a trial for the Leicester Boys and was spotted by Coventry

City, who signed him in 1967. He had loan spells at Oxford United and Northampton Town before moving to Hereford United, where he made 37 league appearances, helping them win promotion to the old Third Division. But his career was ended by rheumatoid arthritis, which began in his left knee and spread, forcing him to retire in 1973 at only 21.

After that he went into the media and gained a higher profile as a sports reporter and presenter for the BBC than he ever had as a player. But that hardly prepared the world for his announcement on the Terry Wogan TV programme that he was the Son of God, or his subsequent career as a public speaker and writer.

Wogan famously pointed out to Icke that the studio audience was laughing at him, not with him, but it turned out not to have been such a bad career move, establishing him in the public mind as the king of weird.

Icke has gone on to sell hundreds of thousands of copies of his books, many DVDs and to fill theatres and lecture halls everywhere, which not many other former Hereford players can say. Perhaps if Ashley Cole had written about "a group of reptilian humanoids, called the Babylonian Brotherhood, [that] control humanity" or "an extraordinary experience with former prime minister Ted Heath; both of his eyes, including the whites, turned jet black and I seemed to be looking into two black holes," rather than his disappointment at being offered only £55,000 per week to play for Arsenal, he would have shifted more than a few thousand copies of his autobiography.

Goalkeepers are usually big men, but Sheffield United's Willie 'Fatty' Foulke, who played over 300 games around the turn of the century, also appearing for Chelsea and Bradford City, filled more of the goal than most. His height was variously estimated as between 6 feet 2 inches and 6 feet 6 inches – at a time when the average Englishman was 5 feet 5 inches – but it was his width that mattered.

He weighed around 13 stones at the beginning of his career, but hit 22 stones at his peak, making him the heaviest player in England history. But being an immovable object was an advantage in the days when forwards were allowed to shoulder-charge goalkeepers, often attempting to take them into the goal along with the ball. C B Fry, the cricketer, who also played football for Southampton, described Foulke as "no small part of a mountain. You cannot bundle him." During a lull in one match, he swung on the crossbar – and broke it.

Foulke only represented his country once – keeping a clean sheet in a 4-0 win over Wales – but his qualities were proved by his medal collection, which included a League Championship in 1897/98, when United had the best defensive record in the league, and two FA Cup wins, both at Crystal Palace. The first was a 4-1 win over Derby County in 1899 and the second 2-1, after a replay, against Southampton, in 1902. After the first match in 1902, Foulke was so incensed by the referee's decision to allow a Southampton equaliser that, naked, he pursued the official, who had to hide in a broom cupboard rather than confront the angry mountain of flesh.

Some clubs seem to attract a number of great goalkeepers, Manchester City for example. Unkind souls and Manchester United fans would say that they have needed them because of the state of their defending. But between 1933 and 1964 they had two of the greats.

Frank Swift was a showman, who relished his close proximity to the crowds behind the goal and believed they should be entertained. He would drop to his knees to implore referees to change decisions and mime firing a gun at forwards as they charged towards him.

He made his debut on Christmas Day 1933 and ended the season with an FA Cup winner's medal although he had to be revived before he could receive it from King George V, having fainted at the final whistle in the final. "Fancy a strapping fellow like me fainting in front of all those people and the King," he said later. He missed only one league game before the outbreak of World War II and helped City to their first league title in 1937. But, City being City, they managed to get themselves relegated the following season.

He had huge hands and his speciality was catching the ball one-handed and throwing it straight out to a teammate, initiating attacks before the opposition could react. He also analysed his own performances meticulously, drawing diagrams of each goal he had conceded to see if he could have done better.

Those enormous paws made 'Swifty' a natural in a wartime role as a special constable with responsibility for traffic control, although on his first day "I got everything so muddled that, on the advice of a colleague, I walked away leaving the traffic to sort itself out. I felt at that moment how many full-backs must have felt when playing against Stanley Matthews."

After the war, he helped City back to the First Division, keeping 17 clean sheets in 35 appearances as they won the Second Division title. He also made his England debut and even captained the side against Italy in Turin in 1948. After retiring he entered journalism and rose to become football correspondent of the *News of the World* and died in the Munich air crash after covering United's European Cup match against Red Star Belgrade. He retired at 35 and his replacement in the City goal was, improbably, a former member of the Hitler Youth and the Luftwaffe who had been decorated as a paratrooper on the Russian front.

Bert Trautmann was captured in France and ended up in a prisoner-of-war camp in Ashton-in-Makerfield, Lancashire. After the war ended, he decided to stay on, and showed true footballer pedigree by getting his first girlfriend pregnant before joining St Helens Town, where he was spotted by City. Eric Westwood, the City captain, was a Normandy veteran, but he defused what could have been a tricky situation by welcoming him into the dressing room, declaring "There's no war in here, Bert. You're one of the team."

However, there were protests among fans, not least from Manchester's Jewish community, at the arrival at Maine Road of this blond, blue-eyed Aryan but the city's communal rabbi supported him and, as friendly as he was big and brave, Trautmann soon won them over.

The bravery was in evidence in the 1956 FA Cup final against Birmingham City, when he rushed from his line 17 minutes from time as a headed pass dropped between him and Brum's Peter Murphy six yards out and Murphy's knee hit the goalkeeper's neck. Trautmann was momentarily unconscious but with no substitutes allowed in those days, carried on until the final whistle, with what turned out to be a broken neck.

Trautmann had, in fact, received death threats after denying Tottenham Hotspur in the semi-final with a challenge that might have been a penalty, and one irate Spurs fan wrote that he would be standing behind the goal with a gun. As it was, Trautmann came close to losing his life through his own courage.

"The vertebra was broken diagonally but the impact pushed the third one up under the second one and held the two pieces together," Trautmann later explained. "A hundredth of a millimetre and I would have been either dead or paralysed, one of the two things. I played on in a kind of fog, grey – I didn't see figures, no nothing. I was very, very lucky."

Footage of the final after the collision shows him rubbing his neck before throwing himself at a forward's feet again and staying down momentarily before gamely getting up again, then rushing out to catch a cross under pressure before the trainer comes on again to apply a wet sponge to his neck. Yet he managed to mount the Wembley steps to collect his medal from the Queen, and ride an open-top bus in a parade in Manchester city centre two days later – still unaware of the extent of his injury.

It was not until the Wednesday after the final that Trautmann's injury was X-rayed and the true extent of the damage revealed. He was put in a head-to-waist plaster cast and told he might never play again, but he was back in action by Christmas the following season, as reigning Footballer of the Year, the first goalkeeper and the first foreigner to receive the Football Writers' Association award. Strangely, he was never capped by West Germany.

Goalkeepers are often individualists and comedians, with a ready-made audience at their backs. Gordon West, Everton's keeper for most of the 1960s, developed such a rapport with the Kop over many Merseyside derbies that they paid him the backhanded compliment of presenting him with a handbag before one game at Anfield. But he was also a joker behind the scenes, once nailing full-back Sandy Brown's boots to the Goodison Park dressing-room floor.

Gary Sprake also experienced a memorable moment at Anfield in the 1960s, but not one he remembered with any fondness. The Welshman was a notoriously accident-prone goalkeeper for the Leeds United team of the 1960s and early 1970s that was one of the most skilful of its time, when it wanted to be. Sprake was a good goalkeeper, his fantastic reflexes earning him 37 caps for Wales along with 507 appearances for Leeds.

But Don Revie's team won fewer trophies than it deserved, and Sprake was not blameless, his error in the 1970 FA Cup final allowing Chelsea to score a barely deserved equaliser when Peter Houseman's speculative long-range shot slipped under his dive. His other televised errors included letting a long-range header by Liverpool captain Ron Yeats dribble between his feet at Elland Road and allowing a mishit lob by Crystal Palace right-back John Sewell to slip through his fingers in the last minute of a 1-1 draw at Selhurst Park.

But the gaffe for which he is most remembered was seen only by a crowd at Anfield in a match on 9 December 1967 that was not televised. It was late in the first half on a snowy day and the ball was cold and wet when Sprake picked up a backpass from Jack Charlton – as you were allowed to do back then – at the Kop end. With Leeds 1-0 down, Sprake was looking to start an attack in the hope of grabbing an equaliser before half-time, and he shaped to throw the ball out to left-back Terry Cooper.

Fatally, when he saw Ian Callaghan moving to close Cooper down, he changed his mind and tried to draw the ball back into his body. "It went over my shoulder right into the net in front of 30,000 people and right in front of the Kop," he later told BBC Radio Leeds.

According to an authorised biography of Sprake, "everyone in the ground knew where it landed. This was probably with the exception of the referee, who was said to have turned to Jack Charlton and asked what had happened and what he should do. With typical dry humour Jack replied, 'I think the silly so-and-so has thrown it in his own net; you'll have to give a goal.'"

Urban legend has it that the Kop spontaneously broke out into a chorus of 'Careless Hands', a hit single of the time for comedian and occasional crooner Des O'Connor. The reality is more prosaic – it was the Anfield PA system that played the tune as the teams came off at half-time, followed by 'Thank U Very Much' by local outfit Scaffold. The Kop choir simply reprised both when Sprake emerged for the second half. Oh, and the title of that biography that Sprake helped with? *Careless Hands*.

"I just wanted to dig a hole and bury myself in it," Sprake said much later. "It's unfortunate people will always remember the mistakes rather than the saves. I know in my own mind how many mistakes I made. The facts speak for themselves. I played over 500 games for Leeds and made maybe half a dozen mistakes. That's not bad, is it?"

* * * * *

A nickname says a lot about a goalkeeper. Peter Bonetti was 'The Cat' for his agility. David James, in contrast, was known as 'Calamity'.

By most standards, James was an excellent keeper. Brave, strong and agile, he won 53 England caps and, until December 2015, he held the Premier League record for clean sheets during a career with Liverpool, Aston Villa, West Ham, Manchester City and Portsmouth. But, like Sprake, he was prone to errors in the biggest games, such as FA Cup finals, internationals and UEFA Cup ties.

His worst howler came in the last FA Cup final at the old Wembley Stadium, for Villa against Chelsea in 2000 when he dropped a free-kick from Gianfranco Zola and Roberto di Matteo scored the only goal of the match. But it had also been his unconvincing punch to the feet of Eric Cantona that had cost Liverpool the 1996 final against Manchester United.

For England, James blundered in the team's opening 2006 World Cup qualifier in Vienna, allowing Austria midfielder Andreas Ivanschitz's slightly deflected shot slip through his arms for the equaliser in a 2-2 draw.

In 2008, with Portsmouth needing a win in Wolfsburg to stay in the UEFA Cup, and the scores level at 2-2, James had the ball passed back to him by defender Sylvain Distin. Instead of taking a touch, James tried to return the ball to his teammate first time. Unfortunately he scuffed his attempted pass straight to the feet of the Bundesliga side's Bosnian striker Zvjezdan Misimović, who rounded the hapless keeper and rolled the ball into the empty net. James being James, he saved a penalty from the same player five minutes later, but the damage was done.

When a player gets a reputation, it follows him around. While with West Ham in summer 2003, James went over to Florida to try out with the Miami Dolphins to see how goalkeeping skills transferred to American Football. A few members of the British media went along for some free downtime on Miami Beach.

At the Dolphins' practice facility, James suited up and was given a chance to have a go at some activities that gave him the best chance to show off the skills he used as a top-class keeper. Kicking was an obvious one, and he also practised throwing the ball with some of the team's quarterbacks. Finally he worked with the wide receivers. Dolphins' head coach Dave Wannstedt explained his thinking: "David, your game is all about catching the ball under pressure." Cue sniggers from watching UK reporters who remembered that Cup Final against Chelsea.

James is also a good-looking guy who was a natural for the modelling world, but of course that also made him a figure of fun. Some of his haircuts were the result of photo shoots. But there was not really much excuse for the 1930s slicked-down matinee idol look, unless all that Brylcreem kept his locks out of his eyes. Or the grown-out bleached Afro. Or the blond braids. Or the Alice band.

James was also among the more intelligent and socially engaged of footballers, and wrote a column for the *Observer*. Unfortunately, nobody likes a smartarse, and when he revealed his ecological concerns, the queue to take the mickey was miles long, not least among his teammates.

For example, while playing for Portsmouth he paid £2,500 to have his Chrysler converted to run on locally produced rapeseed oil (although some might wonder how ecologically-aware it was to live in Chudleigh, Devon, and drive to Eastleigh every day for training – a 240-mile round trip). Unfortunately, the technology still had teething troubles, and when he broke down on the M27 near the training ground, teammates delighted in speeding past in their sports cars honking their horns.

Naturally he was dismissed as a tree-hugger in some quarters, so he decided to go the whole hog and hug a tree for charity. He hit the woodwork at Woodbury Park, near Exeter, to promote National Tree Week.

But almost the strangest episode in his career came in 2005 when, playing for Manchester City against Middlesbrough, with the match tied at 1-1 and City needing to win to beat the Teessiders to a European place, he was sent forward by manager Stuart Pearce. No, not for an injury-time corner but for seven minutes.

Despite having £5m striker Jon Macken on the bench, Pearce took off midfielder Claudio Reyna, sent on reserve keeper Nicky Weaver and pushed James forward. "I sat at home on Saturday night and thought to myself: 'What shall I do if we're drawing the game late on and need to hit it long?'" Pearce said afterwards. "I've got a good striker in Jon Macken, who is really disappointed, but I wanted to unsettle them and in some ways it did. It unsettled everyone... them and us."

Daniel Taylor, writing in the *Guardian*, described it as "leadership that would have been wacky even by Brian Clough's standards. Amazingly the disorder almost paid off. With James charging around like a headless ostrich, his cameo role incorporating a hilarious air-shot and at least two horrendously late but probably well-meant chops at Doriva's legs, the hitherto wretched referee Rob Styles decreed that Joey Barton's centre had flicked off Franck Queudrue's hand for a penalty."

Unfortunately, the penalty, taken by Robbie Fowler, was saved by Mark Schwarzer. Perhaps if James had taken it ...

* * * * *

Goalkeepers have scored goals, of course: usually in penalty shoot-outs or when long clearances have accidentally bounced over the heads of their opposite numbers at the other end. Pat Jennings was the first to score on television, his long drop-kick from his hands in the 1967 Charity Shield for FA Cup winners Tottenham Hotspur against League Champions Manchester United bouncing over the head of Alex Stepney. Jimmy Greaves turned to Alan Gilzean and said: "You realise, Gilly, that this makes Pat our top scorer?"

In the Premier League era, Paul Robinson, also of Spurs, did the same to Watford's Ben Foster, his England teammate, at White Hart Lane in March 2007, from a free kick just a couple of yards outside the Tottenham penalty area. Tim Howard of Everton scored against Bolton at a windy Goodison Park in January 2012 with a first-time clearance from inside his own penalty area. The ball bounced outside the Bolton area but picked up pace and looped over the hapless Trotters keeper, Adam Bogdan.

Stoke City's Asmir Begović did likewise after just 13 seconds of Stoke City's Premier League match at home to Southampton on 2 November 2013, his clearance bouncing once on its way over the head of Artur Boruc. Not surprisingly, it was Begović's first touch of the game and is believed to be the quickest goal ever scored by a goalkeeper.

Some goalkeepers like to try from closer range by going up for last-minute corner kicks. Results can vary. Former QPR and Wales keeper Tony Roberts, then with Dagenham & Redbridge, shot home a dramatic injury-time equaliser in an FA Cup fourth qualifying round tie away to Basingstoke Town in 1991, but was also sent off after a clash with Peter Clarke of Southend United – in the Southend penalty area – in a third round tie in January 2008. Peter Schmeichel nodded one in for Manchester United against Rotor Volgograd, and the Dane almost bettered that only to see his overhead kick in a match against Wimbledon at Selhurst Park ruled out for offside.

But surely no goal scored by a keeper has been as dramatic as the one netted by Jimmy Glass for Carlisle United at Brunton Park on 8 May 1999. It was the last day of the season and Carlisle went into added time of their game against Plymouth Argyle with the score 1-1 but needing to find a winner to stay in the Football League.

Scarborough, their rivals in the bid to escape the drop, had drawn 1-1 at home to Peterborough United and the crowd were celebrating in the sunshine on the pitch at the McCain Stadium, waiting for confirmation that Carlisle had also drawn and that they were safe and the Cumbrians were down.

But their expectations were to be crushed. In the fifth minute of added time, Carlisle won a corner on the right, and Glass, on loan from Swindon Town, loped forward into the penalty area. Scott Dobie met Graham Anthony's inswinging kick with a firm header, Plymouth keeper James Dungey parried and Glass pounced on the loose ball to score with his right foot from four yards. "It fell to me, wallop, goal, thank you very much," he told the media afterwards. All was joy at Brunton Park but on the Yorkshire coast the fans slumped to the turf in despair. Glass had entered football folklore and it was his boots rather than his gloves that would be donated to the National Football Museum in Manchester.

"I always was a frustrated forward," he told Simon Turnbull of the *Independent* years later. "Even when I was a young boy I didn't know whether to go in goal or play up front. I always felt confident running around on the pitch, scoring goals – probably more confident, if I'm honest, than I was playing in goal sometimes.

"People think the goal was a bit of a freak occurrence but I scored a hat-trick the day before in training. After I quit the professional game, I played a bit of Sunday league football up front. I scored 24 goals in 10 games – six goals two weeks running. One of them was straight from the kick-off. I lobbed the keeper."

Glass had begun his career at Crystal Palace before moving to Bournemouth, where he played over 100 matches, some behind the on-loan Rio Ferdinand. Then on to Swindon, where he returned after failing to agree a permanent move to Carlisle. He had brief spells with Brentford, Oxford and Kingstonian before retiring.

"I carried on trying to be a footballer for maybe two, three years – just trying to knuckle down and be the best goalkeeper I could be and get a decent contract and carry on the way I was before. It ended up being very difficult wherever I'd go as a triallist after I'd left Swindon.

"Whereas I just wanted to be a goalkeeper, an anonymous goalkeeper that razzle-dazzled 'em with my skills, everywhere I went I carried the tag of Jimmy Glass, you know, 'That's the one that scored the goal.'

"I couldn't get my head round it. I thought, 'Well, if I'm such a legend, right, how come I haven't got a contract or nobody wants me to play in goal?' And I asked Rodney Marsh. I said, 'Rodney, am I a legend?' And he thought about it, as he does, and he said, 'No, you're not a legend, Jimmy, but your goal is legendary.'

"It made sense from that point on. I stopped wondering why it wasn't working for me after I scored this goal. Now I've come to terms with the fact that the goal is a wonderful, wonderful piece of sporting history and in certain parts of football, and obviously up in Cumbria, it's a legendary goal. But it is what it is. It's a goal. Life goes on and I enjoy it now for what it is."

It is because goals scored by goalkeepers are so rare that they attract so much attention. But a goalkeeper's best chance of glory is by saving penalties. The game stands still, all the attention is on the two players involved, kicker and keeper, and the odds are all against the man with the gloves.

The champion stopper of spot-kicks was Paul Cooper of Ipswich Town, who saved eight of the ten penalties he faced in the 1979/80 season. In the days before YouTube and widely available stats, Cooper used to make mental notes about various teams' penalty-takers. And he also had a technique, as David James recalled in his *Observer* column. "Keepers were not allowed to move their feet in those days, so he used to stand there swinging his arms and leaning to one side to put people off. I remember mimicking him in the playground. It was a bizarre technique, but it worked."

These days, when so many cup ties and matches in the knock-out stages of tournaments are decided by penalty shoot-outs, a keeper has more chances to be a hero – or even a villain. The proof of that came in the 2012 League One play-off final between Huddersfield Town and Sheffield United, which finished goalless after extra time. Steve Simonsen, the United keeper, looked set to be the hero when he saved two of Town's first three kicks. But his teammates failed to take advantage, and it went to sudden death. And eventually all the outfield players had had a go, leaving just Simonsen and Alex Smithies, his opposite number. Smithies smacked his penalty past Simonsen who then put the 22nd penalty high and wide.

Strangely, until Simonsen's miss, all the penalties in the sudden-death stage had been successful, even though the players were not regular penalty takers. Smithies later explained that he had seen video of most of the first five United kickers as part of Town's preparation and so had a reasonable idea of what they might do – but had had no clue where the next six might go.

Two Liverpool goalkeepers, Bruce Grobbelaar and Jerzy Dudek, became famous in shoot-outs in European Cup finals, although in fact Grobbelaar did not make a save in the 1984 match against AS Roma in the Italian capital's Stadio Olimpico. Instead, his antics on the goal line are credited with distracting Bruno Conti and Francesco Graziani so much that they missed their shots.

Grobbelaar later explained what inspired him in an interview with the official Liverpool website. "It came down to Joe Fagan," he said. "He put his arm around me before the penalties were actually taken and he said: 'Listen, we are not going to blame you for not stopping any penalties.' As I walked away, he said: 'But Bruce, try to put them off!'

"That is what stuck in my head and that is another great example of how Joe was a very good tactician. He knew how to press buttons with certain people and he did it with me. I looked at the players who were taking the AS Roma penalties and I did those silly things with my legs against two international players in Conti and Graziani. I wasn't doing that to any minnows, I wanted to put off the best, and unfortunately they came up short and they failed – which was great for us."

Steve Nicol missed Liverpool's first kick, but Phil Neal netted their second and it was 2-1 to Roma when Bruno Conti stepped up. "I remember the second penalty against Conti. He was dancing as if he was on a disco and I thought: 'If you want to dance with me, then we are going to dance 1960s style!' So I put my hands on my knees and when he came up to kick it I crossed my legs. He missed and I thought: 'Hey, this might work!'

The next three penalties all went in, putting Liverpool 3-2 ahead. Then Grobbelaar took centre stage again against Graziani. "The law was you had to keep your feet on the ground before they kicked the ball. That's what I did. The spaghetti legs came about when I went to the back of the net and bit it! The net looked to me like spaghetti so I went and did the spaghetti legs. That's where it comes from." Grobbelaar actually went the wrong way, but the shot hit the crossbar, giving Alan Kennedy the chance to win the trophy, which he took.

Fast forward to 2005 and Liverpool v Milan in Istanbul. After the Reds had fought back from 3-0 down to level the scores, and Dudek had made a stunning save from Andrei Shevchenko in the last minute of extra time to preserve the tie, they probably had the psychological advantage anyway. But they also had the advantage of history. "I just reminded Jerzy of what Grobbelaar did in 1984," Jamie Carragher said. "I said to him: 'Jerzy, you've got to do everything you can to put the penalty takers off.' I mentioned Grobbelaar to him."

"I said OK, but give me a few seconds because I've got a book and I need to study my penalties," Dudek later recalled. He did not exactly do a Grobbelaar, but waved his gloved hands and moved from side to side along his line. Serginho put the first shot high. "When I did the thing with the hands I wanted the player to see me and when he shot over the bar I said: 'OK, it's working, you made him scared – carry on!'"

Dudek then saved Milan's second penalty, from Andrea Pirlo. But the final penalty save, also from Shevchenko, was pure goalkeeping craft, as the notebook revealed that the Ukraine forward had no set side for placing penalties. "I said OK, I have to wait for the last second," Dudek said. "I went right, he stopped but he couldn't stop completely. He wanted to change, to put it in the middle of the goal, but he couldn't. I saved it as if something stopped me from falling down. I was a split second in the air, waiting for this ball and I caught it in my hand and then I saw the people running at me."

Not having to head the ball in the normal course of a match meant that Borislav 'Bobby' Mikhailov, the Bulgaria stopper, who played for Reading between 1995 and 1997, could do something no outfield player would get away with – play in a wig.

Mikhailov starred in the World Cup in the United States in 1994 as Bulgaria beat Argentina and Germany on the way to the semi-final, saving two penalties in a shoot-out against Mexico for good measure. He had begun the qualifying tournament bald, but a couple of games later he appeared from the tunnel with a full head of hair, which seemed to bewilder his teammates as much as the crowd. It was later confirmed that Mikhailov had bought a hair clinic in Bulgaria and was promoting its products. His son, Nikolay, who played for Liverpool and later FC Twente, under Steve McClaren, also had a receding hairline, but did not bother disguising it.

Toupee aside, Mikhailov was voted the second-best goalkeeper in the 1994 tournament. So why, with all due respect to Reading, did he end up at Elm Park around a year later, transferred from Botev Plovdiv for £300,000, washing his own kit and uncomfortable with the physical nature of the British game?

Roger Titford, a Royals fan and regular contributor to *When Saturday Comes*, says: "Legend took root that Mikhailov must have mistaken the video of Reading's Division One play-off final defeat to Bolton at Wembley for an ordinary home game.

"Implausible though the deal appeared, it did finally happen. The work permit unexpectedly took ages and then there was the request to 'call me Bobby' (perhaps Borislav didn't look right on the sponsored car) and the well-known wig, of course. Then somehow he was between marriages and wouldn't move out of a hotel, wasn't quite fit, couldn't kick very far and it all began to smell a bit fishy."

Mikhailov played only 25 league games for Reading over two seasons in which he also managed to be fit enough to represent Bulgaria on 14 occasions – as Titford says, "the kind of internationals-to-league appearances ratio generally found only in Manchester United reserves."

* * * * *

Recent changes to competition rules, allowing substitute goalkeepers, have denied fans a favourite sight on a football pitch – an outfield player having to go in goal. These days, if a keeper is sent off or injured, a specialist usually goes on in his place.

But years ago – or even now when all three substitutes have been used or the sub keeper has to leave – a volunteer would be sought and hastily given the spare green jersey and some gloves before tottering nervously towards the net. The Anfield Kop serenaded Luton Town's Kirk Stephens with chants of 'Shakin' Stephens' when he was forced to go in goal in front of them in September 1982. But Luton escaped with a point in a 3-3 draw.

The stand-ins have included some big names in some big games. Bobby Moore, for instance, took over between the sticks in a League Cup semi-final replay against Stoke City at Old Trafford and even saved a penalty.

Bobby Ferguson, the West Ham goalkeeper, injured his head in a collision with Stoke's Terry Conroy and was led off after being treated for seven minutes. West Ham believed that Ferguson could come back so carried on with ten men. Moore went in goal and survived one narrow escape when a shot from Mike Bernard hit a post. Then John McDowell fouled John Ritchie and the England captain was facing a penalty from Bernard. The kick was poorly hit and very central, so Moore's save was far from spectacular, but he could not hold the ball and the Stoke man knocked in the rebound.

"It flashed across my mind I was another Gordon Banks when I beat out the penalty kick," Moore said later. "I don't think I've ever felt so sick in my life [as] when the ball came back over my head."

West Ham equalised through Billy Bonds' deflected 25-yarder, and took the lead via Trevor Brooking's volley from Bonds' cross. Ferguson came back in time to concede an equaliser to Stoke captain Peter Dobing late in the first half, and Conroy blasted the decider in the second half. Stoke went on to beat Chelsea in the final, the first major honour in their long history.

Ireland striker Niall Quinn went one better than Moore when he played for Manchester City against Derby County at Maine Road on 20 April 1991. Quinn had volleyed City ahead in the first half then went in goal after City goalkeeper Tony Coton was sent off late in the first half for bringing down Derby's Dean Saunders as he went through. It was a clear penalty, and Quinn went in goal to face it. Saunders hit the ball low to Quinn's left, but the Irishman got his 6' 4" frame down to scoop the ball away. Quinn was unable to keep a clean sheet, conceding a second-half goal to Mick Harford, but City won 2-1 and Derby were relegated.

Phil Jagielka is a versatile player, the Everton and England central defender having also appeared in midfield and at full-back for Sheffield United. So it is hardly surprising that he volunteered to take over from Paddy Kenny when the Blades' goalkeeper was injured 30 minutes from the end of a match against Arsenal at Bramall Lane in December 2006 and there was no back-up keeper on the bench. United were 1-0 up through Christian Nadé and Jagielka kept a clean sheet to preserve the win, bringing off a spectacular late save from Robin van Persie.

Rio Ferdinand was another England defender who had to grab the gloves and, like Moore, face a penalty. It happened in an FA Cup quarter-final for Manchester United against Portsmouth at Old Trafford in 2008. Edwin van der Sar had suffered a groin injury and been replaced at the interval by Tomasz Kuszczak, who was sent off for bringing down Milan Baroš in a rare Portsmouth attack. Ferdinand went in goal and his first task was to face the resulting penalty. Although he dived the right way, Sulley Muntari's kick was too well hit, and that goal was enough to knock United out.

East Stirlingshire, though, used what is thought to be a British record of four goalkeepers, including two outfield players, in their final match of the 2002/03 season away to Albion Rovers, who were battling for promotion to the Scottish Second Division and needed to win and hope that East Fife did not.

Starting keeper Chris Todd was taken off injured after seven minutes and his replacement, Scott Findlay, was shown a red card for fouling John Bradford 40 yards from goal after 53 minutes. Forward Graham McLaren took the gloves, but he was also sent off for a foul on Charles McLean inside the penalty area. Midfield player Kevin McCann went in goal for the kick and tipped McLean's effort over the bar. It was all in vain for both sides as Albion won 3-1 but failed to go up as East Fife scored a last-minute winner in their match against Queen's Park.

Chelsea defender David Webb had the more unusual experience for an outfield player of starting a game in goal. Ten days earlier, England custodian Peter Bonetti had been injured after 30 minutes of a match against Coventry City at Highfield Road on 17 December 1971, and Webb replaced him, doing well and only conceding once, to Willie Carr, in a 1-1 draw.

John Phillips, the reserve keeper, started the next match, a League Cup semi-final first leg at home to Tottenham Hotspur, but reported injured on the morning of the following game, at home to Ipswich Town on 27 December. Manager Dave Sexton phoned third choice Steve Sherwood, who had been spending Christmas in Selby, Yorkshire, with his family. But traffic prevented Sherwood from reaching Stamford Bridge until three minutes before kick-off, by which time the teams were already out on the pitch and Webb was wearing the green jersey, having been told to carry on where he had left off against the Sky Blues.

Cheered every time he touched the ball, Webb kept a clean sheet with some ease against an ineffective Ipswich in a 2-0 win. He had only one serious save to make, diving at the feet of Town forward Mick Hill in the sixth minute and deflecting the ball for a corner. In the return match at Portman Road on 1 April, Webb wore the number eight shirt and scored both Chelsea goals in a 2-1 win. In his Chelsea career he wore every number except 11.

Switching permanently to duty between the sticks might have been a good career move. If they can avoid injury, goalkeepers can go on almost indefinitely, as they do not have to worry about losing stamina or speed and tend to hit their peaks later as their experience increases.

John Burridge was on the books of no fewer than 27 different clubs between his debut for Workington, his local team, in 1970 and his final appearance, for Blyth Spartans in an FA Cup tie away to Blackpool on 15 November 1997. Blackpool, you will not be completely amazed to learn, were one of his former clubs – in fact the league club for whom he played the most games, 165 between April 1971 and September 1975 – and the only clubs he played for twice were Blyth and Newcastle United.

However, he was given the boot at Newcastle in 1991 when Osvaldo Ardiles arrived as manager because the Argentinian had a long memory and remembered the Cumbrian motormouth standing on his foot in a match between Southampton and Tottenham and giving him a lecture about the Falkland Islands.

Burridge thought of himself as an entertainer as well as a shot-stopper and, during his finest hours in Crystal Palace's so-called Team of the Eighties, used to perform a lengthy pre-match warm-up routine that included what looked like an early form of break-dancing, some walking on his hands, one-handed press-ups and forward and backward somersaults. He even sat on the crossbar while Palace were beating Ipswich Town 4-1 to move to the top of the old First Division.

He became the oldest player to appear in the Premier League at 43, for Manchester City, and played his last top-flight game against QPR at Maine Road on 14 May 1995. He finally hung his gloves up at 46 and, after struggling to cope with life after playing and checking himself into The Priory, made a new career for himself as a goalkeeping coach, mainly in the Gulf, where he discovered Ali Al-Habsi, later to play in the Premier League for Bolton Wanderers and Wigan Athletic, but also turned down the chance to work for Saddam Hussein's son Uday as Iraq manager. Obviously not all goalkeepers are crazy.

6.

All for One and One for All

"The opposition is in front of you and your enemies are all around you."

Winston Churchill on the House of Commons. But he could just as well have been speaking about certain football teams

As the cliché goes, there is no 'I' in 'team'. But there are usually some pretty big egos, often some clashes of personality, and occasionally – very occasionally – 11 players all pulling in the same direction. Not that the teams where everyone gets on are always most successful.

Some serial trophy-winners have included players who can't stand the sight of one another, adulterers – including some who have slept with teammates' significant others – addicts and alcoholics. Managers are generally well advised to let the players sort the team dynamic for themselves. Team-bonding exercises can go spectacularly wrong.

A Newcastle United trip to Dublin in March 1998 while Kenny Dalglish was manager, for instance, ended up with Alan Shearer putting teammate Keith Gillespie in hospital. The England striker took exception to Gillespie flicking bottle tops at him during an evening out at the Café En Seine in a fashionable area of the Irish capital just off St Stephen's Green.

In his autobiography, *How Not to be a Millionaire Footballer*, the Northern Ireland winger admits that he foolishly asked the bigger and stronger Shearer "if he wanted to take it outside". They emerged into busy Dawson Street, and a number of locals witnessed Gillespie take the first swing, and miss. Shearer did not, and Gillespie fell, hit his head on a plant pot and woke up in a hospital bed.

George Graham had taken more of a hands-off approach with the Arsenal team that won the Football League Championship in 1989 and 1991, whose players were allowed to indulge in drinking sessions that seem incredible from today's perspective.

Younger Arsenal fans will know the Tuesday Club as the title of a podcast hosted by Gunners' fan Alan Davies. But it takes its name from a notorious group of drinkers among the squad in the days before Arsène Wenger introduced Perrier and pasta in place of lager and curry.

Graham regarded the Tuesday binges as valuable in knitting his players together, and they did not prevent Tony Adams, Paul Merson, Lee Dixon, Nigel Winterburn, Perry Groves or Ray Parlour winning a host of honours. Tuesday was the day chosen as the players had Wednesdays off and could still be ready for training on Thursdays. According to Groves, it was not unknown for some players to sink 15 to 20 pints.

"In the morning, George put us through some very tough physical training, running until we were almost sick, followed by some gym work," Dixon recalled in his Friday column in the *Independent* in 2011. "And afterwards we would go to the

Bank of Friendship pub round the corner from Highbury and sink a few beers.

"In those days, players could still socialise in the same places as supporters and there would not be any trouble. There'd be old Jim sitting in the corner smoking Woodbines, and us at the bar downing pints. I was never a heavy drinker – six pints was my limit and I'd be blotto.

"But some of the others, Tony Adams in particular, would carry on all night. I used to join the Tuesday Club once a month, but others like Tony would be there every week. It was an important part of the team, where the strong bonds were formed that took us to a couple of league titles.

"And if you didn't join in, then you would be ostracised. I remember Martin Keown was an example of that. He told me that in his first spell at the club it was expected of him to have a drink with the lads from time to time.

"He is very strong minded and didn't join in with the drinking sessions. He might have a pint but he wasn't part of the group and as a result he was cut off a little. At the time, that must have been very difficult for him. I admired him for having that strength of character."

"We weren't going out and getting pissed all the time, we were going out when we could," Groves said. "Tuesday was our big day, cos we knew it would be out of our system by the time we played on Saturday. The alcoholic thing with Merse and Rodders [Adams] was rubbish – you couldn't be alcoholic and play at that level, no chance. They were just binge drinkers, that's all."

Not every player was able to keep up. On his Tuesday Club debut after joining Arsenal from Liverpool, Jimmy Carter lost bladder control after just four or five pints, relieving himself over Groves' and Merson's trousers. "Merse told him 'you are banned'," Groves wrote in his autobiography, "but he was such a lovely guy we changed our minds."

Fortunately for Groves, Merson and their teammates, the alcohol was also out of their system by the time they played the

The mascots' Grand National. (Gettyimages)

Partick Thistle's new mascot, Kingsley – a giant, child-eating Lisa Simpson? (Gettyimages)

Michael Knighton ball-juggling at Old Trafford. Or looking for UFOs. (Gettyimages)

Cap'n Bob quietens the rowdies at Oxford. (Gettyimages)

A rare shot of Tommy Smith enjoying the company of Liverpool team-mate Emlyn Hughes. (Gettyimages)

Sanchez and Fashanu take on a Liverpool opponent. They'd rather have been kicking each other. (Gettyimages)

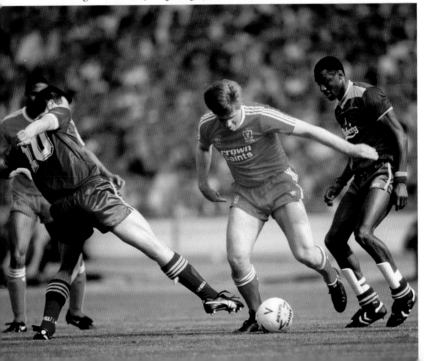

Laurent Koscielny of Arsenal nods the seventh in a tight, defensive 12-goal League Cup tie at Reading. He had earlier scored an own goal.(Gettyimages)

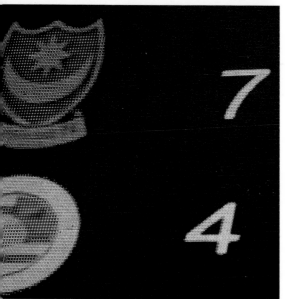

And it's Reading again, this time in the Premier League's highest-scoring game.(Gettyimages)

Steve Morrow about to leave Wembley on a stretcher after Arsenal's League Cup victory celebrations left him with a broken arm. (Gettyimages)

The Nest, Norwich. (Gettyimages)

Celebrity fans: don't give up the day jobs. (Gettyimages)

Cristiano Ronaldo posing with the Millennium Stadium mural that enabled Manchester United to win the FA Cup from the South dressing room. Playing Millwall in the final probably didn't hurt. (Gettyimages)

The Arsenal mural – all-white version. (Gettyimages)

Karl Power gets into the team picture. (Gettyimages)

Ken Baily in costume. (Gettyimages)

Malcolm Allison and the fedora. (Gettyimages)

Egil Olsen sports his signature wellies at Highbury. (Gettyimages)

Not to be sniffed at? Robbie Fowler crossed the line with his goal celebration – as well as snorting it.(Gettyimages)

Gareth Ainsworth at Wembley – thinking he's on stage at Live Aid not on the touchline at the League Two play-off final. (Gettyimages)

David James with some friends. (Gettyimages)

Huddersfield goalkeeper Alex Smithies celebrates while Sheffield United keeper Steve Simonsen has just missed the decisive penalty. Smithies scored his. (Gettyimages)

'Triggs – walkies!' (Gettyimages)

Di Canio – fascist salute or just waving to his mum? (Gettyimages)

John Terry with some players who did win the Champions League. (Gettyimages)

Pedro Mendes appeals in vain that his lob has crossed the line. (Gettyimages)

Two balls on the pitch at Sunderland and Liverpool goalkeeper Pepe Reina can't save either of them. (Gettyimages)

The programme for Sheffield United's home match against Manchester United in August 1992. Manager Dave Bassett (centre) decided to celebrate Christmas four months early in the hope that the Blades could show their traditional New Year form in the first half of a season for once. Brian Deane (left) scored the first-ever goal in the Premier League and the home side won 2-1. (Sheffield United FC)

1989 title decider at Anfield on a Friday evening, winning 2-0 to become champions on goals scored. But alcohol was far from being out of their lives. In May 1990, the same month as he was omitted from Bobby Robson's England squad, Adams crashed his car into a wall after a drinking session, and was later jailed for four months. Incredibly, the Arsenal squad, bolstered late in the season by Adams' release after serving only two months, won the league title again in the 1990-91 season, this time by seven points.

* * * * *

The Tuesday Club was finally ended by the appointment of Wenger and Adams' decision, as Arsenal captain, to ban alcohol in the players' lounge after he had successfully battled his addiction. But Arsenal had twice interrupted a period of dominance by Merseyside, which was surprising because the Team of the Eighties, of course, was supposed to be Crystal Palace.

It was Jimmy Greaves who is believed to have hung that albatross of a title around the necks of manager Terry Venables and his young squad, and you could understand why. The club had won the FA Youth Cup in 1977 and 1978, and with products of those youth teams beginning to break through, Palace won promotion to the old First Division in 1979.

For a while, they swept all before them, and with Vince Hilaire, Peter Nicholas, Dave Swindlehurst and Kenny Sansom living up to their promise, and older heads such as John Burridge, Gerry Francis and Mike Flanagan providing guidance, all seemed set fair.

But they fell away. Sansom was sold to Arsenal, Venables left for QPR, and Palace were relegated at the end of their first full season of the decade they were supposed to dominate, 13 points adrift of also-relegated Leicester. The low point was surely the 3-0 home defeat by rivals Brighton over Easter that sealed their demise, Hilaire marked out of the game by Chris Ramsey, later QPR manager, on his league debut.

However, an entire decade of unbroken top-flight football did eventually come to Selhurst Park, but mainly thanks to a club that was not even in the league when Palace won that 1976/77 Youth Cup. Wimbledon joined the Football League for the 1977/78 season in the days when clubs had to be elected to the Fourth Division, replacing Workington. From the beginning it was the definition of a rollercoaster ride – they went up in their second season, straight back down, back up, down, up and then up again.

Dave 'Harry' Bassett was their third manager in the League, after Allen Batsford and Dario Gradi. He was promoted from assistant manager in 1981 when chairman Ron Noades left for Crystal Palace and took Gradi with him. And that was really when the fun began. Wimbledon through and through, Bassett had played in their 1975 FA Cup run, when they held Leeds to a goalless draw at Elland Road. In fact, it was his foul on Eddie Gray that gave Dickie Guy the chance to be the hero, saving Peter Lorimer's penalty.

It was Bassett's idea to start playing the long-ball game. From the kick-off, the ball would go back to Guy's replacement in goal, Dave Beasant, and the next time it touched the ground – if at all – it would be in the opposing penalty area. "It was ironic that Plough Lane actually had a good playing surface, because the ball hardly ever touched it," Lawrie Sanchez told *The Blizzard*.

Plough Lane was essentially still a non-league ground, and there was no training ground as such. The players trained on the north-west corner of Wimbledon Common near the Robin Hood Roundabout, their base a former transport café. "If we were short of cones at training, we used to pick up cones off the A3, put them in a van and take them back to the training ground," Bassett said.

Nigel Winterburn was signed in 1983 from the more sedate surroundings of Oxford United. "Arriving at training was an eye-opener," he told *Shortlist* magazine. "They were public pitches and the dressing rooms were through a café. You couldn't leave your stuff in there because the café was packed with all sorts. It was Sunday league stuff. We'd take our bags out onto the pitch to train. I used to take my training kit home to wash myself. Oh, and I bought my own boots."

He found that the club tradition of practical jokes was already well established. "The pranks started immediately. I had my shoes nailed to the floor and Ralgex in my pants straight away.

"The manager, Dave Bassett, might not have liked it, but he didn't have a say. We'd travel and it was Dave's bed that more often than not would end up outside his room or, on one occasion, in the swimming pool."

Later, new players went through an initiation that usually involved their clothes being shredded or burnt. Eric Young's clothes were put in his Brighton duffel bag before being set alight. "It caused noxious fumes that made us have to evacuate the transport café because it [the smoke] was going through the building," Lawrie Sanchez recalled.

One player was tied to the roof of a car and taken for a ride around the neighbourhood. When Cork's car was set on fire, though, it was not an initiation, but a way of getting him more money without breaking the budget – he was told to claim on his insurance.

The only new player who seems to have escaped ritual humiliation on his arrival was Mick Harford. "I didn't get the normal welcome," he told *Total Football* magazine in 1998, with the chilly stare that froze the souls of defenders. "I've no idea why. I'm a lovely soft-centred bloke really." Perhaps that was a sign that the club had gone soft. But the Wimbledon of the 1980s thrived on what player and later coach Wally Downes called "very, very, very tough love".

When the Dons reached the second tier of English football, they feared they might struggle, but proved no soft touch. Brighton manager Chris Cattlin, a tough guy himself as a player, thought he might pick "eleven hammer-throwers" for the return match after a spicy encounter at Plough Lane. In

1986, after only two seasons in the second tier, and after only nine years in the league, they were in the top flight.

Gary Lineker famously said that the best way to watch them was on Ceefax, and Ron Yeats, scouting for Liverpool, said that "the ball must have been screaming for mercy." But the received wisdom that they simply kicked and hoofed their way up the league was far from the whole story. They employed a statistician, Neil Lanham, and a video analyst, Vince Craven, who kitted out a room in his house as a video room. "Billy Beane at Oakland came in with Moneyball and all the statistics," Bassett said. "We were doing that in 1981."

And they also invested in coaching qualifications and a youth policy. "In my last season we had 23 first-team players and 13 had played in the youth team," Bassett said. "If that had been Manchester United, people would have been ejaculating all over the stadium."

But it was the players who made the club what it was. When they played their first match in the old First Division, away to Manchester City, on 23 August 1986 seven of the squad had played in the Fourth Division and one of the starting eleven, Steve Galliers, had made his debut in the club's first-ever league game in 1977. Alan Cork had made his debut later the same season and went on to play in the 1988 FA Cup final.

Wimbledon lost 3-1, but won the next four matches and topped the table.

"We were the pantomime villains and it was a great story for people until we hung around," Lawrie Sanchez said. "Everybody loved to see us climbing up through the divisions and being the victorious underdogs. But the Premier League weren't keen, firstly because we basically had no fans. Also, the other chairmen would ask their managers how come this team with no money on small wages was beating the big boys. They all wanted the story to end. But Wimbledon stayed at the top level for twelve years."

Illustrious opponents used to outplaying teams soon found out that they were in for 90 minutes of defending a rain of set plays, high crosses and long throws, contested by John Fashanu, and very few relished it. "Players that I played against said that when they went to Wimbledon, they didn't care about the result," winger Terry Gibson told the BT Sport documentary *The Crazy Gang*. "They wanted to come away without an injury. Can you imagine the advantage that gave us?"

Some of the old gang disliked that documentary, saying that Fashanu and Vinnie Jones had been encouraged to exaggerate the violence and thuggery, but they did not deny that an element of physical intimidation was part of their armoury. Bassett himself described the club as "the borstal of football". "If you had a weakness it was picked up on," Sanchez said. Bobby Gould, who took over from Bassett in June 1987, described managing the team as like being the headmaster of the worst comprehensive school in the United Kingdom.

But the other part of their uniqueness was the team spirit, more usual in a pub team than a professional outfit. For many of the players who had been misfits elsewhere such as Dennis Wise, rejected by Southampton and who went on to captain Chelsea and win 21 England caps, the Dons represented their last chance in the game.

"We'd all come from difficult backgrounds," Fashanu said. "Wimbledon were my family."

Even after the club had left Plough Lane to groundshare Selhurst Park with Palace, their training facilities had improved only marginally. There were still no fences to stop dog walkers ambling across the carefully tended pitches on which Joe Kinnear would coach million-pound players such as Jones, Robbie Earle, John Hartson and the rest. Journalists, who would be able to talk to players freely, were often invited into the players' lounge where punters used to down their full English and mugs of strong tea.

Owner Sam Hammam would sometimes stroll around the perimeter and chat with fans and media. "Wimbledon was a group of people who worked hard and fought against heavy odds for twenty years and came up trumps," he said.

"We represented the little person, the working-class fan who doesn't have a lot but works hard and doesn't give up." Some of the players didn't give up because Hammam had put clauses in their contracts that meant that they had to go to the opera or eat sheeps' testicles if the team lost by four goals.

Even when they reached the FA Cup final in 1988, Wimbledon did things differently. The night before the game, instead of being tucked up in bed early in the team hotel, the squad went to the pub that was used as a base when the team originally played on Wimbledon Common. "Bobby Gould gave one of the players, I think it was Corky, some money. Corky said it was £20, Gouldy says £200. Anyway, we went for a nice quiet drink. Or some of us did."

Wimbledon beat Liverpool at Wembley the next day, and commentator John Motson famously said on the final whistle, "The Crazy Gang have beaten the Culture Club," but by then it was ridiculous to caricature the Dons as minnows. They were coached by Don Howe, mastermind of Arsenal's 1971/72 double triumph, and that season they finished seventh in the top division and had already beaten Arsenal, Manchester United and Tottenham.

Of course, too much high-spiritedness can lead to internal divisions, and Fashanu and Sanchez were clashing personalities who reportedly came to blows in training. Respected tabloid journalist Tony 'Sten Gun' Stenson was once phoned by Sanchez. "He said: 'I want to put a story out that Fash tried to end my career. He tried to break my legs with his karate chops.'" Fashanu said his only regret was not hitting Sanchez sooner. "From the first moment, he knew what I was and I knew what he was," Sanchez said. "For six years they never spoke to each other," Gibson said. "They were in the same changing room but wouldn't even celebrate together.'

* * * * *

Teammates coming to blows is not unusual. There was no need for anyone to phone the media when John Hartson and Eyal

Berkovic clashed at the West Ham training ground in 1998 because it happened in front of TV cameras. Israel midfield player Berkovic was an artist with the ball, but, by many accounts, could be a difficult personality.

During one training session, Berkovic was lying on the pitch after a tackle and Hartson tried to pull him up. The annoyed Israeli aimed a punch at Hartson and the big Welshman snapped and kicked Berkovic in the head. Well, not just kicked but delivered a textbook left-foot volley. "If my head had been a ball it would have been in the top corner of the net," Berkovic is said to have commented.

It was revealing that the other players chose not to look after the injured Berkovic but gather round Hartson to check whether he had hurt his foot.

Soon afterwards, Berkovic was sold to Celtic after agitating for a move. Hammers manager Harry Redknapp was unsure of the player's motive in wanting to head north of the border, and not entirely serious when he told reporters: "I didn't want to lose him, but what can you do when the lad comes to you and tells you how he used to kick a ball around the streets of Tel Aviv in a green and white hooped shirt?"

West Ham and Wimbledon enjoyed moderate success despite internal stresses, but at least two of English football's most decorated club sides included teammates who were barely on speaking terms.

When Liverpool won their first European Cup by beating Borussia Mönchengladbach in Rome in 1977, the central defensive pairing of Tommy Smith and Emlyn Hughes was one of the foundations of their success. Hughes lifted the trophy as captain and Smith scored what proved to be the winning goal, but after his bullet header hit the net, he ran towards the sideline rather than back towards his teammates. "I hated scoring for Liverpool because Hughes would come up and congratulate me," Smith said later. "I hated him."

Part of the reason was Smith's loss of the club captaincy to Hughes after a falling-out with manager Bill Shankly in 1973, but there was also an obvious clash of personalities between the strong, silent Aintree Iron and the more talkative Crazy Horse. "It was my club," Smith said. "I'd been there a damn sight longer than him. Everything in my life was football, especially Liverpool, so why should I let this two-faced little so-and-so spoil my football life?"

Worse still, Shankly's successor Bob Paisley confirmed Hughes as captain even though he knew that many of the players preferred Smith, disliking Hughes' chattiness and what the *Daily Telegraph*'s obituary called his 'parsimony in the pub'. "Some of Emlyn's team-mates weren't that fond of him and one of them, Tommy Smith, absolutely hated him," Paisley later admitted. "Smithy and Hughes never spoke to each other.

'I had to speak to them both when all the trouble was brewing up but it never mattered to me if players got on like a house on fire or if they couldn't stand the sight of each other, as long as they didn't let their personal feelings spill over onto the pitch." As Paisley hoped, their differences did not affect their performances. "Once we were over that white line, we were playing for Liverpool, and our personal dislike of each other did not come into it," Smith said. "As a footballer, he was very good. As a person, he wasn't. Away from football, I did not entertain him, or speak to him off the pitch. Never."

Hughes, who seldom commented on the matter, went further in his professional admiration. "He is the greatest captain I have ever played under," he said. "Although I never particularly got along with him as a man, I had nothing but admiration and respect for him as a captain on the pitch. He had powerful qualities of leadership."

Paisley added: "Their dislike of each other was something we managed to keep within the dressing room. I certainly don't think the fans who were watching them play alongside each other had any idea of the feud that was going on."

But if the fans were ignorant of their mutual loathing, opponents soon got to know about it. When Allan Clarke of Leeds fouled Hughes in a match between the two great rivals of the 1970s, Smith was heard to say: "Maybe that Clarke's not such a bad bloke after all."

And an opponent can explain why, in a match at Anfield, Smith apparently rushed to remonstrate with Chelsea's fearsome Ron 'Chopper' Harris after a foul on Hughes, the man he hated. Was he simply standing up for a fallen teammate, putting team loyalty before personal enmity, as honour demanded? Not a bit of it.

"Chopper's done Emlyn Hughes after 15 minutes and he's gone down squealing," the late Chelsea striker Peter Osgood said. "Tommy Smith sprints in from 20 yards away, but he sprints straight past Emlyn, his teammate, gets to Chopper, hauls him up, and says: 'I could get to like you, Harris.' Nobody hated Emlyn more than Smithy."

Liverpool enjoyed many successful trophy-winning seasons, but no club has ever equalled Manchester United's 1998/99 treble-winning campaign. Yet two of its central figures, strikers Andy Cole and Teddy Sheringham, never spoke. "I would rather sit down and have a cuppa with Neil Ruddock, who broke my leg in two places in 1996, than with Teddy Sheringham, who I've pretty much detested for the past 15 years," Cole told the *Independent*.

It all started with Cole's England debut. "It was early 1995, I had recently signed for Manchester United, and it was my England debut, against Uruguay," Cole said. "I was a sub. I came on for Sheringham [then at Spurs], after about 70 minutes. You'll need to understand what was in my head at that moment to get even close to comprehending my reaction to what happened next.

"I was so nervous it was frightening. This was the culmination of a lifetime of ambition. You hear the cliché, 'It means everything to play for my country.' But trust me, it did. Not just for me, but for my family, my parents especially, who had endured all kinds of hardships to give us the chances we had. Becoming a pro had been incredible. Now the magnitude of playing for England was indescribable. The moment has arrived.

"I walk onto the pitch, 60,000 or so watching. Sheringham is coming off. I expect a brief handshake, a 'Good luck, Coley,' something. I am ready to shake. He snubs me. He actively snubs me, for no reason I was ever aware of then or since. He walks off. I don't even know the bloke so he can't have any issue with me. We're fellow England players, it is my debut and he snubs me.

"You know what my immediate thoughts were? 'Jesus Christ! How many people just saw Teddy Sheringham do that to me?' I was embarrassed. I was confused. And there you have it. From that moment on, I knew Sheringham was not for me.

"Two years later, in summer 1997, after Eric Cantona left United, Sheringham arrived. We played together for years. We scored a lot of goals. I never spoke a single word to him.

"People wonder how on earth we could function like that. Gary Pallister once said to me: 'I know you don't speak to Teddy and he doesn't speak to you, but at least you play well together.' We did, and I wouldn't ever cast aspersions on Sheringham's talent as a top-rate footballer for his clubs and country. I've just loathed him personally for 15 years."

But sometimes, internal rivalries and dislikes just cannot stay hidden, and boil over on the field. David Batty and Graeme Le Saux of Blackburn Rovers came to blows on the field after they collided while going for the same loose ball in a Champions League match away to Spartak Moscow in 1995 and had to be separated by skipper Tim Sherwood.

In his autobiography, *Left Field: A Footballer Apart*, Le Saux denied stories that the rough-and-ready Batty had made a homophobic remark to the *Guardian*-reading defender. Although Rovers were reigning champions, the team was misfiring and frustrations boiled over. "It wasn't the words that got to me, but a combination of four or five things. I was upset at what he said and that he was accusing me of being selfish again. I was upset that we were not doing well as a team and I reacted because of the way he behaved.

"I swung at him, connected and knew immediately that I had broken my left hand. I am not a fighter. I hadn't closed my fist properly. I was in a lot of pain, which just made me feel more ridiculous."

The referee took no action, but when Lee Bowyer and Kieron Dyer of Newcastle went at it during a Premier League game at St James' Park against Aston Villa in 2005, both were sent off. Dyer later explained that Bowyer had complained at not receiving a pass and then claimed that Dyer never passed to him. "The reason I don't pass to you is because you're shit, basically," was Dyer's reply and Bowyer walked over and the fists began to fly. Dyer admitted that his red card had taken him by surprise because he thought you could only be sent off for hitting opponents.

* * * * *

Speaking of violence on the pitch brings us to Don Revie's Leeds United, or at least their reputation as 'Dirty Leeds'.

On their day, few teams could live with Leeds, in the all white kit that Revie had copied from Real Madrid. With artists such as Eddie Gray and Johnny Giles, they could dominate and even humiliate opponents, as an often-repeated period of arrogant possession football during a 7-0 thrashing of Southampton proves.

Yet they finished the Revie era with only two league titles, an FA Cup, a League Cup and two UEFA Cups to show for a decade of sustained brilliance. They finished runners-up in the league five times, and were twice losing FA Cup finallists, and also lost the final of the European Cup-Winners' cup to AC Milan, although there was more than a little reason to suspect that the referee had a red and black shirt on under his jersey in that one.

Part of the reason for their relative lack of success was that Revie seemed more afraid of losing than keen on winning. He gave his players exhaustive dossiers on opponents and built up the opposition to seem better than they were.

Revie was also weirdly superstitious, wearing out lucky blue suits, sporting a lucky tie and carrying lucky charms in his pockets. Before every match he would walk out of the team hotel to the nearest traffic lights and walk back. He thought birds were unlucky, which eventually led him to replace the owl logo on the team kit with a simple LUFC.

"The suit he wore was blue mohair and you could see his underpants through it, it was so worn on the backside," Scotland star Peter Lorimer said. "But he wouldn't change it and it was quite embarrassing. He had to wear his overcoat even in summer to cover it up but when he turned round it was threadbare."

He was controlling, carrying out checks on girlfriends to make sure they were suitable, preferring his players to settle down and get married as soon as possible.

While party animals such as George Best and Osgood would be out enjoying the bright lights whenever possible, Revie kept his players away from temptation before matches with interminable sessions of bingo and carpet bowls – the opposite of Wimbledon's Crazy Gang off the field, whatever might happen on it.

But Revie also ensured that flowers were sent to every wife's bedside when a child was born, and the players grew to regard him as a father figure to the Leeds family. "Our whole ethos was built on loyalty," Lorimer said. "We all fight for each other, we all work for each other. If someone kicks me, he kicks all eleven of us." And they would kick back twice as hard.

For Revie's team were not just unloved but hated for their 'professionalism' – which, to Revie, included appealing for every decision and surrounding referees when Roy Keane was still only kicking inside his mother's womb – and perceived dirty play. Leeds had uncompromising players such as Jack Charlton and Billy Bremner, and even their creative players such as Giles could look after themselves. "I was a creative player, but I got some bad injuries early on and I decided that if this was a jungle we were playing in then it's better to be a lion than a lamb," Giles said.

Then, of course, there was Norman 'Bites Yer Legs' Hunter.

When Brian Clough took over from Revie and tried to change Leeds' style, he is reported to have said to Hunter: "You're a dirty bastard and everyone hates you. I know everyone likes to be loved, and you'd like to be loved too, wouldn't you?" Hunter is said to have replied: "Actually I couldn't give a fuck." When coach Les Cocker was told that Hunter had broken a leg, he asked: "Whose is it?"

Away from the field, Hunter is an affable and self-effacing gent. He once told a special 'Hard Men' issue of *Total Football* that he would have had to rethink his approach completely in the modern game or be suspended every week. "I'd have to stay on my feet, not do what I used to do," he said. "All I ever wanted to do was play football and if I was constantly getting booked and sent off I'd have to change. When I was playing, if you got sent off you'd done something really bad, whereas now they go for nothing. Things used to happen on a regular basis but you never saw them because they weren't on television and they were never reported that much."

Surreally, despite the treatment he dished out to their members on a weekly basis, in 1974 the Professional Football Association made him the first winner of their Players' Player of the Year award.

Leeds had a healthy respect for northern rivals such as Liverpool, but little time for the London clubs and those who followed them, fans and reporters alike – Hunter once bowed extravagantly to the West Ham press box after scoring with his weaker right foot in a match at Upton Park – and reserved a special dislike for the would-be glamour-boys of Chelsea.

The 1970 FA Cup final replay between the two at Old Trafford, won 2-1 by Chelsea after extra time, is reckoned to be one of the dirtiest games ever played, the two teams tearing into each other from the kick-off. Incredibly, Eric Jennings, the referee, booked only one player, Chelsea's Ian Hutchinson despite a series of brutal fouls.

Years later, David Elleray, the respected Premier League and FIFA referee, re-refereed the game on video. Officiating by modern standards, Elleray estimated that he would have shown seven yellow cards to Leeds players and sent off Giles, Bremner and Charlton. But Revie's men would probably have won, as Chelsea would have received 13 bookings, including three each for David Webb, who scored the winner, Ron Harris and Charlie Cooke, whose pass created Chelsea's equaliser in normal time. And Elleray suspected that there might have been more cards as a result of incidents off the ball that the cameras had missed.

Eddie Gray, who had tormented Webb in the first game, seemed to have been targeted for treatment. Webb fouled him repeatedly before Harris took him out with an X-rated kick that effectively put him out of the game and should have seen Harris heading for the showers. Charlton head-butted Osgood after the Chelsea striker had tackled him from behind. Revie's side had led three times, only to be pegged back on every occasion, finally losing it in extra time after 240 minutes of hard slog.

After Revie had left to manage England and the Clough experiment had failed, Leeds tried giving several members of his squad the manager's job in the hope of rekindling the old magic, but Bremner, Clarke and Gray all failed. Giles, whom Revie had anointed his successor before the board appointed Clough, and Jack Charlton, who took Middlesbrough to the top flight and was a successful manager of Ireland, never got the call.

* * * * *

The West Ham team of the 1950s produced a far more impressive crop of managers. Malcolm Allison and a group of players used to meet at Cassetari's Cafe in the Barking Road near the Boleyn Ground and discuss tactics using salt cellars and pepper pots. Allison, John Bond, Noel Cantwell, Frank O'Farrell, Ken Brown, Dave Sexton and others were all regulars.

More recently, Chelsea has been the leading coaching academy among British clubs. When Steve Clarke took over as manager of West Bromwich Albion after ten years as an assistant at Newcastle United, Chelsea, West Ham United and Liverpool, he became the 18th former Chelsea player of the Premier League era to manage at league or international level.

Roberto Di Matteo, Mark Hughes, Ruud Gullit, Gus Poyet, Gianluca Vialli and Gianfranco Zola managed in the Premier League, and Di Matteo, of course, was in charge when they won the Champions League. Why were they so successful? Poyet thinks he knows.

"A lot of foreigners together in a different country, always talking about football," Poyet said. "When you move to a new country and there are a few of you together, either single or with just your immediate family, you need that support. And we were strong characters, most of us, already quite experienced in different leagues, so that knowledge was there to share with each other.

"I think that was also why we were so successful as a team, because we sorted out problems between ourselves, not only with the formation and instructions that the manager gave you. We made so many decisions on the pitch that it is showing in the level people are coaching. And not only as managers – I played with four goalkeepers at Chelsea, and three became goalkeeping coaches.

"The only other [similar] situation I can think of is at Manchester United, with Steve Bruce, Bryan Robson, Paul Ince and Mark Hughes – more or less the same type of group and mentality. Strong, experienced, and they learned a lot from Sir Alex Ferguson. Of course they had only one manager where we had a few, so maybe their influence was more focused on what Sir Alex did."

Where the West Ham players went to a café to talk football and used the crockery and cutlery to make their points, you imagine that the Chelsea players of 2000 would have gathered at a wine bar, using bowls of olives or bottles of balsamic vinegar, but the reality is much less glamorous.

"The place we went to the most was the masseur's room at the [old] training ground at Harlington," Poyet said. "In the morning, an hour or an hour and a half before training, the main group was always there, talking about football situations or problems or fixtures. We would sit around the table that someone was having a massage on.

"The masseur was Terry Byrne, who became David Beckham's personal assistant after the problems he had in Spain [with Rebecca Loos]. It wasn't a spectacular room, but it was one of the best rooms I've ever been in in football."

Poyet had not realised that he was in a finishing school for managers until Vialli was promoted from the ranks to replace Gullit in February 1998. "He was sitting next to me in the dressing room and then the next day he was my manager. I thought: 'Wait a moment, this can happen to me as well if I want it.' So I started to pay closer attention to decisions, training sessions, tactics, fitness, getting ready to think about things a player doesn't."

Poyet is pleased that his friend Di Matteo was the first manager to bring the Champions League trophy to the Fulham Road. "So many managers tried to achieve that trophy that was so important to the club, they won the [FA] Cup or the Double, [Jose] Mourinho, [Carlo] Ancelotti, but Robbie did it in three months. I'd been saying: 'We are managing everywhere, come on – give it to one of us.' I'm delighted that Abramovich made the decision to give the opportunity to Robbie."

Chelsea are dismissed by some as a bunch of foreign mercenaries, but John Terry has always ensured that the team bonds, from the ritual of the song that every newly signed player is expected to deliver a capella to his new teammates to strip penalties.

You mean you didn't know about strip penalties? Let the great man tell the story himself. "A group of us would go out after training had finished and we'd get a five-a-side match going. Then we took turns from the spot. If you missed one you had to take off your shirt. If you missed another, off came your shorts and then your socks, and so on. In the end, you would end up in goal stark naked with everyone booting footballs at you. It was a great laugh."

It must have been the fact that everyone kept their kit on that disoriented him when he missed the penalty that would have won the Champions League final in Moscow in 2008.

Terry, of course, was involved in one of the biggest scandals of them all when he was alleged to have slept with Vanessa Perroncel, the model and ex-girlfriend of his England and former Chelsea teammate Wayne Bridge – and the mother of Bridge's son, Jaydon – although since she had been his ex for some time, much of the outrage seemed manufactured. At any rate, it was all over the papers, and Terry took out a super-injunction in an unsuccessful attempt to keep it secret, and there's no smoke without fire. Bridge publicly refused to shake hands with Terry before a match between Chelsea and Bridge's then club, Manchester City. Terry lost the England captaincy. So of course it had to be true. Didn't it?

Except that Perroncel took legal action against seven daily papers and the *News of the World* and *Mail on Sunday*, who were forced to admit that "we published some personal information about Vanessa Perroncel concerning an alleged affair with the footballer John Terry. We have since been informed she would have preferred this to remain private and it was untrue in any case. We apologise to Miss Perroncel for any distress caused."

However, one genuine football sex scandal was revealed by the Terry stories. In February 2010, during a phone-in on Fox Soccer Channel about the Terry-Bridge affair, former United States forward Eric Wynalda confirmed rumours that USA coach Steve Sampson had dropped captain and former Sheffield Wednesday defender John Harkes from his squad for the 1998 World Cup because he had had a relationship with Wynalda's wife, Amy.

And the Terry family was part of a darker tale in 2011 when Rushden & Diamonds goalkeeper Dale Roberts hanged himself, depressed about an injury but also his fiancée having slept with

Paul Terry, his teammate and John Terry's brother. "I'm not sure he could deal with the embarrassment the story caused him," Adam Johnson, the Sunderland and England winger, and a school friend of Roberts, said. "His death was a combination of the negative press and his leg injury."

* * * * *

But sometimes a team has only positive stories to tell. One remarkable outfit was the Celtic side that won the European Cup in 1967, and not only because they were the first British side to reach the final, let alone lift the famous trophy. "We won the European Cup with what was effectively a Glasgow district XI," Billy McNeill, the captain, told Phil Shaw of the *Independent*. "Apart from Bobby Lennox, who's from Saltcoats, 30 miles away, we were all from within 15 miles of Celtic Park. I don't think you'll ever get a situation like that again. Nowadays, with freedom of contract, we'd have been picked off."

They beat Inter Milan 2-1 in Lisbon, but not, as you might have expected, in Benfica's stadium or Sporting's ground but the Estádio Nacional, opened in 1944 and the traditional home of the Portuguese Cup final. The team became known as the Lisbon Lions after coming from behind to beat the overwhelming favourites, who had put out the holders and six-time winners Real Madrid in the quarter-finals. "I think they thought we hadn't a chance," Celtic forward Steve Chalmers said. "They were laughing at us."

Celtic could have been intimidated by that alone when they lined up in the players' tunnel, but there was also the physical element. The Italians lived in the sun and ate a healthy Mediterranean diet while the Celtic players suffered from a Scottish diet and less-than-ideal dentistry – goalkeeper Ronnie Simpson, striker Bobby Lennox and several others had false teeth.

Simpson refused to wear them during games after almost swallowing them after a collision when playing for Newcastle earlier in his career and would keep them in his cap in the back of the net.

"I kept them there in case I had to meet someone important after the game," he wrote in his autobiography, *Sure It's a Grand Old Team to Play For*. In Lisbon, the others kept their dentures in the cap too.

"The contrast was incredible," McNeill said. "They had all these lovely, lyrical names like Alessandro Mazzola, Giacinto Facchetti. We had Bobby Murdoch and Bertie Auld. They had tanned legs and faces, like models. We were all gums and pale skin. I thought: 'They must think it's a pub team they're playing.' Then Bertie started us all singing: 'It's a grand old team to play for.' The Italians were bemused, possibly even a little intimidated."

Inter were also the masters of *catenaccio*, the stifling defensive style that dominated Italian football. So when Celtic gifted them the lead by conceding an early penalty when Jim Craig fouled Renato Cappellini, converted by Mazzola, the game looked over. But that made Celtic's mind up that they had to play their natural attacking game, and Inter's characteristic caution allowed the team in green and white to build up a head of attacking steam long before left-back Tommy Gemmell levelled with a rocket shot from Craig's pass after 62 minutes. "They had so many players behind the ball that I had no need to stay back," he recalled. "I screamed for a cut-back and the rest is history." Six minutes from time Gemmell set up Bobby Murdoch and Chalmers deflected home his shot for the winner.

But before the Celtic players could think about picking up the enormous trophy, there was an important task – retrieve their teeth! "When the final whistle went, the crowd invaded the field," Lennox remembered. "I've jumped on top of John Clark and I'm hugging him and I've seen the crowd spilling onto the field so I had to sprint to Ronnie's goal and get my teeth out of his bonnet."

"There was half a dozen players ran into Ronnie's goalmouth, got his hat and got all their false teeth in," Gemmell said. "And there they were with their pearlies in in time for the photographs." Auld added: "I wonder how they knew their own?"

Glasgow was a great footballing city at that time. On 19 April 1972, a total of 160,000 people crammed into Parkhead and Ibrox to watch Celtic play Inter again in the European Cup semi-final second leg and Rangers face Bayern Munich at the same stage of the European Cup-Winners' Cup – not the sort of fixture clash that you can imagine the TV companies, UEFA or the Glasgow constabulary permitting these days.

Inter won on penalties after both legs ended goalless, and UEFA rules meant that Bobby Murdoch was forced to take a meaningless final penalty even though Inter had already gone through 5-3 thanks to Dixie Deans missing Celtic's first kick.

But Glasgow was to enjoy European glory, and this time it was Rangers' turn after they saw off Bayern to reach the final of the Cup Winners' Cup. They were a team of hard men, coached by Jock Wallace, a Korean War veteran who was obsessed with fitness, but also made the players rub their heads with a whisky-spirit solution to warm their heads before matches, then cooled them down again with icy water.

Captain John Greig, who grew up in Edinburgh as a Hearts fan but played 755 times for Rangers, said he was "really disappointed that we didn't win the treble every year". He took a painkilling injection on the day of the game that overcame a stress fracture of the right foot that rendered him unable to walk.

They faced Dinamo Moscow, the first Russian team to reach a European final, in Barcelona. Dinamo's players had been fired up, allegedly, by speeches on communist ideology and promises of medals and Master of Sport degrees. But they also had concerns about playing in Spain, where the Soviet Union had opposed Spanish dictator Francisco Franco during the Spanish Civil War.

Perhaps they were also alarmed by the sight and sound of 16,000 Rangers fans who had been enjoying Catalan hospitality for days, but whatever the reason, they froze. Colin Stein put the Scots ahead, and Willie Johnston scored twice to give them a 3-0 lead. At that point, Rangers believed the game was won and relaxed. Dinamo pulled two goals back with four minutes to go and the nerves were stretched almost to breaking point.

A minute from time, a whistle for offside was mistaken for the end of the match and the Scottish fans invaded the pitch. They were eventually cleared, and Rangers, who had been hanging on by their fingertips, cleared their heads and saw out the final 60 seconds.

The fans swarmed back on, ripping shirts and even shorts off their victorious favourites. Johnston claimed that he reached the dressing room wearing only the tie-ups on his socks. But the mood turned sour as Franco's paramilitary *Guardia Civil* waded into the celebrating fans.

"When the game finally did finish, the mood among supporters was of jubilation and relief because we had let a 3-0 lead slip away," midfield player Tommy McLean told BBC Sport in 2007. "There was a feeling of euphoria. It was not violent at all. I still can't understand why the police were so heavy-handed. They had cleared the pitch quickly earlier without any trouble and the later reaction was over the top."

Eventually the decision was taken to present the trophy in an office rather than risk stoking up more reaction from the supporters. "It leaves a wee bit of a sour taste," McLean said. "To have the presentation cancelled after such a high-profile win and then not be given the chance to defend it was tough."

"I always visualised winning a European trophy, picking up the cup and being able to go around the park showing all the supporters, who had travelled halfway over Europe to see it," Greig said. "But I walked into a room, and there was a big table. The UEFA committee stood at the back of it, the cup in the middle and they said 'Rangers Football Club, winners', handed me the cup and I walked back along a corridor. I think it was a bigger disappointment for the supporters. I'm just the captain, but we were winning it for thousands of people."

Dinamo appealed the result on the grounds that the pitch invasion had disrupted the match, but UEFA upheld Rangers' win – although they were banned from European competition for two years, reduced to one on appeal, so could not defend the trophy.

Generally, for all their travails, British teams have a fairly proud tradition in Europe. Step forward Aston Villa. No, not for beating Bayern Munich in the 1982 European Cup final in Rotterdam with that shinner from Peter Withe, but for two moral victories over German opposition on foreign soil.

On 14 May 1938, England disgracefully – albeit under orders from Sir Neville Henderson, the British Ambassador in Berlin – gave the Nazi salute during the playing of the German national anthem before a friendly at Berlin's Olympic Stadium.

The following day, Villa, on a tour of Germany, played a German Select XI, which included players from the recently annexed Austria, and were also advised to give the Nazi salute. However, they refused, to the outrage of the local press, before beating their hosts 3-2.

In the book *Kicking and Screaming*, by Rogan Taylor, Villa midfield player Eric Houghton recalled: "We had a meeting about this and George Cummings and Alec Massie and the Scots lads said, 'There's no way we're giving the Nazi salute,' so we didn't give it!"

But Foreign Office diplomats insisted that Villa did not repeat this insult at their next tour match, in Stuttgart. "It did leave a bit of a nasty taste in the mouth for them, us refusing to give the Nazi salute," Houghton said. "The next time they said we'd got to give the Nazi salute, you see."

So in Stuttgart, both teams gave the Nazi salute. Or did they? "We went to the centre of the field and gave them the two-finger salute and they cheered like mad," Houghton said. "They thought it was all right. They didn't know what the two fingers meant."

7.

Die Hard

*"If Cantona had jumped into
our crowd, he'd never have
come out alive!"*

Millwall midfield player Alex Rae

FOOTBALL would still exist without the fans, but it would
not be the same. Imagine Liverpool without the backdrop
of the Kop, an Old Firm game at an empty Parkhead or
Ibrox, or any Newcastle match played minus the Toon followers
draped in black and white – those that aren't bare-chested in
January, anyway.

Fans are the consciences of their clubs. They may be the first
to hurl abuse at players when they make mistakes, but they also
pay their money at the turnstiles, in the club shop, and to travel
the length of the country to watch their teams at the far-flung
corners of football.

They are often the ones who call clubs to account and
march in protest against greedy owners and unfair practices.

When the Brighton board sold the Goldstone Ground, their fans went to Blackburn to picket the home of the chairman, to Hull to deliver a giant Valentine's Day card to John Prescott MP, who was to rule on the new board's stadium planning application, and tramped hundreds of miles delivering leaflets for a council referendum, or election material for the Seagulls Party, formed to stand against councillors who opposed the stadium plans.

They are the ones who provide the terrace humour, even in these days of all-seater stadiums. After Galatasaray supporters produced their infamous 'Welcome to Hell' banners before a home game against Manchester United, British fans came up with perfect answers. Leeds United, who had lost two of their own, Christopher Loftus and Kevin Speight, to stabbings in Istanbul before the first leg of a UEFA Cup semi-final, responded with a banner at Elland Road for the second leg reading 'Welcome to Civilisation'.

Liverpool took theirs to Istanbul for a Champions League tie against Galatasaray at the Ali Sami Yen stadium in 2002. It read: 'Welcome to Hell my arse! If you think this is Hell, try The Grafton on a Friday night.' Mystified locals were probably unaware that The Grafton was Liverpool's oldest nightclub, famed for its 'grab-a-granny' night where, according to *The Times*, "innocent young scallies find themselves at the mercy of predatory Liverpool divorcees."

Fans operate at varying levels of obsession and fanaticism – 'fan' is, after all, an abbreviation of 'fanatic'.

At one extreme, there are those whose love of their clubs consumes their every waking hour and who name their offspring after clubs, players or even entire teams. Like the parents of Anthony Philip David Terry Frank Donald Stanley Gerry Gordon Stephen James Oatway, named after the QPR team of 1973. You would think that would put him off football forever, but far from it. He is better known as Charlie Oatway, who played for Cardiff City, Torquay United, Brentford and Brighton but, sadly, never QPR.

A little less serious are those who buy season tickets, follow their teams around the country and have souvenirs around the house. One Wolves fan built an old Waterloo Road stand seat and turnstile into a home-made bar. Some Arsenal supporters dressed as grim reapers when the bulldozers moved in to demolish Highbury's old home end, the North Bank, and at least one managed to get a crush barrier home, and it now stands at the end of his garden. A Crystal Palace fan confessed online to having gone one better, breaking into Selhurst Park before the building of the Holmesdale Road Stand and removing not only a crush barrier from the old terrace but also one of the goalposts at that end.

Some go only to home matches and manage to find better things to do when the team is on the road than stick a scarf out of the window of the car and head off down the motorway to pay rip-off prices at away grounds and service stations either side of watching their team lose from the worst seat in the house. And those are just the lucky ones who do not brave the replacement bus and train cancellation adventure that is weekend or late-night travel on National Rail.

Most, though, are typical Manchester United fans. In other words, if asked who they support, they would say Manchester United, or, more likely, 'Man United' – by which, despite the sound of it, they do not mean that they are humanists who revere the entire race brought together as one in some type of eternal Coca-Cola commercial – or 'ManYou.'

The odds are that they do not live in Manchester, or anywhere near it. In fact, asked to point on a map to the home of Coronation Street, the Stone Roses and the Peterloo Massacre, most would struggle. And before anyone dismisses this as the sour grapes rantings of a paid-up member of the 'Anyone but United' brigade, the facts are unarguable.

Manchester United's official Facebook page has over 86 million likes. Even allowing for multiple clicks by locally based supporters and members of the Glazer family, that is a number far greater than that of the entire population of Greater

Manchester, which is around 2.73 million. Even with the mass immigration so feared by UKIP, 86 million is actually more than the number of people who live in the entire UK.

These 'fans' have never been to a United game anywhere, let alone at Old Trafford. So cheer up, Stretford End regulars, we don't mean you. And further good news for you is that the 'I Fucking Hate Man United' Facebook page has only 74,000 likes, although that is around 64,000 more than 'George Osborne, Politician'.

Even if the majority of these 86 million are only armchair fans, that is a hell of a lot of armchairs, and a hell of a lot of satellite TV subscriptions worldwide. But most fans, whether we like it or not, are of this type.

It takes a lot to get them out of those armchairs, but their local club suddenly becoming successful or building a comfortable new stadium can do it. Such fans are condemned by rivals or those who have previously braved the rain, snow and unspeakable toilet facilities as 'plastic fans'. But it could be worse. For one season, Arsenal had an entire end of fans who were made only of paint.

The Arsenal Mural made its debut in August 1992, after the old North Bank had been demolished and a new stand was being constructed. It was, in some ways, a brainwave to cover an enormous hoarding behind the goal, 75 yards wide and 18 yards high, with images of a crowd rather than play games in front of a building site – and, with Highbury's reputation as one of the quieter grounds, there was no noticeable drop-off in volume.

The first league match in front of the mural was a 4-2 home defeat by Norwich City on 15 August, and it was not only the result that caused displeasure. Unfortunately, the painters of the mural had omitted to include any black or ethnic minority faces among the crowd, which was misguided on any level, and especially for an inner-city club with the greatest proportion of black and mixed-race supporters in England.

The painting had been altered by the time the team played their next home game, against Sheffield Wednesday on 29

August, only to fall foul of complaints from children's charities that the mural showed children sitting with adults who did not appear to be their parents. None of the children were sitting next to women, and there weren't enough females in any case, so men were repainted as women.

Sadly, the 8,000 painted fans had little to cheer as it was not until 28 September that Arsenal scored at the mural end, Ian Wright heading home Kevin Campbell's cross for the only goal of a match against Manchester City. At least none of the fans at that end had left early and missed it.

* * * * *

For many years, the England team's most famous fan was a man from Dorset named Ken Baily, a sort of all-purpose, self-appointed England cheerleader. Whether he deserved the other epithet often attached to him, 'much-loved', is open to debate. His distinctive outfit of top hat, red tailcoat and Union Jack waistcoat seemed to be everywhere in the 1960s, '70s and '80s, and was more tolerated with raised eyes than appreciated.

He was not only to be glimpsed at England (or Bournemouth) matches, but also at other occasions when the patriotism quota could, in his opinion, do with taking up a notch or two – royal visits, for example. In an obituary in the *Independent* by Leigh Hatts after Baily's death in 1993, it was reported that he had once turned up in Australia to greet the Queen. "'What are you doing here?' asked the Queen on spotting Ken Baily among a crowd in a Sydney street. 'I'd go anywhere for you, Ma'am,' replied Baily." Prince Philip's reaction went unrecorded.

Something of an athlete in his early years, Baily entered the Guinness Book of Records for running the most recorded miles and once ran all the way to North America by going round and round a ship's deck. He also carried the Olympic torch when the games were held at Wembley in 1948.

His trips to sporting events were financed by an inheritance, and he did not confine himself to football. It was he who covered the chest of famous Twickenham streaker Erica Roe in 1982, with a Union Jack, of course.

But the ultimate recognition came when Baily became a Subbuteo figure. He was part of a 'Mascot and Bench' set, along with a manager and two substitutes, and when England played Portugal at Wembley in 1969, Subbuteo Ken Bailys were given away free with the match programme. To workers used to hand painting nothing trickier than some Stoke City or Sunderland stripes or Celtic hoops, that waistcoat must have been a bugger.

Other clubs have their own distinctive fans. Portsmouth's most notorious is unquestionably John Westwood (or John Anthony Portsmouth Football Club Westwood, to give him his full official name). A regular at the Fratton End, he is notable for the amount of Pompey-tattooed flesh on display, a blue and white checked stovepipe hat, a similarly patterned waistcoat, PFC engraved on his teeth, a blue wig and a bell, drum or bugle. Or all three.

The din created by Westwood and his acolytes even came to the notice of Sir Alex Ferguson before Manchester United played a Premier League match at Fratton Park in November 2009. Ferguson was banned from the touchline for the game and there was some concern that he would be unable to convey instructions from the stand to the bench because of the cacophony to his left.

"I have got the communication lines for the game in place," he said at his pre-match press conference. "The only problem is that it's such a noisy place, Fratton Park. It's one of these old stadiums – it's a bit rickety that stand nowadays. The directors' box is towards the home end where all that noise comes from – the drums and whatever the hell they have got going on at that place. But it's a good racket. It's a terrific football stadium really. The atmosphere is always great there. You have to deal with that so it should be a very hard game for us."

A number of papers contacted Westwood for his reaction, and he was delighted to learn that he might be able to unsettle Ferguson. "If we can stop any line of communication between

Fergie and his team, we will do it," he told the *Sun*. "We're famous for our noise and once the fans see Fergie's comments they will make even more. Fratton Park is a proper, old-fashioned ground and it's nice to think the fans have a part to play.

"I used to take a couple of big bass drums into the ground until I was stopped because of health and safety rules. But if anything, the snare drums are even noisier."

The club were to be relegated at the end of the season after going into administration yet still reached the FA Cup final, and Westwood noted: "Portsmouth is the best soap opera going. Never mind EastEnders, this is Fratton Enders."

But before the Wembley trip, Westwood fell foul of authority – the Sports Grounds Safety Authority, to be specific. In March 2010 it was reported that the club had threatened to ban Westwood for persistent standing, in contravention of the rules that required fans to sit in seated areas. Apparently he was blamed for hundreds of other fans standing at the Fratton End.

Westwood released a statement through the Football Supporters' Federation, saying: "We want to make as much noise as possible in support of our club. Playing instruments sitting down is not an option and singing is far more natural standing up. After all you stand for hymns in church and for the National Anthem, even in football grounds."

Most people asked what Westwood does for a living might guess that he works in a pub in the roughest part of Portsmouth docks or has some other occupation in which engraved teeth and club tattoos are a given – in a circus, perhaps. In fact he runs an antiquarian bookshop in Petersfield, which is a Royal Warrant Holder as a picture framer and supplier of art materials by appointment to Her Majesty The Queen's Royal Collection Department.

If most fans would not go as far as John 'yadda yadda' Westwood in displaying their loyalty, then all of them would surely love to be out there on the field playing for their team.

Lol Cottrell managed it, turning out for his beloved Liverpool at Anfield. A bakery delivery driver, he was given his big chance in 1977 by Esther Rantzen in her programme, *The Big Time*, which also launched the singing career of Sheena Easton.

The idea of the show was that decent amateur actors, athletes, chefs and others would be allowed their chance on a professional stage. Cottrell played to a good standard in local football and was chosen to be allowed to take part in Tommy Smith's testimonial match against an international XI that including Bobby Charlton, Norman Hunter and Alex Stepney. Smith helped train him, he was given advice by the other Liverpool players as well as Denis Law, Jimmy Hill and Bill Shankly, and opponents said afterwards that they had assumed he was a reserve player given an outing. He certainly did not stick out as inferior.

But the programme was unable to supply the happy ending it had no doubt wanted. With the score at 3-3 late on, Liverpool were awarded a penalty and Cottrell was given the chance to score in front of the Kop. Unfortunately, Stepney saved the kick. A sympathetic referee 'spotted an infringement' and ordered a retake. But Stepney, dourly refusing to enter into the spirit of the moment (he later claimed it was 'a matter of professional pride') saved again.

Cottrell knew he would be playing for Liverpool, but West Ham fan Steve Davies had no inkling that he would end up playing for his team when he went along to a Hammers pre-season friendly away to non-league Oxford City. He had gone with his wife and a friend, and was giving striker Lee Chapman some stick when Harry Redknapp, then West Ham assistant manager, made him an offer no fan could refuse.

"There's a guy next to the dugout, and he's got West Ham tattooed all over his arms and neck, he's got the earrings," Redknapp told Sky's *A League of Their Own*. "After two minutes, he started on me, 'We ain't got that Lee Chapman up front have we? I ain't coming every week if he's playing.' Half-time I made five substitutions, and we only had the bare eleven out – I was running out of players. Then we got another injury, so I said to this guy in the crowd, 'Oi, can you play as good as you talk?'

"He looked totally confused. So I told him he was going to get his dream to play for West Ham. We sent him down the tunnel and he reappeared ten minutes later all done out in the strip. He ran onto the pitch and a journalist from the local Oxford paper sidled up and asked 'Who's that, Harry?' I said 'What? Haven't you been watching the World Cup? That's the great Bulgarian Tittyshev!' The fella wasn't bad – actually, he scored!"

Not exactly – the goal was disallowed. The US-based football magazine *Howler* tracked Davies down and got the story first hand. "I didn't come out of Oxford's half," laughs Steve. "I was playing up front with Trevor Morley, goal-hanging! It was fucking quick football. This was a step up from Sunday league, to say the least.

"I got a few touches, including a pass from Alvin Martin; I remember he called out my name in his Scouse accent. I was blown away. 'Stevie!' he shouted, and he sent the ball pinging to my feet. It had such pace on it, nearly knocked me over.

"It didn't feel natural at all – that's what people always ask. I was just trying to stay calm. After the first five minutes, my legs were shaking; I was playing for West Ham! After that it was just 'get on with the game' kind of thing. I was running on adrenaline, and I was more worried about fucking up."

And his 'goal'? "Suddenly, we were on the attack. The ball went out wide – I'm sure it was Matty Holmes on the wing – and we pushed forward. I had two defenders in front of me and I was just sprinting forward, I think. I just hit it. I hit it like nothing else. Know what I mean? I belted it. It was like time stopped still – it was the greatest moment of my life. I was two yards offside. I ran up to the ref and told him, 'You bastard, you spoiled my dream!'"

Manchester United fan Karl Power did not get to play for the Red Devils, but in 2001 he managed the next best thing, appearing in a United pre-match photo with the team, in full kit. It happened before a match against Bayern Munich in Germany, and was organised with his friend and fellow fan Tommy Dunn. Dunn had become an old hand at getting into places he shouldn't, having found that carrying a video camera was a passport to the great football stages. Security men assumed he was an accredited media man and allowed him into the dressing room area and, on one occasion, into a car with Sir Alex Ferguson. It was his idea to put Power in the team photo because he looked the part.

"It must be the biggest and best football sting of all time," Power told the *Sun*. "We've videoed players in hotels and got ourselves into official press conferences before all the biggest games in Europe.

"It was during a match against in Barcelona in Spain that we first hatched the plot. We got onto the pitch and it was so easy we thought we could go one better.

"We were planning to do it for this year's final in Milan but we doubted United would get there, so we knew it was Munich or bust. We planned it like a military campaign and brought three United kits with us – red, white and blue. Then we found out where the team were staying and got one of the directors to tell us what colour they'd be wearing.

"We then went back and rehearsed it all in our hotel room. We got a taxi to the ground and pretended we were with a TV crew, and the gatemen let us in. We managed to get down to pitchside and waited for the players to come out of the tunnel. Then with 20 minutes till kick-off, we saw an opening where there were no stewards and walked all the way round the running track and ended up behind the goal. We sat with the photographers watching the warm-up. Then, when the teams walked out, I went to the players' entrance and knew nothing was going to stop me."

Dunn and Power later told Simon Hattenstone of the *Guardian* that they had studied pre-match rituals and knew that the moment had come when the last United player shook hands with the final German player. There are two versions of the photo – one a conventional team shot, only with one extra player on the end of the back row next to Dwight Yorke, and a second in which Roy Keane and Gary Neville spot the interloper – but too late.

Power, of course, did not stop there. He has walked out to bat for England at Headingley, knocked up on Centre Court at Wimbledon before a Tim Henman match, sneaked onto the winner's podium at Silverstone before Michael Schumacher could get there and performed a haka before an Italy-England rugby international.

Another, slightly more drastic, way of getting on the pitch with your heroes is to have your ashes scattered on the hallowed turf. The practice used to be more commonplace, but many clubs get so many requests that they no longer accommodate them. Tottenham, for example, refuse because "the chemical reaction caused with the ashes and mixture of fertilisers and pesticides used on the playing surface cause a level of burning to the polypropylene system used to strengthen the pitch and can cause disease to the playing surface." Others allow scattering around the perimeter or at memorial gardens at the ground, but not on the playing surface.

QPR are reckoned by scattering-ashes.co.uk (yes, really) to be the club who are most sympathetic to the last wishes of fans. They will arrange for mourners to be met at Loftus Road by the club chaplain by appointment on any non-match weekday, visit the dressing rooms and walk down the tunnel onto the pitch. The ashes – a coffee jar's worth is the maximum amount permitted – are laid on a tray in the Loft End goalmouth before prayers and a ceremony. Afterwards, the chaplain gathers the ashes, looks after them until the pitch is dug up and re-seeded in late May, and scatters them himself.

Huddersfield Town offer a bespoke funeral service, the Terriers Funeral Plan. "While many funerals remain quite traditional, some are increasingly becoming a celebration of life, and that includes sporting interests, and we are often asked if people can use our branding in one form or another," Town commercial director Sean Jarvis told the *Huddersfield Examiner*. "It's still a bit of a taboo subject but there's no reason why that should be. The only certain things in life are death and taxes and the sooner we start planning the better. Our commercial deal means the club receives a benefit from plans sold so even when Town fans pass on they can leave a small legacy to the club. This isn't for everybody but it's another service we can offer."

The deal includes a coffin in Huddersfield Town colours and club crest or traditional quality veneered coffin with home shirt and name printed on the back, a blue and white floral football bouquet with condolence card from Huddersfield Town, the club song, 'Smile Awhile' played at the funeral service, the use of a suite at the stadium (catering not included), and announcements at a game and in the programme. Ashes, of course, can be scattered around the pitch. Birmingham City have a similar arrangement with a local funeral firm.

* * * * *

Then there is the 92 club. They are the fans who have seen matches at all 92 Premier League and Football League grounds. But with clubs moving to new stadiums, membership can be quite a complex matter.

For example, the website of the club, which was formed in 1978, states that: "To qualify, on the day your 92nd ground is visited, you must have visited the current grounds of the other 91 League clubs." So if you have seen a game at Roker Park but not the Stadium of Light, too bad. And if you've been to Upton Park, you've got two years to tick the London Stadium off, or you're out.

Several people have done the 92 slightly differently, visiting all the stadiums in 92 hours, a distance of around 2,222 miles, usually for charity. Various routes have been tried: when Wolves fans Natalie and James Allen did the trip in 2014 in aid of Cancer Research UK and the Georgina Cancer Ward in Dudley, West Midlands, they began and ended at Molineux. They headed north through Shrewsbury, Stoke and Crewe before doing the Lancashire clubs. Then up to Carlisle, across to Newcastle and down through Yorkshire. From there it was the East Midlands and East Anglia. Round the M25 to the south coast and along to the West Country. And finally, on a marathon final day, along the M4 and M40 taking in South Wales, the Thames Valley and into London, then back up the M1 and M6.

Two Portsmouth employees, kit men Barry Harris and Kev McCormack, have also done the 92 as Pompey have slid down through the divisions, reaching the magic number at Cambridge's Abbey Stadium in March 2015. Harris's first trip in the job was to Blackburn in the 1966/67 season, while McCormack is an ex-Royal Marine who first got the job under Alan Ball, used to have a half-time cigarette lit and ready for Robert Prosinečki and was given his FA Cup medal in 2010 by manager Avram Grant.

Who is Britain's number one football fan? When interviewed in April 2011, Tottenham Hotspur supporter Brian Buck had attended 10,000 games, which works out as spending 625 days at matches, not allowing for injury time, half-time or extra time and penalties.

He had missed only one match at White Hart Lane since 1968, he had visited 3,000 different grounds in the UK since watching his first game, between Cambridge United and Colchester United reserves at the Abbey Stadium, in 1956, when he was four years old. Game number 10,000 was at the same ground, a 3-1 win for Cambridge Regional College FC – a feeder club for Cambridge United – against Brantham Athletic in the Eastern Counties League, then known as the Ridgeons League, on 19 March. It was his 350th game of the 2010/11 season.

"I'll do this until my dying day," he told the Mirror website. "I hope to make 20,000 but that's some task. I hope I can make it to 15,000 at least. I attend Premier League games but enjoy watching with three men and a dog the next day. It gives you a greater understanding of the game. I haven't seen anybody as good as Pelé since Santos played Fulham in 1973. Recently I think David Ginola has been one of the greatest."

But for devotion to the England team, it would be hard to beat Brian Wright, a Coventry City fan who missed only one competitive match played by the national team in 26 years, and that was only because England fans were banned from a match against Turkey in 2003. He takes a mascot called Rooneyshrek – you can imagine – to most games.

His dedication has been recognised by the FA. He is guaranteed tickets for any England game he applies for, he was invited to meet Fabio Capello, the head coach, in 2010, and the following year got to visit the squad at a training session before a friendly against Holland at Wembley.

"At the South Africa World Cup I went up Table Mountain, visited Nelson Mandela's cell on Robben Island and went cage diving with great white sharks. The 90 minutes are sometimes the worst part of the trip – England can really put you through the wringer."

The dark side of fandom is hooliganism, and an entire branch of the publishing industry has grown up around those who like to remember themselves as hard cases rather than the hangers-on they almost certainly were.

But in 2015, a football club chairman warned that some retired hoolies were planning to relive their glory days, which conjured up images of grandfathers hitting each other with their walking sticks before beating a hasty retreat in their wheelchairs – a sort of *Last of the Summer Wine* with braces and Stanley knives.

But in fact, the geriatric rascals planned to play the roles of generals sending their younger troops into battle.

Dave Doggett wrote in the Cambridge United official programme: "Unfortunately football clubs still attract an undesirable element of society that appear determined to ruin the enjoyment of real supporters of football clubs. Our promotion to the Football League appears to have encouraged our 'risk' from the 1980s to come out of retirement.

"Many of them are grandparents trying to encourage the next generation to join their 'gangs'. It sounds pathetic but unfortunately it is reality. We are working closely with police. Hopefully the reality of the potential consequences will dissuade some of our younger supporters from becoming involved with these undesirables.

"Our football club is too important to so many to allow a few to ruin our great sport."

Finally, there are the celebrity fans. Some are genuine, but others, such as former Prime Minister David Cameron – supposedly an Aston Villa fan who could not remember which claret and blue team he was meant to support and wrongly guessed West Ham, for which he should have been voted out of office there and then – much less so. Villa are also allegedly followed by Prince William and Tom Hanks, who once said the club's name sounded nice and the sort of place he might like to go on holiday. Not too familiar with the greater Birmingham area.

When Villa played Arsenal in the 2015 FA Cup final, though, Villa were put in the shade by the Gunners' celebrity glitter. They have the edge in the Royal Family, with the Queen a fan according to 'royal sources' but also Cesc Fabregas, who told a Spanish radio station that he had chatted to Her Majesty at a reception for the Arsenal team at Buckingham Palace. The Queen Mother had, it seems, been an admirer of former Gunners legend Denis Compton. Prince Harry is also supposedly a Gooner, as are Idris Elba, Spike Lee and Jay-Z, Billy Beane of Moneyball fame, and Piers Morgan (of the Wenger Out persuasion).

Chelsea had a reputation as a club followed by stars in the 1960s and nowadays their supporters include Jeremy Clarkson, Omid Djalili, Mark Ronson, Will Ferrell and author Joanna Trollope, while other London clubs claim Adele, Kenneth Branagh, Jude Law and JK Rowling (Tottenham) and Russell Brand, James Corden, Keira Knightley and Ray Winstone (West Ham). Katy Perry apparently lost her love of the

Hammers when her marriage to Brand ended. So not a real fan at all, then.

As you would expect, Manchester United have attracted a lot of celebrity attention, and they cover the range of devotion discussed earlier. True fans include Olly Murs, Usain Bolt and Mick Hucknall, while somewhere at the other end are Rihanna, Megan Fox and Drake. Ricky Hatton and Liam and Noel Gallagher are, of course, City fans.

Actors Liam Neeson, Kim Cattrall and Mike Myers are Liverpool fans, as are Gary Barlow, former world tennis number one Caroline Wozniacki and NBA superstar LeBron James, while Evertonians include Dame Judi Dench and, possibly, Sylvester Stallone. Well, Sly once visited Goodison and waved a blue scarf on the pitch – so he is probably as much of a fan as Michael Jackson was of Fulham, notwithstanding the statue of the King of Pop that then-owner Mohamed Al Fayed built at Craven Cottage after his sole visit for a match against Wigan in April 1999. Actor Keith Allen is a genuine Fulham fan whose devotion goes back to the days of Johnny Haynes and Tosh Chamberlain, but for some reason no statue of him has been erected down by the Thames – even though he sang and wrote the lyrics for England's unofficial 1998 World Cup song 'Vindaloo' by Fat Les.

Adrian Chiles and Frank Skinner are ardent West Brom fans, and Skinner even insisted on his Saturday morning show on Absolute Radio beginning at 8am so that he could be sure to get to 3pm kick-offs at The Hawthorns. Crystal Palace seem to number a large number of comedians, including Jo Brand, Eddie Izzard and Mark Steel. Insert your own punchline, as they say.

No one knows whether celebrity support has any effect on a team's performance. Mohamed Al Fayed insists that the removal of his Jacko statue by new owner Shahid Khan in 2013 led to Fulham's relegation in 2014, but manager Felix Magath probably had more to do with it. If he had steered the team to safety, the former Hamburg legend would probably have been forgiven for outlandish ideas such as treating injuries with old German folk remedies – defender Brede Hangeland was told to rub alcohol-soaked cheese known as quark on a troublesome thigh and speak to a loved one while it was working its magic.

"I merely suggested it could be worth trying the old wives' tale of applying quark to the injured area," Magath later told German news agency DPA. "I would never tell a doctor what to do. I don't have a guilty conscience. I don't want to sound arrogant, but I am convinced that English football has something to learn from German qualities. Sadly they're not that prepared to listen." Perhaps he should have used Cottage cheese instead.

However, one club seems to have benefited from royal backing, and from beyond the grave too.

Leicester City's all-time win rate in the top flight was only 32 per cent until the remains of King Richard III, which had been discovered under a car park in the city and identified as the last of the Plantagenets by University of Leicester experts, were reburied in the city's cathedral in 2015.

The Foxes were bottom of the Premier League before the ceremony on 26 March 2015, seven points adrift of safety and without a win in eight league games. They won seven of their remaining nine games to finish 14th, six points clear of danger, and continued their excellent form into the 2015/16 season. With their win rate almost doubled to 63.8 per cent, they took the league title to deliver one of the greatest shocks in football history.

No wonder their stadium is called the King Power.

8.

Foam is where the Heart is

"Everybody's Got Something To Hide Except Me And My Monkey."

Beatles song title

L IKE players, they perform before the fans on the pitch at every match in colourful outfits. Like players, they are cheered by some, derided by others. But not many players have married one another on the field, ripped a rival's ears off or been elected mayor of the town they represent. Club mascots, on the other hand, have done all these things and more.

Mascots have beaten professionals in player-of-the-year votes, been guests at their creators' weddings and appeared in national newspapers clad in lingerie. But these foam creations have also been involved in shadier activities. So much so that in November 2001 the Football League announced that it intended to draw up a code of conduct for mascots following a series of fights and pitch invasions, before settling for writing to clubs asking them to be mindful of their representatives' behaviour.

Perhaps the most notorious mascot, and certainly one of the breed's serial offenders, is Cyril the Swan. The nine-foot Swansea City mascot's antics have resulted in more than one four-figure fine from the League and even a touchline ban – usually a sanction reserved for errant managers and coaches.

Swans have a reputation for aggressive behaviour, and Cyril certainly lived down to it in 2001 when he tore off the head of Zampa the Lion, his Millwall counterpart, and kicked it into the crowd at the Welsh club's old ground, the Vetch Field. He was reported to have told Zampa: 'Don't fuck with the Swans.'

But Cyril's charge sheet does not end there. He has also been accused of throwing pork pies at visiting West Ham fans, and pushing over a rival mascot, a woman in a dog suit, before the Mascot Grand National, of which more later. And he has also fallen, er, 'fowl' of the authorities for his over-enthusiastic goal celebrations.

He was first reported by Steve Dunn, the referee, for running onto the pitch to join players' celebrations after a goal in an FA Cup tie, also against Millwall, in 1998, and charged with bringing the game into disrepute. The club banned him for two games and considered building him a nest well away from the touchline, but his natural exuberance got the better of him again when he clashed with Norwich City director of football Bryan Hamilton after celebrating a Swansea goal.

Not that his misdemeanours ever seemed to affect his relationship with the public. He was voted the nation's favourite mascot by readers of *Match of the Day* magazine, has appeared on the BBC National Lottery Draw from the Vetch Field, trod the boards in the pantomime *Aladdin* at Swansea's Grand Theatre, took part in *Night Fever*, the karaoke show on Channel 5, and released a CD of, inevitably 'Nice Swan, Cyril'.

And the club has always backed their man. Or rather, their swan. They arranged for him to be represented at his first

Welsh FA hearing by Maurice Watkins, the Manchester United lawyer who defended Eric Cantona for his two-footed lunge on a Crystal Palace fan in January 1995. Two national newspapers also launched campaigns to defend Cyril while Swansea City were inundated with messages of support for the under-fire mascot.

Naturally Cyril has his own presence on Twitter, and is also among a number of male mascots to have tied the knot with a female counterpart. He wed Cybil the Swan, in April 2005 at the Vetch, with the congregation mostly being too diplomatic to point out that Cybil looked more like a duck than a swan. Love is blind, though. "She is the love of my life and has made the Swan I am today," 'Cyril' said. "All my antics are well and truly behind me. To be honest I couldn't afford the fines."

A staged marriage between two rubber animals is one thing, but true love blossomed for real between the human beings inside Crystal Palace mascots Pete the Eagle and Alice. They had been bird and wife for three years on the pitch at Selhurst Park before Lee McBride/Pete made an honest woman of Kate/Alice at a Palace-themed wedding in 2006.

Kate was first to climb into the feathery suit, in October 2001. "Alice was introduced during the 2001/02 season as a way of making Palace more family-focused," Lee told the *Croydon Advertiser* in 2012. "There was an advert in the match-day programme asking for someone to be a mascot, so Kate contacted the club, had a game's trial and has been Alice ever since.

"I became Pete when the previous handler retired from his mascot duties in the summer of 2003 and the club asked Kate if she knew anyone who would want to take on the role. Having been a Palace fan all my life, I couldn't turn it down and I've been Pete for more than nine years now, so I'll be ready for my testimonial next summer!"

Worst moment? "Paul Peschisolido, who was playing for Sheffield United at the time, once stuffed a football in Alice's mouth," Lee said. "And Kate also nearly had her head knocked off when we played Millwall once, as she ran across the part of the pitch where the players were warming up and they ran into her."

McBride's predecessor in the Pete suit was Keith Blackwell, a Kent headmaster, who once featured in a soft drinks commercial that highlighted how much embarrassment he caused his teenaged son by dressing up on match days as an eagle. "It's every football fan's ambition to be with the team on the pitch," he said. Even dressed in foam? "It means you can meet your heroes, which I have done."

Just as a swan is the obvious mascot for Swansea, anything but an eagle would have been missing a trick for Crystal Palace, who have been nicknamed The Eagles since Malcolm Allison changed it from the more historic Glaziers in 1973. Others are less comprehensible unless you know your history – for instance, H'Angus the Monkey of Hartlepool.

Legend has it that a monkey was washed ashore from a nearby wreck nearby during the Napoleonic Wars, and the somewhat unsophisticated locals, never having met any foreigners, thought it might be a Frenchman. The fact that the poor innocent creature could not speak or understand English did not exactly count in its favour and they sentenced it to death and hanged it.

Unlikely, for sure – but an appropriately named monkey was the perfect mascot for the club known to just about every rival fan as the Monkey-Hangers. And, perhaps in an attempt to prove there were no longer any hard feelings between primates and Hartlepudlians, in 2002 the people of the north-eastern coastal town made H'Angus their first directly elected mayor.

Choosing to stand as H'Angus rather than Stuart Drummond, the man inside the monkey suit, he told the local paper: "People have said for years that a monkey could be elected in Hartlepool. Now we're going to find out." His manifesto included free bananas for school children and his slogan was: 'H'Angus gives a monkey's.'

He must have done a decent job, as he was re-elected twice. But what is most remarkable about his first, narrow election victory is that H'Angus had a far from spotless past. He was thrown out of an away game at Scunthorpe in November 2000 for suggestive behaviour towards a female steward during the half-time lottery draw – fans wore 'H'Angus is innocent' T-shirts at the next home match – and again at Blackpool in 2001 after a half-time routine involving an inflatable doll in a Hartlepool kit. Rugby-tackling photographers was mild by comparison.

A primate can be forgiven for not knowing how to conduct itself in civilised society – just look at King Kong in New York. But there was surely no such excuse for Bury's Robbie the Bobby, named after Sir Robert Peel, the founder of the modern police force, who was born in the Lancashire town in 1788. Robbie conspicuously failed to behave in a fashion worthy of his illustrious and law-abiding namesake when he was sent off three times in the 2001/02 season, the first in which Jonathan Pollard, a plumber and amateur boxer, had occupied the suit.

First he mooned at Stoke City supporters. Within weeks he had ripped off the ears of Peterborough United's rabbit mascot. And finally he got into a fight with Cardiff City's Bartley the Bluebird at a vital relegation match, a ruck that took several stewards to break up.

Some reports allege that Bartley, a large furry bluebird with a yellow beak, threw the first punch, which Robbie had not seen coming, even though he was wearing boxing gloves, so obviously expected some type of pugilism. "I was just having a bit of a laugh when I was thumped in the face. I wasn't going to take it lying down and we had a bit of a scrap," he said. "When I realised Bartley wasn't playing, I clouted him a couple of times and then ripped his head off," Pollard told the *Manchester Evening News*. "I think I broke his nose and I'm sure he lost a tooth or two."

Cardiff later replaced Bartley with a boy and girl pairing of Bartley Blue and Zoe Lou. Pollard was finally dismissed in 2007 after one controversial incident too many, being spoken to by police and stewards during an FA Cup tie against Lincoln

City following complaints from referee Howard Webb and one of his assistants. The man who took over the Robbie role, Anthony Bersz, suffered an immediate but less serious mishap when he was unable to retrieve his street clothes from a locked cupboard after his debut against Brighton and had to go home in character.

If Pollard's behaviour was shocking coming from a mascot made in the image of a man associated with law and order, perhaps a Wolf has some historic excuse for reacting adversely to the sight of three little pigs.

In November 1998, Wolfie, the Wolverhampton Wanderers mascot, found himself on the Ashton Gate pitch with three porkers representing Coldseal, one of Bristol City's sponsors, and, so one version of the story goes, tried to 'borrow' a ball they were kicking after his own had been booted out of the ground by a fan.

If Wolfie expected the pigs to react as timidly as those in the original nursery rhyme characters, he had another think coming. Two of them went on the attack, and after a certain amount of huffing and puffing, as well as the throwing of fairly unconvincing punches on both sides, Wolfie was forced to retreat.

No houses were blown down thanks to the peace-making efforts of City's stewards and their own City Cat mascot. "Maybe Wolfie was taking his role a bit too seriously," an anonymous little pig was quoted as saying. The altercation later featured on BBC's *Have I Got News for You*.

Wolves were tight-lipped about Wolfie's identity, saying only that he had been doing the job for two years, but his natural predatory instincts got the better of him again later that season when he was reported to the FA by a fan after a fight with Baggie Bird, the mascot of Black Country rivals West Bromwich Albion.

Wolves called it 'harmless fun', but an Albion fan, Noel Bishop, told the *Birmingham Post & Mail*: "I was gobsmacked when, during the warm-up, Wolfie ran up behind Baggie Bird and kicked his legs from under him. The shocked Albion mascot picked himself up and was remonstrating with Wolfie, who pushed him on his behind again. It looked like he was trying to start a fight but Baggie Bird walked away to avoid further trouble. However, the 3,000 Albion fans in the ground were going crazy, especially when Wolfie goaded us with a wave.

"I was so angry I've now reported him to the FA for crowd incitement and bringing the game into disrepute. I hope the powers-that-be take action because his behaviour could have sparked off serious crowd trouble."

It certainly seems to be the sight of a rival that causes mascots to see red, or tangerine in the case of Oldham Athletic's Chaddy the Owl, who launched an apparently unprovoked attack on Blackpool's Bloomfield the Bear, pulling off his boots and hurling them into the crowd.

"I was in the press box and they were play-fighting, when Chaddy waded in and seemed to be kicking ten bells out of Bloomfield Bear," Blackpool press officer Matthew Williams told the *Oldham Evening Chronicle*.

However, Chaddy, who twice won the Mascot Grand National, claimed there was another side to the story, and that Bloomfield had tried to damage his beak. "Ninety per cent of mascots are top guys," he said. "But some of them think if they can floor Chaddy the Owl they can be in the newspapers." Well, of course: today Boundary Park, tomorrow the world.

It does not always take another mascot to cause trouble. In March 1998 Gavin Lucas lost his job as Aston Villa's Hercules the Lion over an incident of sexual harassment. At half-time during a Premier League game against Crystal Palace, Hercules hugged and kissed Miss Aston Villa, Debbie Robins. He maintained it was all meant in jest and was done in good spirit, but the club felt he had overstepped the mark and sent him packing.

"I growled and then grabbed Miss Villa around the waist with my paws and pulled her around a bit," he explained. "It was a bit of a grapple and a bit of a hug. Then I gave her a kiss, but it wasn't much of a kiss because I still had my lion's head on. Debbie took it in good spirit. She was enjoying herself. She's an absolute corker, but there was nothing sexual in it." How he must have hoped his fiancée believed that last bit. "She knows I was sacked, but she doesn't know why. I hope she'll be all right about it though because she's bound to find out now."

One man was sacked for becoming too thin to fit the chunky image of Bradford City's mascot. Lenny Berry had entertained the Valley Parade crowd for 19 years as the corpulent, briefcase-carrying, bowler-hatted City Gent before diabetes forced him to lose weight in 2013, dropping to a svelte 10st.

Previously, when taunted by rival fans with chants of 'Who Ate All the Pies,' Berry would pull an enormous pie from his briefcase, which was a hard act to pull off convincingly for a now-lightweight figure, whose replica shirt size had dropped from XXXL to M.

The City Gent was said to be modelled on the club's portly former chairman, Stafford Heginbotham, so ditching the mascot would probably have been a no-brainer when information came to light suggesting that Heginbotham might have had a sinister involvement with the Bradford fire. And the club already had three another mascots, chickens reflecting their official nickname of The Bantams.

That, though, was not yet an issue when Roger Owens, a City director, told the *Daily Mirror*: "The main issue was his physical appearance, which was much changed from the original concept of the then-chairman, the late Stafford Heginbotham, who styled the City Gent on himself.

"We agreed that action needed to be taken. It was also agreed that Lenny be formally contacted, by letter, to put our various points to him and to suggest that the club obtain a Sumo-type suit with character head piece to represent the Gent. The Football League had told us that only animal or human mascots were now appropriate if they wore an anonymous headset."

Not acceptable, it seems. "Lenny was given a deadline to respond, which was extended and then not complied with. Lenny advised me that he would cease his role as City Gent with immediate effect. The board has now decided that we are adequately covered by Billy Bantam and the City Gent name lives on in the excellent club fanzine. We will not replace the City Gent as a mascot."

Lenny said he was gutted. "I play the part of the mascot through my face and my eyes. I've always had a good rapport with fans. I've been through the Bradford City fire. I've been through everything down there. I don't want the club getting hurt, I love the club. If you cut me open I'd be claret and amber. It's not the team and it's not the club, but I am disappointed with the way it's been dealt with. Over the years I've done a lot of fundraising as well as cancer charities. I've taken part in mascot races and other events. I will still be at Bradford City as a season-ticket holder, but it is really sad."

There was better news for Donny Dog of Doncaster Rovers, reinstated after being dismissed for posing in lingerie. Donny, it must be pointed out without delay, is an attractive mother-of-three named Tracy Chandler, who was distraught when she learned via an email from the club that they intended to replace her when photographs of her on a bed with Donny Dog's head appeared in the *Sunday Sport*.

"I was in the *Sunday Times* magazine and another reporter asked if I would do a cheeky shot and I said I would if it was for charity," she told Jim White of *Sky Sports News*. And not just any charity, but the NSPCC, a charity supported by Rovers.

"They said my services as Donny Dog were no longer required as I had 'disgraced the club'. I had to give the suit back. I was in bits over that. I felt as if I was losing my best friend. Being Donny Dog meant the world to me. I put everything into it. Time, money and effort. I've got some brilliant fans and they all want me back. I've been inundated with emails. I can't tell you how overwhelmed I've been by all the support that everyone has given me."

However, John Ryan, the Doncaster chairman, had a change of heart. "The *Sunday Sport* and a mascot designed for children is not an ideal mix," he said. "We were just a bit concerned about the sexualisation of young children. I think some people thought it was inappropriate and I think it was in a way, but I've seen the pictures and I think she looks very nice."

* * * * *

Perhaps a mascots' union would have prevented matters getting that far, but according to Richard Cutcher, formerly Rammie the Ram of Derby County, mascots do have their own very exclusive chatroom and try to maintain very strict standards, even if, as we have seen, they sometimes fall short. Cutcher later became a journalist and looked back on his gap-year experience at Pride Park for the *Daily Telegraph*.

"Derby County has a long standing relationship with Burton Albion and I was fortunate enough to strike up a camaraderie with their mascot Billy Brewer, who quickly began guiding me through this weird and wonderful world," he wrote. "Billy introduced me to a VERY private mascot forum where the men and women inside the costumes can contact each other and exchange experiences, ideas and event information. The site quickly became my go-to webpage each morning.

"Mascots take their roles extremely seriously. Some individuals have been playing the part for 20-odd years and there are strict, unwritten rules regarding anonymity for past and present protagonists (rules that, admittedly, I'm breaking by writing this piece).

"I remember one scandal, when a handful of Football League mascots appeared on *The One Show* sofa – costumes on, but heads off – chatting away with an over-excited Adrian Chiles. All hell broke loose in our forum and for a short while we were a profession divided. Weren't these headless, out-of-character mascots degrading their roles? And why were they talking? The vast majority of mascots are mute: to speak while in costume is to sin.

"Yes, mascots should be, and are, objects of fun and entertainment (I'm fully aware it is hard to take seriously a football-playing ram, a sword-wielding pirate [Sheffield United's Captain Blade], or a big pink shrimp [Sammy, of Southend United]). However, to be effective they probably shouldn't sit on a sofa with a human head poking out the top."

Cutcher's year as Rammie was not all plain sailing. On one occasion he mocked Brian Howard of Reading, who had stayed down after a clash of heads and was later discovered to have broken his jaw. He wrote a letter of apology to Howard, but he was not the only mascot to make the same mistake. York City's Yorkie the Lion was formally warned by the Football League when he collapsed, feigning injury several times over while an opposition player in the penalty box received extensive treatment for what turned out to be a broken leg.

But overall it was a positive experience. "No other supporter gets as close to the pitch as you, and no other supporter gets to lead their heroes out of the tunnel at the start of the game (officially, Robbie Savage had that honour as captain – but I think we both knew who was in charge). The real hairs literally stand on end.

"Mascots are a strange and diverse group. Many are part time, combining match day duties with a more conventional profession outside of the world of football. Others will be part of the football club's day-to-day framework, taking part in community activities, coaching children and working with local charities. As Rammie, I was a full-timer. When I wasn't in the costume at Pride Park (now the iPro Stadium) or making a visit to a Derby fanatic's birthday party, I was marketing and selling Rammie appearances."

He also recalled "a mascot pageant where I was fortunate to meet Children in Need's Pudsey – possibly the most recognisable mascot in this country," and filming a video in London with other mascots before the 2010 World Cup – "the first time I met Arsenal's legendary Gunnersaurus Rex. He remains my favourite living dinosaur today."

Ah yes, Gunnersaurus. Why a dinosaur? Most clubs' names or nicknames suggest a cuddly animal or some other character who could be modelled in family-friendly foam and latex, but not all. Arsenal's cannon emblem is somewhat aggressive and their name suggests nothing at all suitable, which gave them a problem that they solved by holding a competition in the hope that a fan could come up with something.

Hence Gunnersaurus Rex, the brainchild of Peter Lovell, then 11, who won the Pepsi Junior Gunners' competition in 1994. A Jurassic Park obsessive from a long line of Arsenal fans, he put his two loves together. "It was just one of those eureka moments where the name suddenly came to me – Gunnersaurus Rex," he said much later. "So I started to flesh out this big, friendly-but-cool dinosaur that I thought really embodied – at least at the time – the ferocity and power of Arsenal Football Club.

"It was a one-take drawing; it happened really quickly, it wasn't something that I put a great deal of time into. And I thought, 'God, that's *perfect*', and coloured him in and then started to write out a little bit about him."

A few weeks later, a rather excited and somewhat informally punctuated letter arrived from the Junior Gunners that read: "WELL DONE PETER – you are the winner of our mascot competition. Your design will be made up and used at every home game!! Wow this is history in the making!"

Gunnersaurus' first appearance was to be at the home game against Manchester City at Highbury on 20 August 1994. "They invited me to the inaugural mascot ceremony where I ran around the pitch with Gunnersaurus and got to meet the guy inside. And for the next 20 years I've watched in awe as my little Gunnersaurus Rex has gone on to become a loved and idolised part of Arsenal.

"It's the most immensely flattering and wonderful thing. Wherever I go and meet an Arsenal fan, it doesn't take me long to drop in that I designed Gunnersaurus. I have a drink bought for me everywhere because he's such a wonderfully loved character. It's the proudest thing I've ever done.

"Being 11 years old and designing a Premier League mascot gave me real self-affirmation. To have that injection of confidence – no art A-Level teacher was ever going to tell me that I sucked at art because I could always say, 'How many Premier League mascots have *you* designed, mate?' So I'm grateful to Arsenal for the concept of the competition, for giving it to a young audience."

But the story does not end with Peter milking his claim to fame in a quest for free drinks. We move on to his wedding in August 2013, when, like the T-Rex in Jurassic Park, Gunnersaurus reared his scaly head once again.

"Unbeknown to me, my wife, my best man and my family contacted Arsenal. So I did my speech and my best man did his, and at the end he told the Gunnersaurus story. And I'm like, 'That's great, I didn't think the story would come up today.' Then there was this amazing reveal where these curtains opened up and in runs Gunnersaurus Rex with a signed letter from Arsène Wenger and all kinds of cool stuff – I was just blown away.

"There were a lot of Arsenal fans there and none of them had any idea it was going to happen, so it was a wonderful moment. And it was made even more special when I learnt that the gentleman inside the dinosaur is the same guy who ran around with me as an 11-year-old! So not only is Gunnersaurus a great icon and mascot for Arsenal, he's provided this guy with his calling as well. I had one of those wonderful hit-home moments where the significance of an 11-year-old's drawing on a kitchen table really came through. It was a beautiful moment, a beautiful day."

Peter's pride is almost father-like – he refers to Gunnersaurus by his full name of Gunnersaurus Rex and says the dinosaur "feels like my son who I don't get to speak to very much.

"He's not only the coolest mascot in the Premier League, he's the most powerful, he's the most fun, and I think the most adored.

"We've got this awesome, much-loved icon. I was nearly in tears when I saw him hugging Cesc Fabregas after his last game at the Emirates [in 2011].

"It's the most rewarding thing. Whenever I watch Arsenal – and whatever the results – I see him and feel like a proud Fathersaurus."

His creator may claim that Gunnersaurus is football's best-loved mascot, but surely no other mascot has run the same gamut of experiences and emotions as Pottermus of Stoke City, a blue hippopotamus who has been there, done it and got the T-shirt – which would have been infinitely preferable to what happened as he helped Graham Kavanagh celebrate a goal against Charlton Athletic in February 1998.

According to the *Stoke Sentinel*, Kavanagh "collected Kevin Keen's short free-kick and dispatched a perfect shot into the far corner." But as the mascot joined in the revels behind the goal, "poor old Pottermus went for a hug and ended up on his backside after being drop-kicked by the goalscorer. It ended up on the next edition of Chris Evans's *TFI Friday* on Channel 4."

The fans, though, liked Pottermus – perhaps more than they liked the players in that dire 1997/98 relegation season. In fact, he came seventh in the fans' player-of-the-season vote ahead of 27 players who had appeared during the campaign, and second in the vote for man of the match in a home defeat by Huddersfield Town. When Kyle Lightbourne was substituted, supporters chanted: "Bring on the Hippo." Pottermus came second in the man-of-the-match vote again a couple of home matches later, a 3-0 defeat by Tranmere Rovers.

Two seasons later, Pottermus was again on the same level as the Stoke players, sent from the touchline by referee Phil Richards during a match against Bristol City for apparently confusing a linesman, who kept mistaking him for a defender. It is not recorded which of the Stoke back four that day was a doppelganger for a large blue-headed hippo, even one wearing the red and white stripes.

And in November 2000 Pottermus took a leaf out of Cyril the Swan's book by decapitating a rival – in this case, Nuneaton Borough's Brewno the Bear – during a first-round FA Cup tie at the Britannia Stadium. The *Sentinel* reported that "the Bear was cavorting in front of the away end when Pottermus approached and seemed to be joining in the fun. Then the well-rounded Stoke man swiftly lobbed off the head of his rival and sprinted away. Brewno gave chase but he was never going to get his bonce back quickly. Pottermus, after all, was two-time Mascot Grand National champion. The race continued down the length of the then-Sentinel Stand, our hero pursued by a bear with the head of a man."

* * * * *

Which brings us back to that Mascot Grand National, in itself a sometimes controversial occasion. It was first staged in 1999, but in 2010, it faced a mass boycott over accusations that ringers were infiltrating the ranks of official mascots, many wearing far more streamlined outfits than the traditional large-footed football club costume.

The *Lincolnshire Echo* reported that Lincoln City's Poacher the Imp was among a number of football club mascots who would be pulling out of the one-furlong obstacle event at Huntingdon Racecourse, along with Preston North End's Deepdale Duck, Captain Blade of Sheffield United and AFC Wimbledon's Haydon the Womble, over the presence of serious runners from charities, newspapers, companies, rugby clubs and amateur teams such as Saffron Walden Town, represented by Wacky Macky Bear.

"Basically, these are guys who are coming just for the win," Poacher, alias Gary Hutchinson, said. "We asked for football mascots to be given a fair race but weren't accommodated."

Captain Blade agreed. "The race is being taken over by ringers. You have got to tell these people to stop ruining it for us and get it back to what it was before – a load of blokes going down and earning money for charity, having a laugh and entertaining people."

This was not the only instance of solidarity between mascots. Deepdale Duck was escorted away during a match between

Preston North End and Derby County after Stephen Bywater, the Derby goalkeeper, complained to the referee. Captain Blade stood up for his colleague by appearing at the South Yorkshire derby with Doncaster the following weekend holding a placard reading: 'Free the Preston One.'

Did the boycott work? A spokesperson for the racecourse said: "I think in an ideal world they would like us to limit the race to football mascots. But we would be limiting charities from entering and the amount of money that could be raised."

In the end, Mr Bumble of Barnet won the event, but it was not held the following year and moved to Kempton Park in 2012, when Mr Bumble triumphed again. But in 2013 Barratt Homes' mascot won and football was the loser.

But where mascots compete, controversy always seems to follow. Dorking's town mascot, Dorkers, was disqualified from an egg and spoon race in a mascots' race organised by the Rotary Club of Horsham. Dorkers, it seems, had been running. Not so, according to a Friends of Dorking spokeswoman, who claimed he had been 'strutting.'

And even hero mascots can become villains. Burnley's Bertie Bee earned YouTube fame for bringing down a male streaker where Turf Moor stewards had failed, but was sent to the stands by referee Simon Hooper on another occasion for offering a pair of spectacles to another match official. Pictures were later posted online of a penitent Bertie in a jail cell.

The glasses probably seemed like a good idea at the time, which is more than can be said about Dunfermline Athletic bear mascot Sammy the Tammy's brainwave of dressing as a tank and 'firing' at fans of Fife rivals Raith Rovers. The stunt was obviously planned well in advance as sounds of shellfire came over the East End Park PA system. Novelist and Raith fan Ian Rankin tweeted: "The Dunfermline mascot has appeared, driving a cardboard tank and 'firing' away at the fans. Not subtle."

The police later offered Dunfermline officials 'a word of caution in relation to the way the mascot presented himself,' but at least there was no risk to life and limb, in contrast with an earlier incident in which Sammy sledged down a gangway in the busy Norrie McCathie Stand during a match against Ayr United.

The stunt was an apparent tribute to recent Olympic skeleton bob gold medallist Amy Williams, and was carried out despite a warning from the stadium announcer who correctly foresaw that the sledge could veer into the seating area. A club spokesman told STV News: "He has been warned about it and told not to do it again. Obviously, we were a wee bit worried, health and safety-wise, in case he'd hit somebody on the way down."

One mascot famously attracted negative headlines at its very first appearance. When Partick Thistle allowed a Turner Prize-winning artist, David Shrigley, to design a replacement for Jaggy MacBee, the result was Kingsley, a nightmarish, monobrowed vision of Lisa Simpson as if re-imagined by Edvard Munch, painter of *The Scream*. The club made the most of the papers and websites all over the country, but reactions were overwhelmingly negative. BBC's *Newsbeat* sought the expert opinion of none other than Stuart 'H'Angus' Drummond, who was unimpressed. "Oh dear, what were they thinking?" he said. "Rule number one for mascots is to give children plenty of hugs. This thing looks like it is going to eat them."

Finally, a word for a mascot who is not linked to a particular club, but took part in a crossbar challenge at Goodison Park to the amusement of Gwladys Street regulars. Mr Testicle, the mascot for the Male Cancer Awareness Campaign, is more or less what his name suggests: a pair of hairy gonads on legs. "Everton have shown that it's a Premier League club with balls," a spokesman for the charity said. "With so many supporters, the majority of them being men, Everton is looking after its supporters by ensuring they are aware of male cancer."

Mr Testicle – he's the … well, you get the message.

9.

Just About Managing

"There's only two types of manager. Those who have been sacked and those who will be sacked in the future."

Howard Wilkinson

THE manager, head coach, call him or her what you will, is the person who steers the ship and carries the can. He or she should be an intelligent, knowledgeable, committed motivator, tactically astute yet capable of giving a half-time team talk that sends his men or women back out on the field ready to die for the cause.

He or she must be calm, except when the situation calls for tea cups to be thrown, know when to put an arm round a player's shoulder, and when to put a boot up their backside.

In short, he or she must be a natural leader. It is a role that calls for the wisdom of a Confucius, the diplomacy of a Dalai Lama, the dignity of a Nelson Mandela, the psychological insight of a Sigmund Freud, the inspirational qualities of a Churchill, the strategic genius of a Patton and the inner strength of a Gandhi.

With any luck, the manager of your team will have about half of those qualities.

In the worst case, they'll have the wisdom of a Paul Gascoigne, the diplomacy of a Basil Fawlty, the dignity of a Lee Evans, the psychological insight of a Homer Simpson, the inspirational qualities of an Iain Duncan Smith, the strategic genius of a General Custer and the inner strength of a marshmallow.

The job description can vary from club to club. Not every manager has an army of analysts and video researchers to prepare reports on opponents. At different times and different clubs, managers have had to combine their basic coaching duties with those of chief scout, kit washer and even painter and decorator around the ground. Some managers love to get out on the training ground pitch, others stick to the office and only emerge to deliver a rousing pre-match team talk.

You would think that the most basic and straightforward job of a manager is to pick the team, but even that can prove tricky. When Stuart Pearce was put in temporary charge of Nottingham Forest in December 1996, after Frank Clark had resigned with the club at the bottom of the Premier League, his first match was at home to Arsenal. He sat down to select his starting line-up the night before, juggling names until he had eleven that he was happy with, and showed it to his wife to see what she thought. She pointed out that he had not included a goalkeeper.

Once the team crosses the white line, there is only so much a manager can do. Players can find it hard to hear instructions – by accident or design – and there may be only seconds during a break for an injury in which a manager can relay rapid instructions for a tactical change. Quick thinking is vital, such as that demonstrated by Partick Thistle boss John Lambie after being told by the physio that Colin McGlashan had had a knock on the head and did not know who he was. "Tell him he's Pelé and get him back on," Lambie replied.

The pressure can do strange things. Alan Pardew, then Newcastle boss, got so worked up on the touchline that he chinned Hull City midfield player David Meyler during a Premier League relegation battle, and made an ageist remark to his Manchester City counterpart Manuel Pellegrini. Leicester's Nigel Pearson insulted a fan, wrestled an opponent and called a journalist 'an ostrich'. Steve McClaren's English developed a strange Dutch twang when he managed in Holland. Ron Atkinson went and sat in the wrong dugout for his first game in charge of Nottingham Forest.

One of the first managers to become as nationally famed as any of his players was Bill Shankly at Liverpool. There are so many stories about the Scot that some are certain to be apocryphal, and Shankly even had to correct one of them himself – the notorious tale that his idea of a wedding anniversary celebration was to take his wife, Nessie, to a Rochdale game. "Utter rubbish," he claimed. "Of course I didn't take my wife to see Rochdale as an anniversary present. It was her birthday. Would I have got married in the football season? Anyway, it was Rochdale reserves."

Everyone knows the most famous Shanklyism, the one that goes: "Some people believe football is a matter of life and death, I am very disappointed with that attitude. I can assure you it is much, much more important than that." But did he ever say those exact words? In a TV interview in 1981, he was asked whether he regretted sacrificing family life for football and replied: "I regret it very much. Somebody said: 'Football's a matter of life and death to you.' I said, 'Listen, it's more important than that.' And my family's suffered. They've been neglected."

And when asked about the Everton-Liverpool rivalry that sometimes split families on Merseyside, he said: "I am not saying they love each other. Oh, no. Football is not a matter of life and death, it's much more important than that. And it's more important to them than that. But I've never seen a fight at a derby game. Shouting and bawling, yes. But they don't fight each other. And that says a lot for them."

Shanks was always proud of everything Liverpool, once inviting journalists to stroll around new signing Ron Yeats ("Go on, walk around him. He's a colossus!") and even taking one of them into the dressing rooms to demonstrate a new toilet cistern. "You know it refills in 15 seconds," he is reported to have said. "It's a world record." So when the club acquired a German-made machine that supposedly helped players avoid injuries by sending small electric impulses through muscles, Shankly was as pleased as Punch.

Tommy Smith recalled a demonstration, using Jimmy Melia, who was in the treatment room for his daily rub-down, as the guinea pig. But when Bob Paisley, then the physio, turned the dial to one, then three, and finally all the way up to ten, nothing happened, and Shankly was furious – until he noticed that the machine was not turned on at the plug socket. "'Christ, Bob, you haven't even turned it on!' He flicked the switch and poor Jimmy, still on a maximum setting of ten, nearly hit the ceiling," Smith said. "Sparks were coming out of his ears. His hair would have stood on end if he'd had any. We all ran out, exploding with laughter."

Shankly liked to use psychology as well as tactics to beat opponents. Before a game against Manchester United in 1967, he personally welcomed all the visiting players into the ground, telling them all how well they looked – except Bobby Charlton, who was known to be a worrier. "Bobby, son, good to see you," he said. "But by God, if ever there was a man who looked ill, it's you, Bobby! You look like you're sickening for something. If I were you I'd see a doctor as soon as you set foot back in Manchester."

The United team that eventually took the field showed one change to the side that had beaten West Ham in their previous game. Manager Matt Busby announced that Bobby Charlton was unavailable after being taken ill.

Visitors did not always get such a warm and personal welcome. "I might say to the old guy on the Anfield door: 'Here's a box of toilet rolls,'" Shankly said. "'Hand them to the opposition when they come through the door.'"

Paisley remembers another piece of kidology before a European Cup tie against Anderlecht of Belgium in 1964. "Before the game, in the dressing room, Bill talked to the lads. He said, 'You've read about Anderlecht having all these internationals and how good they are. They can't play. They're rubbish. I've seen them and I'm telling you, you'll murder them, so go out there and do it.' The boys went out there and murdered them. They won 3-0. And after the game, Bill burst into the dressing room and said: 'Boys, you've just beaten the greatest team in Europe.'"

Shankly loved to play football himself, sometimes joining in kids' games in the park across the road from his house, and usually taking part in the five-a-side games in training. Once his side claimed a disputed goal and Shankly turned to Chris Lawler, the famously quiet and reserved first-team right-back, who was injured and watching from the sidelines. "Chris, you were watching," Shankly shouted to him.

"Yes."

"Speak up, Chris, I can't hear you. Did you think that was a goal, Chris?"

"No."

"Good God, Chris," Shankly replied. "This is the first time I've heard you speak to me and you tell me a bloody lie!"

He had a love/hate relationship with Everton, even coaching some of the Toffees' youth team players after retiring. But he was merciless to the city rivals in public. Famously he referred to Merseyside as having "two great teams, Liverpool and Liverpool reserves". But Shankly could wax lyrical on subjects other than Liverpool, and he was always full of praise for his former Preston teammate Tom Finney, who, he said, would be "great in any team in any era even while wearing his overcoat". When asked in the 1970s whether Tony Currie of Sheffield United compared with Finney, he replied: "Aye, he compares all right. But Tom is getting on for 60."

The legend of Shankly probably persists because he is so indelibly associated with one club and was almost universally loved by its fans. In contrast, Tommy Docherty, also a former Preston player and teammate of Finney's (he once called Lionel Messi "an immature Tom Finney"), coined the saying about having more clubs than Jack Nicklaus. "I look out for all the clubs I've played for or managed," he said in 2015. "It usually takes me a couple of hours every Saturday night!"

But among the 12 clubs he managed were some pretty big ones, including Chelsea and Manchester United. Admittedly, he was in charge when United were relegated to the old Second Division in 1974, but he did take them straight back up as well as winning the FA Cup in 1977 before losing the job not because of bad results but an affair with Mary Brown, the wife of the club physio. "I'm the only manager to be sacked for falling in love," he said.

A player with Celtic, Arsenal, Preston, Chelsea and Scotland, he began his career in the dugout at Stamford Bridge after he retired as a player and he built a young attacking side around Ron Harris, John Hollins and Peter Osgood that won the 1965 League Cup and lost the 1967 FA Cup final. "Chelsea is my club," Docherty says. "I won't have a bad word said against them. I love the Bridge. I go five or six times a year and they're brilliant to me."

United, he feels, still have a problem over the Brown affair. "Only a couple of years ago, I phoned up for a couple of tickets for one of the games," he said. "My daughter wanted to see one of the matches. And they invoiced me for £88 – charged me for it! It seems to be that [how I left] still hangs over me. I wouldn't cross the road now to watch Man United, because of two tickets. What's that to them?"

He also took charge of Rotherham, QPR (twice), Aston Villa, Porto, Scotland, Derby, Preston, Wolves, South Melbourne, Sydney Olympic and Altrincham as well as United. But like his fellow Scot Shankly, Docherty had a one-liner for every occasion. On managing Scotland, he said: "On my first day as manager I had to call off practice after half an hour, because nobody could get the ball off wee Jimmy Johnstone."

He quit the Scotland job to take over from Frank O'Farrell at United with a brief to rebuild an ailing club, but he later admitted that it had been a mistake to walk out on a national team full of talented players such as Billy Bremner, Kenny Dalglish and Johnstone. "That was the biggest mistake I made," he told BBC Scotland, and he made a few, including turning up for his first day at Derby in a Manchester United tracksuit.

"I should never have gone to Manchester United, I should have seen my job out with Scotland at the World Cup and then, if Man United were still interested, I could have gone then. It was partly greed and partly stupidity. But I was concerned I might miss the chance.

"I think we would have done great [at the World Cup]. I was getting a bit too strong at the SFA and I don't think they liked that either. I had a contract with Scotland and they could have held out and said to Man United, 'We want some compensation.' But that wasn't asked for. I think they were quite glad to get rid of me."

At Old Trafford, he had to contend with complex club politics and Sir Matt Busby as a continual presence in the background. "I don't think Henry Kissinger would have lasted 48 hours at Old Trafford," he said later. Docherty knew that he had to move on legends such as George Best, Bobby Charlton and Denis Law. Charlton was allowed to retire, Best to leave – "George just kept on going missing at the time – Miss America, Miss Canada, Miss Great Britain" – and Law was allowed to go to Manchester City, in defiance of Busby's wishes, with a £5,000 pay-off to boot.

Law repaid the favour with the backheeled winning goal for City at Old Trafford that set the seal on United's relegation. "That's the amazing thing about football. Ex-players come back to haunt you," he told Ian Herbert of the *Independent* in 2014.

"One minute I had got the United job and I was standing in the centre of the pitch, looking around and humming the lyric 'You Were Meant For Me.' The next minute I knew I would always be known as the man who took United into the Second Division."

He took them straight back up, and his signings of wingers Steve Coppell from Tranmere Rovers and Gordon Hill from Millwall were truly inspired. Or were they? Both were recommended by Jimmy 'Spud' Murphy, previously Busby's assistant, who, like Busby himself, was still around the club and phoned Docherty after watching one of Tranmere's traditional Friday evening home games in 1973. "Tom, it's Spud," Docherty recalled Murphy saying. "'Buy Coppell, Tom. Buy Coppell or you'll lose him.' I'd never seen either of them."

* * * * *

Despite his achievements, Docherty will never be the most-remembered manager at any of his clubs, overshadowed by Mourinho at Chelsea, Busby and Ferguson at Manchester United and a certain Brian Clough at Derby.

Clough managed five clubs: Hartlepools United, as they were then known, where he became the youngest manager in the league, Derby County, Brighton & Hove Albion, Leeds United and Nottingham Forest, with distinctly mixed results in some cases. He lasted only 44 days at Leeds, and left Brighton more or less where he had found them, in the lower reaches of the third tier. But he took Derby from the old Second Division to the League Championship and Europe, and did even better at Forest, with not only promotion and the title in successive seasons but also back-to-back European Cups. The only major trophy that eluded him was the FA Cup.

He started as he meant to go on. "I was sacked twice at Hartlepool but I refused to go," he said. And he took the unprecedented step, for the manager of a Fourth Division club of the time, of hiring an assistant – Peter Taylor, a gifted talent-spotter.

He was interviewed for the England manager's job, but the FA were scared of appointing a man with so much to say for himself and went instead for the safer option of Ron Greenwood. "I'm sure the England selectors thought if they took me on and gave me the job, I'd want to run the show. They were shrewd, because that's exactly what I would have done."

He referred to himself as 'Old Big 'Ead' in order to remind himself not to get too self-important, but it did not always work. "Rome wasn't built in a day," he once said, "but I wasn't on that particular job."

Of course, a player could disagree with Clough, but it would not do him much good. "I ask him which way he thinks it should be done, we get down to it, we talk about it for 20 minutes and then we decide that I was right," he explained.

Michael Dunford worked behind the scenes at Derby and owed a long career in football administration to Clough, whose invitation to work for the Rams showed his belief in the personal touch. "My father was a beat copper, around the area of the Baseball Ground, and Cloughie knew him," Dunford told *Backpass* magazine in 2013. "In 1969 I was at college and wanted to be a draughtsman. One day Cloughie said to my father, 'What's young Michael doing? Tell him to get off his backside, he can come down here and help us in the box office.' I went down and loved it. They said if I passed my exams I could come full time and I did."

But he also saw the other side of Clough. "Stuart Webb, who came as secretary and ended up being managing director, had told me I mustn't give the safe keys to anyone. Brian came in and said, 'Young man, give me the safe keys,' and I said: 'No, Mr Clough, I'm sorry. I've been told by Mr Webb that I mustn't.' He said: 'Well, I think you'd better get on your bike, you're sacked.'

"I went home and told my dad. Being a policeman he said: 'He can't do that.' What did he even want with the keys? I don't think even he knew. He was probably testing me. Two days later I was back.

"Later on we laughed about it but it wasn't pleasant at the time."

Players and supporters would also find out that Clough was among the most unpredictable of characters. "Once a couple of fans came in to renew their season tickets and he overheard them saying that Peter Daniel should be playing at centre-forward instead of John O'Hare. Brian said: 'Excuse me, gentlemen, would you just repeat that?' So they did. He said: 'That's why you're that side of the counter and I'm this side, earning a lot of money. Now bugger off.' And they did, but he went out of the directors' entrance after them, caught up with them, took them into his office, poured them a drink and bought their season tickets for them."

Clough famously treated Trevor Francis, Britain's first £1m player, as a tea boy at Nottingham Forest. But he had previously done the same to the entire Derby squad. "Once we drew Wolves in the Cup at home in January, freezing weather, and he was desperate to play the game," Dunford recalled. "This was before heated pitches. So we had everyone bar the players covering the pitch with straw bales, putting braziers out, everything, trying to thaw it out. And we got the game on.

"He told the players to report to the ground on Saturday morning at ten o'clock, which was much earlier than usual. Then he said: 'Have a look out of the tunnel. Then get down to the kitchen. You're making teas and coffees for the next hour for all the staff out there who are getting this pitch ready for you to win this game.' So there were Roy McFarland, Colin Todd, international footballers, coming out with teas and coffees. Brian followed them, carrying the required bottle to give everyone a nip of brandy.

"Cloughie was by far the best man-manager I saw in operation. He believed in the personal touch. Towards the end I saw him at a game at Pride Park and he asked after my father. I said he was going to be 80 on 9 July, and it was March and he said

'Give him my best wishes.' My dad went down to stay with my grandparents in Newquay and on 9 July, a birthday card arrived there from Brian Clough. I was amazed that he'd remembered, but how he'd found out the address I can't imagine.

"But that was him – always keeping you guessing. One morning he told the staff to shut the reception and get everyone – tea lady, groundsman, about ten people – on the two coaches used to take the players to training, each employee sitting next to a player. Instead of going to the training ground, some of us who had a decent sense of direction could tell that we were heading east. We ended up at the south shore in Scarborough. He got everyone out and walked them up to the north shore, with the players all complaining and muttering, 'What are we doing here? What's all this in aid of?' Then he told everyone to get into a fish and chip shop he'd booked for lunch. Afterwards he got us all back on the coach and we went back to Derby."

Garry Birtles, spotted by Taylor playing for Long Eaton United and fitting carpets as a day job, was never the tea boy. Clough had other duties in mind for the forward. "I was his squash partner," he told the *Nottingham Post* in 2015. "When I was in the reserves I used to get dragged off the training pitch covered in mud and have to go across to Trent Bridge to play squash with him."

Birtles remembers being ordered to shave before being allowed onto the bus to the 1980 European Cup final against Hamburg in Madrid – 'He could see I was nervous and wanted to take my mind off the game' – and the team being encouraged to drink beer on the journey to the previous year's final against Malmo in Munich. And Clough got the squad so drunk on the eve of the 1979 League Cup final that some players could hardly stand up. Yet they came from a goal down to beat Southampton 3-2.

"People say they couldn't have played for Brian Clough because there was a fear factor, but what a load of rubbish that was. It was a great place to go into every day because you never knew what was going to happen next. It was always lively, it was always funny. Some days you would go in thinking you'd be getting a hard session and you'd end up doing nothing at all, he'd send you home after a cup of tea."

Many have compared Clough's methods to those of José Mourinho, who seems to court controversy in order to take the pressure off his players. Not surprisingly, Mourinho is a Clough fan. During Euro '96 he visited Nottingham and was amazed. "I walked all the way (around the city) and when I saw the stadium I thought: 'Are you kidding me – this club won the European Cup? Twice?'

"We all probably remember Clough's best quotes. 'I wouldn't say I am the best football manager there is,' he used to say, 'but I am in the top one.' I love that line. He had all that self-esteem and big self-belief. He was very confident about himself, and from what I know about him he was very comfortable with the attention. Maybe because Brian Clough was such a huge personality, with so much charisma, everyone remembers his quotes and the stories and a few people forget his talents.

"He didn't win two European Cups with Nottingham Forest just because of his charisma. History cannot delete what he and Nottingham Forest did – their results, the cups, the achievements, absolutely unbelievable achievements. I have huge respect for what they did. I think if Brian Clough was around today, we would get on."

He isn't, of course, thanks to the drinking that finally killed him. But he even had a memorable line about that. "Walk on water? I know most people out there will be saying that instead of walking on it, I should have taken more of it with my drinks. They are absolutely right."

The only modern manager to rival Shankly, Docherty and Clough for quotability is Ian Holloway, who has delighted members of the media at Bristol Rovers, QPR, Plymouth Argyle, Leicester City, Blackpool, Crystal Palace and Millwall. The Bristolian links ideas in a surreal fashion with few nods to political correctness, most famously when asked for his opinion of Queens Park Rangers' workmanlike victory over Chesterfield.

"To put it in gentleman's terms," he said, "if you've been out for a night and you're looking for a young lady and you pull one, some weeks they're good-looking and some weeks they're not the best. Our performance today would have been not the best-looking bird but at least we got her in the taxi. She wasn't the best-looking lady we ended up taking home but she was very pleasant and very nice, so thanks very much, let's have a coffee."

Holloway seems equally to be a connoisseur of standards of male beauty, judging by his comments on Cristiano Ronaldo: "He's six foot something, fit as a flea, good-looking – he's got to have something wrong with him. Hopefully he's hung like a hamster. That would make us all feel better. Having said that, my missus has got a pet hamster at home, and his cock's massive."

With such a way with words, it was surprising that Holloway once invited a QPR supporter to give the pre-match talk in order to let the players know how much the club meant to the fans. After all, most fans are unlikely to say: "I couldn't be more chuffed if I were a badger at the start of the mating season," after beating Cardiff City. Nor to celebrate promotion by saying: "Every dog has its day, and today is woof day! Today I just want to bark!"

Nature, reality TV, even Hollywood movies – Holloway's inspiration is drawn from the whole of human experience. He once compared QPR's financial situation to "the film Men in Black. I walk around in a black suit, white shirt and black tie where I've had to flash my white light every now and again to erase some memories, but I feel we've got hold of the galaxy now. It's in our hands."

Not that he claims mastery of space–time on other occasions. Once, asked to predict a result, he said: "I can't see into the future. Last year I thought I was going to Cornwall on my holidays but I ended up going to Lyme Regis."

Some managers can be monosyllabic, especially after a poor result, but that is seldom a problem with Holloway. At least one journalist, having called Holloway when he was in charge of Bristol Rovers, was tempted to put the phone down with a deadline looming. When managing Millwall to a 2-2 draw away to Bournemouth in 2014/15, Holloway arrived in the press room already in full flow, continued talking as he sat down for the post-match press conference, got up mid-sentence to leave and departed still talking, his voice dying away as he headed back out towards the other side of the ground to the team coach.

In October 2007, Holloway, then in charge of Plymouth Argyle, was persuaded to record a series of pre-match and half-time scenarios on the Carling Pub Football website. This was for a team losing at the break: "As for you two muppets up front, what are you doing? You're like Statler and Waldorf off the balcony. 'Huh, this show's rubbish.' Well, this game's rubbish, sort your life out. What have we spoken about all summer, about being the Romans? They didn't conquer Europe by breaking their ranks, forgetting their jobs. Useless, sort it out, my missus could do better, so could my kids. So could my gran."

* * * * *

Some managers are remembered for their words; others, like Malcolm Allison, for their actions. 'Big Mal' was one of the most colourful managers of the 1970s, although he made his name as a coach in the previous decade at Manchester City, where the avuncular Joe Mercer could temper his protégé's excesses. On one occasion, Mercer was flagged down for speeding and, as he wound down the window, said: "OK officer, what has Malcolm done now?"

Allison, who deliberately failed his 11-plus so that he would not have to attend a rugby-playing grammar school, played for the West Ham team that became a coaching academy. He and Mercer were a successful partnership who won City a league title, the FA Cup, the League Cup and the Cup-Winners' Cup.

But when Allison was given sole charge, his unwise signing of Rodney Marsh upset the balance of the team.

Allison moved on to Crystal Palace, where, again, there was no one to curb his excesses. He oversaw a period of upheaval, beginning with relegation from the top division. He changed the club's nickname from Glaziers to Eagles, the colours from claret and sky blue to blue and red, and gave the players tracksuits with bizarre monikers on them – Don Rogers was 'Troublemaker', Charlie Cooke 'The Card Shuffler' and Allison himself 'The Judge'.

Midfield player Martin Hinshelwood recalled the period immediately after relegation for *Backpass*: "I was only 20 and thought: 'We aren't going to be in this division too long.' And we weren't – we went straight on down! We were more of a collection of individuals than a team. The smaller clubs would come to Selhurst, with a big crowd and a nice pitch, against Malcolm Allison and those big names, and it would be their cup final.

"But Malcolm wasn't frightened to try things and what other people thought never worried him. He made the pitch bigger, because we had great wingers, but after we lost a couple he made it narrower again. We had a spell training at 3 o'clock in the afternoon, because that's when we played – and then at 7.45 before an evening game. After we beat Chelsea at Stamford Bridge in the FA Cup fifth round, the coach broke down at Thornton Heath on the way back. It was close enough for us to have walked from there but Malcolm took us into a pub and ordered champagne."

Allison strode onto the Stamford Bridge pitch afterwards wearing a fedora, which had actually made its debut on Doncaster railway station en route to the third-round tie at Scarborough. "We were changing trains and Malcolm came down the platform and said: 'Look at this, boys.' We turned round, saw him in the fedora and thought: 'What the – ?'

"He wore it at Scarborough, where we scraped through, wore it at Leeds – he loved it because he would put it on and stroll over to the home fans and wave to them and they would give him so much abuse. At Sunderland in the sixth round he walked over in front of the Roker End before kick-off in it, waved to them, signalled 3-0, and there were things flying at him. We actually won 1-0. He was like Mourinho is now. He was almost taking the abuse onto himself rather than the team, but sometimes you'd be thinking: 'Malcolm, don't do that – it just makes everyone more determined to beat us.'"

Allison had other unusual ideas. He invited Fiona Richmond, the glamour model and actress, to training. "We were in the bath afterwards and she came in, took her top off and jumped in," Hinshelwood said. "You can imagine some of the lads' reaction. And it got in the papers as well. After that I wasn't allowed out for a week."

But while at Palace, Allison was conned by a professional. He had been informed by Arnie Warren, the chief scout, recently arrived from QPR, about a young defender named Kenny Sansom that Palace would do well to sign. The story, as recounted in Sansom's autobiography, goes that Allison went to Ray Bloye, the Palace chairman, who owned a chain of butchers' shops, and told him about the young prospect – but there was a catch. "'His dad wants five hundred notes tonight to seal the deal and then we can sign him tomorrow.'" Allison and Bloye set off around Bloye's shops, "raiding the tills of five-pound notes until they came up with the full amount needed to secure my dad's signature on the dotted line."

What Allison did not know was that George Sansom had left home to pursue a life in East End gangs when his son could barely walk and had had nothing to do with Kenny's upbringing or football education yet had somehow got wind of the signing and inserted himself into the deal.

Other managers have tried to be as unconventional as Allison, with varying results. As a player, mostly in the top division with West Ham and QPR, Martin Allen was an aggressive midfield player who earned the nickname 'Mad Dog'.

"I was nasty," he said. "Intimidating. Horrible. Right through my whole life." As a manager, mostly in the lower divisions – he has taken charge of Barnet on four occasions, despite calling them 'two-bob' and comparing the new ground to a scene from *Prison Break* – his nickname stuck as his reputation for an unconventional approach grew, often overshadowing his considerable effectiveness.

His mantra was FIFO (Fit In or Fuck Off) and at Brentford his players were given a booklet listing fines – from £5 for taking a newspaper into the treatment room to £50 for ordering room service after 9pm. It was also during his time at Griffin Park that his habit of leaping into rivers came to prominence. First he swam in the Tees near Darlington before an FA Cup tie away to Hartlepool, and then jumped naked into the Solent in advance of the following round at Southampton. At Gillingham he took his squad for an early morning run along the beach before veering off into the sea.

Allen was not the only manager whose methods included plenty of cold wet stuff. John Beck almost took Cambridge United into the top flight in the early 1990s with a team that included future Premier League players Dion Dublin, Steve Claridge, Liam Daish and Alan Kimble. Pre-match rituals included a soaking in the showers with buckets of icy water.

Unexpectedly for a man who had been a cultured midfield player under Dave Sexton at QPR, Beck took the long-ball game to another level at Cambridge. He ordered his players to hit the ball towards the corner flags, where the Abbey Stadium grass was left purposely long to hold it up, and win throw-ins that would be aimed towards their mountainous forwards. The player who kicked the ball furthest was paid a bonus. The team would train on the pitch in midweek, making the central areas a mudheap that tested visiting teams with aims of passing the ball.

And it was not just the playing surface that he doctored to give Cambridge an advantage. Before kick-off he would have the away dressing room flooded, the heating turned up to uncomfortable levels, and too much sugar put in their tea, while the balls they used for the pre-match warm-up would have been soaked to make them heavier than normal.

Beck's methods were described by critics as 'anti-football', but they worked up to a point. Beck took Cambridge from the fourth tier into the play-offs for a place in the inaugural season of the Premier League, but they were beaten 6-1 on aggregate by Leicester City. "Beck will always say we got so far because of him and his methods," Claridge said later. "I maintain it was in spite of them. I believe he stopped us being what we really could have become."

Football in general seemed to agree as Beck's name became synonymous with the type of tactics the game was trying to leave behind – until, in a stunning move, Beck joined the FA in 2013, working with coaches taking the B licence. It was, said one former player, like putting Dracula in charge of a blood bank.

* * * * *

Speaking of long-ball teams, when two Norwegian fishing magnates who had bought Wimbledon from Sam Hammam were looking for a replacement for Joe Kinnear in June 1999, they thought they knew the very man to take over as manager: Egil Olsen, former manager of the Norway national side, whom he had led to two World Cups – they beat Brazil 2-1 in France in 1998 – and second place in the FIFA World Rankings.

At first, the eccentric Scandinavian known as 'Drillo' – a Norwegian word roughly translated as 'Dribbler' in reference to his style as a player – amused fans and media with his trademark Compo-style turned-down wellies, worn to combat arthritis, apparently. He walked to the training ground, never driving anywhere, and donned them instead of boots. The club shop at Selhurst Park even stocked Olsen wellies at £9.99 a pair.

He was a committed Marxist and a well-read man with a wide range of interests and an encyclopaedic knowledge of geography. At one midweek press conference, he refused to answer questions until the press had named the ten largest countries in Europe (your scribe saved the day with Ukraine or we might still be there). A fierce anti-tobacco campaigner, he would berate smokers in Wimbledon high street. He was an accomplished poker player and even impressed his players, early on, with some impressive card tricks.

Eccentricity is fun if the team wins, but always held against you if not – just ask Christian Gross, whose brandishing of an Underground ticket to demonstrate his new credentials as a Londoner on his introduction as Tottenham Hotspur manager must have seemed a good idea at the time. When he failed to galvanise Spurs into a winning team, it was held up as evidence of hopelessness. After all, what sort of manager uses public transport?

Olsen did, as did his assistant Lars Tjærnås, once seen getting off at the wrong Shepherd's Bush station to watch a match at Loftus Road. Whatever the reasons, his new system of quick breakaways, a lone striker and, most controversially, zonal marking, which worked for Norway, caused the Crazy Gang to struggle. Everyone who remembers a certain photo of Vinnie Jones and Paul Gascoigne knows that the Wimbledon tradition was very much man-to-man marking. Goals were shipped from set plays and when the lone striker was Trond Andersen rather than John Hartson, while Carl Cort and Marcus Gayle played wide, goals at the other end were few.

Part of the problem was a difference in footballing cultures. Olsen was intellectual and analytical and spoke a technical language which his players did not understand. Their drinking and practical joking were alien to his ideas of how professional athletes should conduct themselves. Norwegian ex-Don Ståle Solbakken commented: "A brain surgeon shouldn't have to work with peasants."

The team stopped playing for him, whether by accident or design. The last straw was a 3-0 defeat away to Bradford City with three games to go, hardly helped by a dreadful miss from Jason Euell, an even worse penalty decision by referee Jeff Winter, and the dismissal early in the second half for foul and abusive language of Hartson – which went unnoticed by the baffled Olsen until pointed out by his recently appointed assistant, Terry Burton.

Olsen was sacked, long-time club stalwart Burton took over and the players believed they could pull out of their nosedive down the table and save themselves from the drop by winning their final two games. Sadly, they had lost the winning habit, took only a single point and were relegated.

Another strange 'Did that really happen?' foreign presence in the British game was Avram Grant. The Israeli first appeared as Portsmouth technical director, although his precise role – under Harry Redknapp, over Harry Redknapp or irrelevant to Harry Redknapp – was never clear to the media, who occasionally glimpsed him refereeing training matches while Redknapp and his coaches looked on.

Nevertheless, Chelsea saw enough in the Israeli to offer him a similar unspecified role at Stamford Bridge. So vague was his brief that, when he was promoted to manager, despite having no formal UEFA coaching licences, captain John Terry had no idea who he was. Yet a man whose career seemed to be based on the Peter Sellers movie *Being There* came within one penalty kick of winning the Champions League.

Unfortunately for the gloomy-faced coach, his main claim to fame instead of European glory will be the discovery in December 2010 while he was back at Portsmouth overseeing their relegation from the Premier League – a feat he was to repeat at West Ham – that he had visited FuFu's, a Thai massage parlour on a nearby industrial estate. And he was not exactly discreet, turning up wearing a club tracksuit.

Sadly, the *Sun* had initially drawn back from naming him for fear of legal action, depriving the world of the back page headline 'Rumpy Pompey' which was all ready to roll. But the story came out, and with it an insight into Grant's marriage to his Israeli TV presenter wife Tzofit.

The *Mail Online* website claimed that she had laughed when hubby telephoned her to break the news. "It's nobody's business what he does with his body," she said. "He can get Thai massage anytime and anyhow. He loves massages, also Australian massage and Japanese massage, as well as having massages from Thai women.

"What Avram and I say behind closed doors is nobody's business. Not even our definition of what it means to live as a couple. If I suspect that my husband actually went to a brothel, that's just between me and him. I swear on my children's lives that I am not mad at him. If I am mad, it is because he does not get massages every day." The *Mail* also revealed that, while she had been happy to live in London with Grant and attend matches when he was Chelsea manager, she drew the line at Portsmouth – 'a great manager stuck in a crappy team' was her verdict. "She would never, never live in a town like Portsmouth," the *Mail* quoted 'an Israeli friend' as saying. "It's not nearly glamorous enough for her. She has to be in the centre of things, she needs to be talked about. I know she hoped something would happen in London to get her on British television, but it never did, she thinks because her English was not good enough."

A shame, perhaps. British breakfast TV might have been livened up a treat by a presenter whose previous early-morning stunts included drinking a whisky glass of her own urine, donning a bathing costume to join a male guest in a bath of spaghetti and tomato sauce, and immersing herself in melted chocolate as a skin treatment.

* * * * *

Grant is such a lugubrious character that it is difficult to imagine him giving him a rousing speech at half-time, which is when most people assume that managers really earn their money. Usually we know very little of what happens in the dressing room, with players reluctant to break the *omerta*. But when former Chelsea, Millwall, Gillingham and Leyton Orient defender John Sitton launched into an impassioned rant during Orient's defeat at home to Blackpool, he forgot that cameras were filming a documentary on the East London club, *Orient: Club For a Fiver*. What followed has passed into legend and onto YouTube.

Sitton was appointed joint caretaker manager of Orient in April 1994 with Chris Turner, the job being made permanent in the summer, although financial problems at Brisbane Road (which he later called 'the circus upstairs') meant that he had to fulfil a number of roles while drawing only the salary of a youth-team coach.

The squad was halved and players' wages were paid by the PFA for a time, perhaps helping to explain the tensions that boiled over during the half-time team talk at Griffin Park when, with Orient 3-0 down to Brentford, Sitton informed the players that the owner would like to sell most of them and replace them with cheaper options, "and he might be right," before sending them back out onto the pitch after only five minutes in the dressing room.

But that was nothing compared to what happened after 45 minutes of the home game against Blackpool on 7 February 1995. With Orient 1-0 down, he began almost calmly but then sacked Terry Howard, a popular player with the Os fans, before turning to two other players. "You, you little ****, when I tell you to do something, and you, you fucking big ****, when I tell you to do something, do it. And if you come back at me, we'll have a fucking right sort-out in here. All right? And you can pair up if you like, and you can fucking pick someone else to help you, and you can bring your fucking dinner. 'Cause by the time I've finished with you, you'll fucking need it."

Orient failed to pull the goal back, and won only one of the next 15 games. Sitton and Turner were sacked and the team finished bottom of the table. The documentary, which had failed to show any of Sitton's work with the youth team or his junior coaches, never mind hours on the training ground with his back four, was effectively career-ending.

"I felt ostracised after the Channel 4 documentary, made an outcast, treated like a leper," Sitton later told *Pitch Talk*. "I struggled to get back into football, the only thing I'd known for 23 years, since the age of 14, 12 maybe. I didn't want that feeling so it was time to get my head down, study and get a real job, become a licensed London cab driver. It cost me any prospects of a future career and parts are significantly embarrassing, but I thought games were being played with my livelihood and you can't go through life squeaking like a mouse."

Another famous half-time team talk took place on Boxing Day 2008, and while we do not know what Phil Brown said to his Hull City team during their defeat at Manchester City, we have some finger-pointing body language as a clue, as Brown sat his players down in a circle on the Etihad pitch and conducted proceedings in front of the visiting fans – and the TV cameras – with his team 4-0 down.

"Our 4,000 travelling fans deserved some kind of explanation for the first-half performance and it was difficult for me to do that from the confines of a changing room," Brown said. "We owed them an apology. I thought it was nice and cold and I thought I would keep the boys alive because they looked as if they were dead. It wasn't a knee-jerk reaction. It was definitely the right thing to do. If it meant bruising one or two egos, so be it.

"I was told it meant I had lost the dressing room and that I had exposed the club to ridicule. But the bigger picture was that we had won at the Emirates, we had won at White Hart Lane, we had won at St James' Park and lost 4-3 at Old Trafford. People choose to forget that."

Lost his marbles more than the dressing room, to most people. And certainly his judgement. Hull were busy sliding down the table after those early-season results Brown mentioned, although they did escape relegation, albeit only because Newcastle lost on the final day of the season.

But there was a pay-off to the Manchester madness. When Hull visited the Etihad the following season – which ended in relegation this time – they drew 1-1. And when Jimmy Bullard scored the equaliser, he sat his teammates in a circle in front of the Hull supporters and wagged his finger at them all in turn in joyful mockery of Brown's team talk. "I couldn't deliver my post-match speech I was laughing so much," Brown said later.

Brown had also gone barmy on the field when he took the microphone after Hull had rather luckily avoided relegation from the Premier League on the last day of the 2008/09 season and serenaded the KC Stadium crowd with a rather dodgy version of the Beach Boys' 'Sloop John B'. At least it wasn't 'My Way'.

With a few exceptions (see chapter 11) singing managers should be banned. But usually they are the ones doing the banning. Paolo Di Canio banned ketchup and mayonnaise from the Sunderland canteen and told players not to sing in the showers. Fabio Capello refused to let England players' wives and girlfriends visit the team hotel on the eve of games so that their sleep would not be disturbed. Did it work? Not judging by results on the field. George Best never played in a World Cup finals, but he was an expert on sex. "I certainly never found it had any effect on my performance," he once said, although he did add: "Maybe best not the hour before."

David Moyes banned chips at Manchester United's Carrington training ground. Ireland manager Giovanni Trapattoni banned mushrooms from the pre-match menu. Neil Lennon banned beanie hats at the Bolton training ground, although he wore one himself. "If they want to keep warm, they should run around," he said. Harry Redknapp banned somersault goal celebrations after Lomana LuaLua broke his ankle performing a backflip.

Redknapp also grabbed the headlines in 2003 when he announced that he was cancelling Christmas for his Portsmouth players after a damaging league defeat against Southampton and that his players would be training on 25 December. Not a bad headline, of course, but really Harry was just trying to impress the fans. All players train in England on Christmas Day because there is a full programme of games on Boxing Day.

Managers ban things because they fear the sack, the one thing that all managers know awaits them. Sometimes it is dressed up in words such as 'left by mutual consent' but everyone knows that the boss has got the bullet.

Leroy Rosenior found out that he had been sacked just ten minutes after being appointed manager of Torquay United in 2007 – gone in 600 seconds. Rosenior was put in charge of the Gulls by chairman Mike Bateson just before he sold 51 per cent of the Devon club to a consortium, who wanted their own man.

That broke the British record previously held by Dave Bassett, who took charge of Crystal Palace for four days in 1984 before deciding it had all been a horrible mistake and going back to Wimbledon. The ink had not dried on his contract for the simple reason that he had not got around to signing one.

Kevin Cullis was manager of Swansea City for a week in 1996, the former Cradley Town chairman and under-16s coach lasting as long as it took the Swans' hardened pros to sniff out his lack of experience. 2-0 down at Blackpool at half-time in Cullis's second game in charge, they took matters into their own hands, with striker Dave Penney making team changes. Not that they helped, as Swansea lost 4-0.

Cullis's remarkable story was recalled by Chris Wathan for *Wales Online*. The former road worker had been recommended to new Swans owner-chairman Michael Thompson. Fans had been led to expect Trevor Francis, Mike Walker or even Ian Rush, but instead got Kevin Who? The club's own match programme got his name wrong ('Mr Keith Cullis').

After the Blackpool game, previous owner Doug Sharpe announced that Thompson's takeover was off and Cullis was history – or at least a small footnote in it. Cullis claimed he learned he had gone when he phoned the club information line (although why he was doing so remains a mystery) and later sued the club, eventually settling out of court. "People laugh at it now when I tell them but it was a disgrace," caretaker manager Jimmy Rimmer said. "It is one of the worst things I have experienced in football. It should never have happened, he should never have been there."

By comparison to Cullis's stormy week at the helm, Micky Adams' 13 days at Swansea were a marathon before he decided that money promised for team building at the Vetch Field was an illusion.

Some people have forgotten completely that Paul Hart took charge of QPR for 28 days before falling out with star player Adel Taarabt and leaving by good old mutual consent. Steve Coppell resigned after 33 days as manager of Manchester City in 1997, blaming stress. And this is a manager who managed Crystal Palace on three occasions.

Paul Gascoigne got his chance at Kettering Town in October 2005 when chairman Imraan Ladak was looking for a big name to galvanise the club and lead them into the Football League. Sadly Gazza's path led to the drinks cabinet and he was out again after 39 days.

All these short stays and long weekends make Brian Clough's 44 days at Leeds seem like an age, but perhaps it was a surprise that he lasted that long. Clough had never had a good word to say for his new players when at Derby, accused them of winning their medals by cheating in his first team meeting and was forced out when they held their own meeting with directors and even mild-mannered Paul Madeley dismissed him as "no good".

But Leeds did manage to set one record when Neil Redfearn managed the team three times in three years, twice as caretaker and once as permanent manager – if the concept of permanence had any meaning at Elland Road under owner Massimo Cellino.

Maybe the weirdest sacking was that of Paul Sturrock by Southend United in March 2013. The board offered to let him come back for one day two weeks later to take charge of the Johnstone's Paint Trophy at Wembley – after all, he had got them there. But Luggy, as the big-eared Scot is known in the game, refused.

Good for him.

10.

The Big Chair

"The only sure way to make a small fortune from football is to start with a big one."

BBC business correspondent
Jeff Randall, 2003

SOMEONE has got to captain the ship, set the agenda, point the club in the right direction. Oh, and pay the bills. Which is where the owners, chairmen, chief executives and directors come in.

Quite often there is an overlap in their roles. At smaller clubs they may all be one person. Some of them are women. Many of them are disliked by fans. Rather like referees, the best ones are probably those you don't notice.

Indeed, for much of the history of British football, owners and chairmen were largely unknown outside their communities. Frequently they were local businessmen who sought kudos among rivals and colleagues. It was only when football started to become significantly commercialised that clubs began to be

211

seen as national and international status symbols and potential sources of revenue than short cuts to bankruptcy.

One of the first chairmen to become nationally-known was Bob Lord, who ruled Burnley from 1955 to 1981. Unfortunately, his notoriety was less a result of his presiding over a club that punched above its weight and was the first to invest seriously in training facilities, but because Lord, an abrasive, humourless local butcher, had a gift for falling out with reporters, rival chairmen, the FA and the Football League, and even his own star players.

He insisted that Jimmy McIlroy, one of the key performers in the club's title-winning side of 1959/60, be sold because he was too friendly with another director. He said that Manchester United's players had behaved like 'Teddy Boys' in a match against Burnley only weeks after the Munich Disaster and blamed a journalist for reporting it. At one point in 1966 he had banned three national newspapers and six individual journalists from the Turf Moor press box.

Most outrageously, Lord, who refused to allow cameras into Turf Moor for many years, told a Variety Club dinner in 1974 that "We have to stand up against a move to get soccer on the cheap by the Jews who run television." Leeds United chairman Manny Cussins said he would walk out of the Elland Road boardroom if Lord attended Burnley's match there, but Lord, instead of apologising, ordered his fellow directors to stay away from the game.

In Lord's day, which began in the time of the maximum wage, it was possible for a club from somewhere as small as Burnley to win major honours. Nowadays, with wages and transfer fees at stratospheric levels, the ideal owner of a football club would be a lifelong fan who happens to be extremely wealthy, and follows a few simple rules: hire a good manager, give him lots of money to spend, keep ticket prices down, and don't wear a replica shirt in the directors' box.

Stoke City are held up these days as a model for good relations between board and fans, but even there Peter Coates, the chairman, has admitted that he worried about "going to the grave hated by fans" at the end of his first spell in charge. And only a very few fortunate clubs have had such benefactors.

"Sack the Board" is a common refrain at football grounds when things go wrong, but a futile one. If you could sack them, then what? Finding someone else willing and able to bankroll a football club is easier said than done.

For example, Ken Bates was vilified by some in Yorkshire for his southern background when he took over at Leeds United, and his answer was simple. "I said: 'You've got a problem then, haven't you? Nobody in bloody Leeds wants to run Leeds, do they? I see all these bloody millionaires with money coming out of their ears, talk about long pockets and short arms."

Given the choice of a less wealthy fan or a billionaire with no previous links to the club, many would choose the latter, because money rather than local pride buys the best players. But there are no guarantees – just ask supporters of Blackburn Rovers, who benefitted from the best of all possible ownership models when lifelong fan Jack Walker bought them and delivered the Premier League title, and then suffered from the disastrous buyout in November 2010 by Venky's, an India-based poultry company who had plenty of money but little apparent understanding of club, town, area or even the way football worked.

The fact that Venkateshwara Hatcheries Private Limited, to give them their full name, decided to call the new holding company that paid the Walker Trust £23m for Rovers 'Venky's London Limited' was not a good sign. Did they even know where their new acquisition was based?

In one way, the purchase made sense – according to the 2011 census, the Blackburn and Darwen district has a large Asian/Asian British population: 41,494, or 28 per cent of the total. "Blackburn Rovers fans will be delighted to add to the family a huge Indian and Asian fan base," Balaji Rao, a Venky's director, said when the takeover was announced. But any delight was followed quickly by dismay.

The decision to sack the experienced Sam Allardyce as manager a month later was an act of supreme folly, and the explanation – that he was not the man to take them into the Champions League – was laughable. "We want good football and Blackburn to be fourth or fifth in the league or even better," Mrs Anuradha Desai, the Venky's chairwoman, said. "The fans should trust us because this is in the best interests of the club."

The reasons for the actions of the Indian poultry farmers and Shebby Singh, their 'global advisor', are as hard to solve as the mystery of why the chicken crossed the road. After talk of bringing in Diego Maradona as manager, they gave Big Sam's job to first-team coach Steve Kean, his number three and with no previous managerial experience. They tore up the blueprint for running a town club in a Premier League of big-city outfits that club chairman John Williams had almost perfected. They decided Williams was surplus to requirements, along with managing director Tom Finn.

They somehow survived a relegation scare with a last-day win at Wolves, but ignored the warnings. After Kean said that Venky's' financial backing meant an end to selling the club's best players, Phil Jones left for Manchester United.

With Venky's board members staying at their headquarters in Pune, Kean was left to take the abuse from unhappy fans, and the atmosphere at home games was poisonous. His unwillingness to face the reality of the club's dire situation only made the situation worse, but Mrs Desai supported him. Forcing him to fly backwards and forwards to Pune for meetings cannot have helped him, however much value they added to his air miles account.

After a home defeat by local rivals Bolton Wanderers in December dropped Rovers to the foot of the table again, deputy chief executive Paul Hunt, the highest-ranking official still at Ewood Park, wrote to Mrs Desai, warning her that the team was going down if Venky's did not replace Kean and possibly into administration if they did not invest at least £10 million.

The letter was leaked to the influential Sporting Intelligence website. "He [Kean] has lost the crowd and, as a result of this evening's game, he has lost the dressing room as well. It is a shame and disappointing but we must act now to save the club," Hunt wrote.

Instead, key players Christopher Samba and Ryan Nelsen left in January, while Michel Salgado was not included in the squad for fear that a contract extension might be triggered. Jason Roberts was frozen out like a microwaveable chicken drumstick, joining Reading and scoring the goals that won them promotion to the Premier League while Rovers were relegated from it, but Kean somehow kept his job. When the drop was confirmed by a 1-0 home defeat by Wigan on 7 May 2012, 26,144 were in attendance. But not one of the owners.

* * * * *

The problem with Venky's was not that they were foreign, but that they ran the club poorly. Some foreign owners can be sympathetic. Markus Liebherr's purchase of Southampton, based in a port city where he sold many of the cranes that his Swiss company manufactured, was a good fit, and as a devout Christian he was delighted to learn that the Saints had begun as the church team from nearby St Mary's. The Liebherr family has continued to back the club with sensitivity and a sure hand even after his death.

Some, though, can have little interest in the club they own. A few miles down the M27 from Southampton, Portsmouth once had an owner who never paid a visit to Fratton Park and may, in fact, never have existed at all – despite passing the Premier League's Fit and Proper Persons Test.

It all began when Milan Mandarić, the owner who had led them into the Premier League in 2003, sold half the club, and then the whole lot, to a businessman named Alexandre 'Sacha' Gaydamak – he described himself as French, although he was the son of an Israeli businessman of Russian descent.

Sacha himself owned a few pizza franchises in Belgium and Switzerland, but no businesses that anyone could discover on the scale necessary to purchase a Premier League football club, and certainly not to bankroll the big-money stars that were signed by manager Harry Redknapp and won the 2008 FA Cup.

However, his father, Arkady, was very wealthy indeed. The only trouble was that he was wanted by Interpol in Paris in connection with some arms dealing in Angola and could not set foot in Western Europe for fear of being arrested. Sacha always denied that his dad actually owned the club, until Arkady rather inconveniently answered suggestions in Israel that he was in financial difficulties by naming Pompey among his assets to the *Haaretz* newspaper.

But when Arkady was sued in an Israeli court for $17 million, his assets were frozen and suddenly, by an amazing coincidence, Portsmouth ran out of money. Players, and eventually the whole club, had to be sold. Enter, in August 2009, Sulaiman al Fahim, who had been involved as a front man for Sheikh Mansour's takeover of Manchester City and now fancied owning his own club. He turned up in the Fratton Park directors' box wearing a replica away shirt but after only 43 days he was hitting the road himself. Wages went unpaid and chief executive Peter Storrie publicly doubted al Fahim's ability to finance the club, putting together his own consortium.

The main backer and effectively the new owner was named as one Ali al-Faraj. Journalists rushed to Google the name, quickly identifying a Saudi oil entrepreneur. But it was not him, and although photographs of two different mystery men in the directors' box, both captioned Ali al-Faraj, appeared in two newspapers, they turned out to be of Mark Jacob, a Spurs-supporting London lawyer representing the new consortium, and Gary Double, the club's press officer.

When home match after home match passed without an appearance, he was dubbed Ali al-Mirage. However, behind the scenes all appeared to be a surprising and almost unprecedented miracle of Arab-Israeli co-operation, with a disbarred Israeli lawyer and convicted fraudster named Daniel Azougy, whom even the Premier League refused to allow in their offices, in charge of finances.

What could possibly go wrong? Plenty. Some of the money had been 'borrowed' from a Hong Kong-based businessman named Balram Chainrai, who supposedly got tired of waiting to have it repaid and in February 2010 exercised a clause making him the new Pompey owner, the fourth within a year. You could say that al-Faraj disappeared at this point, if he had ever appeared.

There was a twist, though. It turned out that Chainrai had been one of the men who sued Gaydamak in Israel, forcing the sale of Portsmouth, but had never received the money the courts had ordered Sacha's dad to pay – and that Azougy was also owed money by Gaydamak. The club had, in effect, been a football all along in a game between Gaydamak and his creditors, who saw Portsmouth, and all the money from the Premier League TV deal and potential player sales, as a way of getting their cash back.

The slight problem was that in all this in-fighting and dealing nobody connected with the club bothered paying the Inland Revenue, instalments on transfer fees, or the players' wages. The League refused to pay Portsmouth their share of the TV deal, using it to settle the club's football debts direct instead.

Pompey went into administration, owing millions to local businessmen, the St John Ambulance and even the Boy Scouts. A dry cleaner in Havant kept the boardroom banqueting cloth in lieu of payment. The club somehow reached the 2010 FA Cup final but were relegated, and would have gone down even without the ten-point deduction imposed by the League for entering administration.

Was al-Mirage a real person? Some people believe the name was an alias for Chainrai. His alleged brother Ahmed al-Faraj turned up in the Fratton boardroom, but Ali himself remains a mystery. A passport in that name was apparently shown to the Premier League but whether its owner had even heard of Portsmouth Football Club is very doubtful.

The whole Portsmouth ownership saga took football reporters out of their normal comfort zone in the press box into unfamiliar territory, such as the High Court in London. And it was there, while waiting to be invited into the press seats at one of Pompey's many liquidation hearings, that they bumped into a familiar figure – Peter Ridsdale, who was dealing with winding-up orders in his role as chairman of Cardiff City.

Ridsdale had made his name as chairman of Leeds where, along with manager David O'Leary, he was the face of a successful team that reached the 2001 Champions League semi-finals. 'Publicity Pete' was always available to the media. When I called Leeds' press officer asking to speak to Ridsdale, I was told he was on holiday, "but he will speak to you."

Ridsdale was not one of those chairman who fail because they are outsiders who understand very little about the clubs they control, or their supporters. He found new ways. A boyhood Leeds fan who had been an Elland Road regular, he left the club he loved £78.9m in debt when he resigned in March 2003. Revealingly, he said, as he sat alongside then-manager Terry Venables to announce the sale of Jonathan Woodgate to Newcastle in 2003, that Leeds had "lived the dream".

Lived Ridsdale's dream would have been more accurate. He appeared to revel in his popularity with fellow fans in the good times as Barcelona, AC Milan and Real Madrid came to Elland Road to play the expensive Leeds team he had assembled. But everything – including the rented goldfish in the boardroom that became a symbol of the reckless spending at Elland Road – was financially unsustainable. "The Leeds programme has a team-sheet so glossy that it is impossible to write on," David Hopps reported in the *Guardian* in 2005. "They should have given Peter Ridsdale chequebooks like that."

Sadly, the best tale about Ridsdale – about Seth Johnson's wage negotiations – has been denied. The story goes that Johnson had been on £5,000 per week at Derby County and his agent, Leon Angel, said they would ask for £13,000 at Leeds. Ridsdale is said to have offered around twice that, and mistook their looks of amazement for disappointment and said: "Okay then, £35,000, but that's as high as we'll go." Ridsdale called it 'a myth' and Angel has said: "We negotiated and I can tell you we didn't get everything we wanted. In other words, it was a perfectly normal negotiation."

But it was still a disastrous deal for Leeds, who had paid Derby an eyebrow-raising £7m for a decent, but hardly world-beating, defensive midfield player. Johnson was often injured and played only 59 times, but still triggered bonuses that cost the Yorkshire club £250,000 every 15 appearances up to a maximum of £1.25m. When appearance number 60 loomed on the horizon, new chairman Ken Bates refused to make the next payment. "He's cost us £230,000 a game," Bates said. "Both himself and Derby must have been laughing their socks off at that deal. What sort of value is that for this club and its fans?"

But other stories have been confirmed, such as agent Dennis Roach submitting an invoice for £200,000 for 'translation services' and Ridsdale paying it although Roach did little more than attend a meeting between the club and Olivier Dacourt's English-speaking agent. We know this because Ridsdale wrote a book about his time at Elland Road entitled *United We Fall* (and, to his credit, donated the royalties to St Gemma's Hospice in Leeds).

Ridsdale had been smart enough to become a member of the board of Burton's by the age of 40, but his acumen deserted him at Elland Road and the fan took over, as he admitted to the *Daily Telegraph* when his book came out in 2007: "'I always thought I was a good, hard-nosed businessman until I read my book again and I thought: 'I wasn't actually.'"

David Batty, who came through the Leeds youth system and won the league title with the club in 1991, reflected on the Ridsdale era in an interview with 'Moscowhite' on the website www.thecitytalking.com.

"It was so close, yet so far, wasn't it?" Batty said. "But then if they'd qualified again for the Champions League the following year, would they have just spent even more? It seemed one or two buys too many, just for the sake of it, just because they could. Everybody jumped on the bandwagon and enjoyed the ride. The players were getting rewarded, and you're going to say yes to it, aren't you? That's just how it goes – if someone offers you a wage packet you take it. I was the union man, and when Gordon Taylor came from the PFA I saw the wages the lads were on, and it was just unbelievable. I couldn't believe it. They still compare to what players are getting now – massive money."

Professor John McKenzie, Ridsdale's successor as Leeds chairman, found evidence of 'indulgent spending' that included 70 company cars at £600,000 a year and air travel for directors at £70,000 – as well as the goldfish. "Leeds United may have lived the dream, but I inherited the nightmare," he said.

In October 2012, while 'Chairman of Football' – whatever that means – at Preston North End, Ridsdale was disqualified from acting as a director of any company for seven and a half years after a company he owned while working for Cardiff City, WH Sports Group, went into liquidation in April 2009, owing £442,353 in unpaid tax and VAT.

But was it fair that Ridsdale was blamed for much of what happened at Leeds long after he left? "When Leeds got to the play-off final in 2006 under Ken Bates, I got no credit and nor should I have done because it was nothing to do with me," said Ridsdale. "But what is startling is that when they get relegated, the year after, it is all my fault. I suggest you examine the creditor list when they went into administration in the summer and tell me how many of those creditors were there when I was and you will find it is very, very few."

Bates, of course, had previously been Chelsea chairman after buying the London club for £1 in 1982, taking on debts of £1.5m. His most notorious plan was to install electrified fences around the pitch at Stamford Bridge to keep the hooligans in line because 'it worked on his farm'. The Greater London Council refused permission.

On the plus side, Bates won a ten-year battle to buy back the decaying ground, which was in separate ownership, and rebuilt it. He eventually restored the swagger to the club that had gone missing since the days of Peter Osgood and Alan Hudson. Glenn Hoddle, Ruud Gullit, Gianluca Vialli and Gianfranco Zola arrived in the Fulham Road and success followed in the form of two FA Cups, the Cup-Winners' Cup and a League Cup. He became godfather to Dennis Wise's son. "He'll always have a laugh and a joke with you," said Chelsea defender Graeme Le Saux. "At your expense, obviously."

On the minus side, Bates was autocratic and self-opinionated. He banned club legends Osgood and Ron Harris from the ground, as well as barring Matthew Harding, the wealthy fan who had invested £26m in the club, from the boardroom. "Has any chairman since Mao had more faith in his own opinions than Ken Bates?" wrote Sir Alex Ferguson in his 2000 autobiography. "If laying down the law was an Olympic sport, the Chelsea chief would be staggering under the weight of gold medals."

You disagreed with Bates at your peril. The electric fences plan may have been blocked, but, like Bob Lord, he kept various journalists and entire papers out by banning them when they wrote something that he took exception to.

Christopher Davies of the *Daily Telegraph*, the respected former chairman of the Football Writers' Association, was one. Bates accused Davies of leaking a story to the paper's *Peterborough* column about a lunch before a Chelsea game in Monaco that Bates had invited journalists to attend, giving them the impression that he would pay. However, it turned out to be the journalists who were expected to settle the bill and attempt to get around £200 past their expenses departments.

Bates could not sue, because the story was true, and in any case the column had learned of the incident independently and only approached Davies for confirmation. Nevertheless, Davies was banned from Chelsea *sine die* – or rather, as he says, beyond *die*. "He banned me for life," Davies recalls. "I said: 'Can we include the afterlife as well?'"

Bates's construction of Chelsea Village, including restaurants, apartments and a hotel at the famed Shed End (inevitably dubbed 'Bates Motel') was not universally welcomed, player-manager Hoddle unhappy that it meant a shorter pitch. But it also helped the debts eventually climb back up to around £80m. The club could not afford to pay compensation due to Roberto di Matteo when he was forced to retire through injury.

Debt repayments of £23m were due when Bates sold Chelsea to Roman Abramovich for £140m in 2003. Pini Zahavi, the agent who brokered the deal, claimed later that Bates had made £19m from the sale.

But while Leeds chairman he remained as blunt as ever – so much so that some suspected him of having secret Yorkshire blood in his veins – and as controversial, using his programme notes as he had done at Chelsea to fire off broadsides at business and football rivals, and any group in society that he disliked.

Melvyn Levi, a former director, whom Bates claimed owed the club money, sued him for libel over remarks in the programme and took him to court again for harassment after Bates issued a wanted notice for Levi over the Elland Road PA system and asked Yorkshire Radio to broadcast an appeal for information as to his whereabouts.

"When I stopped writing [the programme notes] at Chelsea, programme sales fell by 10 per cent," he said in 2010. "At Leeds, it's the first page people turn to. The media call me controversial because I talk straight."

After having Ridsdale and Bates running their club, Leeds were surely entitled to a quieter life. Instead they got Massimo Cellino, whose whimsical hiring and firing of head coaches led to the quip from talkSPORT's Colin Murray, "only three Leeds managers until Christmas".

Cellino, an agricultural trader, had also owned Cagliari of Serie A, where he honed his skills in dismissing head coaches –

36 in 22 years. He became known as 'Il mangiatore di allenatori' – the manager-eater. He also played guitar in a rock band, and got up on stage at Leeds' annual end-of-season awards with indie band The Pigeon Detectives and played lead guitar in a cover version of Hendrix classic 'Hey Joe'.

Even before Cellino had completed his takeover of Leeds he had sacked a manager, Brian McDermott, being forced to reinstate him after Ross McCormack, the captain, had called *Sky Sports News* to protest on air. He once said: "It's very hard when you have to tell someone you like they are fired. My dream is to keep a coach 20 years." Some lasted nearer 20 minutes.

David Hockaday, a left-field choice to replace McDermott, having managed no higher than Forest Green Rovers, survived for only six games, four of which he lost. Hockaday had seemed a strange appointment, but when Cellino was asked why he picked Darko Milanić to succeed him, he said: "I don't know. The coaches are like watermelons. You find out about them when you open them. His particular qualities? He's good-looking, what can I tell you?" McDermott, Hockaday and Milanic were followed by Neil Redfearn, Uwe Rösler and Steve Evans.

The Football League, however, looked askance at his conviction back in Italy for tax evasion and realised that they had finally found someone who would fail their Fit and Proper Persons Test, although an independent QC overturned the decision on appeal.

* * * * *

Speaking of the Fit and Proper Persons Test brings us onto Darren Brown, who was jailed for four years in November 2004 for ransacking Chesterfield FC and driving the Derbyshire club to the edge of ruin. He took over in 2000, three years after the Spireites had reached the FA Cup semi-final and taken 23,000 fans to Old Trafford, when only a controversial decision by referee David Elleray denied them victory over Middlesbrough.

Brown, 29, the youngest chairman in the league at the time, also owned the Sheffield Steelers ice hockey club and the Sheffield Sharks basketball team, and started to invest in the team.

The club was top of League Two when the FA began an investigation into its finances. A Football League tribunal found that Chesterfield had presented a false contract for striker Luke Beckett to a transfer tribunal, so that it would set a lower fee, and failed to accurately declare gate receipts. They were fined £20,000 and deducted nine points, but were still promoted.

By now Brown had transferred ownership of the club to an associate named Andrew Cooke, who offered it to the newly formed supporters trust, the Chesterfield Football Supporters Society. This must have seemed a generous gesture until they found that the ground had been used as security to guarantee a loan, the previously stable club owed £2m, and that £439,000 had been loaned to Brown's UK Sports Group.

Derbyshire Police and the Serious Fraud Office found that Brown had taken a total of £790,000 out of the club to pay his own and the Steelers' debts but also on the proverbial 'lavish lifestyle', including a new house, three luxury vehicles and even a £2,500 lawnmower.

It was the Brown case that finally convinced the League to establish the Fit and Proper Persons Test for club directors, but the irony is that Brown, who had no previous criminal or serious debt record, would almost certainly have passed it. As a footnote, while in jail he received another sentence of almost four years for five separate fraud charges regarding another company and Cooke was also jailed, for 30 months.

Brown was by no means the only club owner to end up behind bars for his football misdeeds. Ken Richardson, the self-styled 'benefactor' of Doncaster Rovers, was jailed for four years in 1999 for conspiracy to commit arson after paying Alan Kristiansen, a former SAS man, and two other men £10,000 to burn down the main stand at the club's Belle Vue ground in June 1995. He had had plans for a new stadium turned down by the local council and saw the fire as a way of forcing the issue. Unfortunately, Kristiansen left his mobile phone at the scene and the trail swiftly led to Richardson. Not criminal but equally ill-advised was giving control of team affairs to a former Stockport County manager. Manager of the Stockport club shop, to be exact.

Other owners have been to jail before or after their spells in charge of clubs, or both, in the case of one-time Darlington owner George Reynolds. After doing time for safe cracking and burglary, Reynolds set up a kitchen business, Direct Worktops, and his net worth of £260m put him 12th in the *Sunday Times* rich list for 2000.

That enabled him to buy Darlington, but sadly, his stewardship of the Quakers was less successful. A low point came when Reynolds' wife, Susan, 24 years his junior, suggested to a fans' forum that the team were not always trying their hardest, and only tended to impress when contract renewals were coming up; the squad, led by skipper Craig Liddle, immediately walked out to cheers from the supporters.

Reynolds then moved the club from Feethams, their idyllic town-centre ground next to a cricket field, to a 25,000-seater out-of-town stadium named after himself. Bland and ridiculously over-ambitious for a club with Darlo's modest average gates, it drove them into administration in 2004.

Darlington dropped out of the league and after exiting administration with no Creditors' Voluntary Agreement, were told by the FA that they would be treated as a new club and relegated to the ninth tier of the football pyramid. Oh, and they couldn't call themselves Darlington FC any more. Darlington 1883, the reconstituted club, now ground-share at Bishop Auckland's Heritage Park, 12 miles from Feethams.

Reynolds, though, was also on the move – back to jail. In 2005 he was found guilty of cheating the Inland Revenue out of £650,000 and sent down for three years. His firm had collapsed with debts of £3.4m but Reynolds had used money from his company's legitimate director's expense account to pay for luxury cars and houses in Spain and Hampstead, and paid himself a salary of more than £100,000 per year while declaring a tax liability of only £14.

Mrs Reynolds is not the only owner's wife to have addressed a club's players with unfortunate consequences. Irena Demin, the wife of AFC Bournemouth's Russian owner, Maxim Demin, was reported to have given part of the half-time team talk in a 1-0 home defeat by MK Dons in 2012. But that was only the start of the story. Eddie Mitchell, the chairman, who had brought Demin – and, as it happens, his considerable wealth – to Dean Court, went on BBC Radio 5 Live to defend her, only to have the interview terminated when he used inappropriate language to Mark Chapman, the host, on three occasions while denying that Mrs Demin's address had been a team talk as such.

"She's a very passionate person but she's not very football intelligent," Mitchell said. "She watched the first half and asked me if she could come into the players' tunnel and wish them all the best. They came in and they were 1-0 down and a bit (expletive deleted) and I can understand that. She can't speak a lot of English, she speaks mainly Russian, she just wished them well, they're a great bunch of boys.

"She and her husband have put a lot of energy and a lot of money into the club ... and I believe that she is entitled to express her opinion," he added. Chapman then asked if he would be so accommodating if a season-ticket holder asked to do the same. Mitchell replied: "That's a load of (expletive deleted)." After insisting that the Cherries were a family club who invited fans into the boardroom, Mitchell continued: "Just because we've been (expletive deleted) in the past it don't mean we're going to be any more, mate." And with that he was removed from the airwaves.

Mitchell, a local property man, later apologised publicly to the BBC, saying: "I'm a passionate man and unfortunately that manifested itself in the language I used during the interview." The FA warned him about his future conduct and fined him £1,500 – £500 per expletive.

Mitchell's passion came out on other occasions. He had to be prevented by stewards from confronting disgruntled supporters after a 3-0 home defeat by Chesterfield in 2011. After the final whistle, Mitchell went onto the pitch to talk to fans, then returned with the PA announcer's mic, and said to one fan: "Why don't you jump over the fence and come and have a chat with me? Come on then. One to one?" Days earlier he had made a public apology for telling critics at a fans' forum that those who disagreed with his management style should "go and support Southampton".

Giving the microphone to owners can be hazardous. Just ask Delia Smith, the much-loved TV cook who became a director and later co-owner of Norwich City. She made the football headlines with a notorious half-time address to the fans at Carrow Road during a match with Manchester City in February 2005 in which the Canaries threw away a 2-0 lead. Delia, incensed at the crowd's quietness and, perhaps fortified with a little cooking sherry, boiled over. She went pitchside at the interval, grabbed the PA announcer's microphone and roared: "For the best football supporters in the world, we need a twelfth man. Where are you? Where are you? Let's be 'aving you. Come on!"

The cameras zoomed in and captured a Delia who looked slightly more ruffled than the calm presence that viewers of her cookery programmes were used to. "My message to the fans at half-time was a totally spontaneous appeal from the heart aimed at trying to do everything we could to get behind Nigel Worthington and the team," she told the club website. "Maybe in the heat of the moment I didn't choose the best words." Chelsea fans visiting Norwich later that season chanted: "We've got Abramovich, you've got a drunken bitch." Harsh.

Such a spectacle would surely never have happened at nearby Ipswich Town, which was far more discreetly run under John Cobbold, even though he was from the brewing dynasty and, perhaps not coincidentally, an alcoholic. He became football's youngest-ever director, at the age of 21 in 1948, and chairman when still only 29. He was on the board when Alf (later Sir Alf) Ramsey was given his first managerial job, and he appointed Bobby (later Sir Bobby) Robson, albeit as third choice. He presided over a league title win, an FA Cup final victory, a UEFA Cup triumph and many seasons of European football.

Mr John, as he was universally known, was an Old Etonian, grandson of the ninth Duke of Devonshire and nephew of PM Harold Macmillan, although he stood for parliament unsuccessfully on three occasions as a Conservative candidate for Ipswich. It was he who established the club's reputation as one of the most welcoming in Britain. Under his successor, David Sheepshanks, the media were welcomed into the boardroom after European games and even given club fleeces to wear 'on tour'.

It was also Mr John who, when questioned about whether a poor run of results constituted a crisis, memorably replied: "There is no crisis at Ipswich until the white wine runs out in the boardroom." His younger brother, Mr Patrick, when invited to meet Labour Prime Minister, James Callaghan, before the 1978 FA Cup final against Arsenal, said: "I would much prefer a gin and tonic."

* * * * *

Another Mr John – Elton – bought his boyhood club, Watford, starting the trend of owners who were more famous than their clubs. He was an exemplary chairman, overseeing the club's rise from the Fourth Division to the First. Robert Maxwell did something similar at Oxford United, although Captain Bob failed to win the love of fans in quite the same way. But then proposing an amalgamation with Reading under the name Thames Valley Royals was never going to capture the hearts of Oxford fans.

Maxwell had saved Oxford from bankruptcy by buying it in 1982, and also had some shares in Reading. News broke of the planned merger on Saturday 16 April 1983, just before matches were due to start. When the Oxford players heard about it, manager Jim Smith imaginatively claimed: "We're only doing it so we can buy [Reading striker] Kerry Dixon. All your places are safe."

In the end, the deal was scuppered from the Reading end when shareholders voted against it. After a flirtation with the possibility of buying Manchester United, Maxwell concentrated his football energies on Oxford, who reached the old First Division under Smith in 1985 and won the League Cup in 1986.

Fans remember the autocratic Maxwell expecting all to tremble before him as his minions in his other companies did, but football follows its own rules. During one match he attempted to calm fighting fans at the London Road end of the Manor by entering the stand and standing, arms outspread. The battles, however, raged on around him unabated. Even Cap'n Bob, as was proved later, could not walk on water.

In 1987 Maxwell demonstrated his loyalty to United by stepping down as chairman to take control of Derby County, installing his son Kevin at Oxford. He also tried to buy Watford from Elton John the same year, which prompted Tommy Docherty to quip that Maxwell had wanted to buy Brighton & Hove Albion but gave up when he learned that it was only one club. It was also behind the Football League introducing rules preventing major shareholders of any club from owning more than two per cent of another.

Whereas the Maxwell family seemed to want to buy a whole collection of clubs, another famous ownership dynasty, the Oystons, are indelibly associated only with Blackpool. Owen Oyston was chairman first until he was jailed for rape and indecent assault in 1996. His wife Vicki took over before stepping aside in favour of son Karl.

Oyston oversaw the rebuilding of Blackpool's antiquated Bloomfield Road ground and an against-all-odds promotion to the Premier League in 2009/10 – they were pre-season relegation favourites. And Ian Holloway's low-budget attacking team came close to surviving in the top flight when they led

Manchester United 2-1 at Old Trafford on the final day of the season only to lose 4-2.

The club should have been in good shape after being in receipt of Premier League TV riches, and then parachute payments – a windfall estimated at around £90 million. Supporters were unhappy about the Oystons' proud boast that the club was in the black, criticising what they saw as lack of ambition, and wondering why there was so little investment in the team.

They objected especially strongly when the club reported back for pre-season training in 2014 with only eight players on the books, none of whom were goalkeepers. Oyston told them to judge at the end of the season, and when it was obvious that the Tangerines were going to be relegated, they did.

Protests included the throwing of tangerines and tennis balls onto the field in a match at home to Burnley, flash mobs in the village where the Oystons live, and flares, fireworks and smoke bombs. When fans called on fellow supporters to lay scarves and other memorabilia around the statue of Stan Mortensen at Bloomfield Road before the final game of the season, against Huddersfield Town, the statue was inexplicably removed. Instead they invaded the pitch and held a sit-down protest, causing the abandonment of the game.

The Oystons have not done much to garner sympathy. In December 2014, text messages became public in which Karl called supporter Steve Smith a 'retard' and an 'intellectual cripple' and told him to 'enjoy his special needs day out'. Club president Valeri Belokon called for Oyston to resign and Wonga, the shirt sponsors, said: "The comments were unacceptable, something we'll be making clear to the club."

Were the remarks less serious than those made by Newcastle United chairman Freddie Shepherd and his deputy, Douglas Hall, when recorded by the *News of the World*'s fake sheikh in 1998? Both resigned after calling the women of Tyneside 'dogs', deriding fans for buying their overpriced replica shirts and referring to Alan Shearer as 'Mary Poppins'.

Whatever the relative merits of the two cases, Oyston did not resign, although he apologised and the FA banned him from all football activity for six weeks and fined him £40,000. Oyston was also ordered to attend a mandatory education session and warned about his future conduct.

But be careful what you say about the Oystons. They are fond of taking legal action, even against Blackpool fans. And whatever you do, don't call them asset-strippers. Joey Barton did, was sued and reportedly paid a five-figure sum to the Oystons as an out-of-court settlement. "It's simply not true we have asset-stripped or misappropriated football generated funds," Owen Oyston told the *Blackpool Gazette* in 2014.

Other chairmen and owners have felt forced to go to law to answer their critics. Sir Alan Sugar successfully sued the *Daily Mail* for libel when they claimed he had been 'miserly' in his running of Tottenham Hotspur.

Sugar had certainly tried to run the club on sound business lines, which was admirable but unusual in football, and frustrating for fans keen to see him flash the chequebook. Yet Sugar sanctioned the signings of major players such as Jürgen Klinsmann and David Ginola – both reportedly persuaded to join over coffee and/or dinner on his yacht in the south of France – and allowed George Graham to break the club's transfer record for Sergei Rebrov.

The *Mail* lawyers called Teddy Sheringham in their defence, who said he had left Spurs for Manchester United because Sugar would not pay the going rate for top players. "The sort of players we were buying were £1million or £2million and the top players were going for £6million or £7million," he said in court. "That was the sort of price I was hoping the club would spend."

Perhaps it was not surprising that the court found that spending millions of pounds did not constitute miserliness. That definition only exists in football.

Sugar took over at Tottenham in partnership with Terry Venables in 1991 after beating a certain Robert Maxwell to buy out Irving Scholar. But he fell out with El Tel, sacking him in 1993. Ossie Ardiles followed, then Gerry Francis, Christian Gross and Graham, who finally delivered a trophy, the League Cup.

The gift for a soundbite that Sugar has shown on *The Apprentice* was also in evidence at Spurs. 'Carlos Kickaball' to describe a foreign mercenary footballer was one of his, and when he famously fell out with Klinsmann when the German left for Bayern Munich in 1995, Sugar pulled out the signed Tottenham shirt the German striker had worn in his final match for the club in a TV interview. "I wouldn't wash my car with it now," he said. "There you are, you can have it if you want."

* * * * *

But of all the football cases to end up in the courts, perhaps none was more remarkable than the one in which Queens Park Rangers' director Gianni Paladini allegedly had a gun pulled on him in the Loftus Road chief executive's office.

A former Napoli youth team player, Paladini retired through injury and settled in England and became an interpreter and agent, representing Fabrizio Ravanelli, Benito Carbone and Juninho. He was initially welcomed onto the QPR board in 2003 as a potential saviour of a club in financial difficulty. However, doubts surfaced about his intentions and the true level of his assets. In fact, far from having the wealth required to bankroll an ambitious club, Paladini had had to remortgage the family home in Solihull to raise the £650,000 money to buy an eventual 14.7 per cent of QPR. And in summer 2005, dissatisfaction at Paladini's influence at the club reached such a level that, he claimed, a rival tried to force his resignation from the board at gunpoint.

A matter of minutes before the opening match of the new season, at home to Sheffield United, David Morris, another shareholder, asked to speak to Paladini in the chief executive's office. Six other men then entered the room, at which point, Paladini said, the gun was produced.

"I was petrified," he told the *News of the World*. "One of them was holding my wrists and another was pointing a gun. They shouted at me to sign a piece of paper resigning from the board. Of course I signed it – but I have no intention of leaving the club. They tried to push me out of the ground, but I managed to break clear and run into the boardroom, shouting for help."

The police were called and entered Morris's private box at Loftus Road just after half-time. They arrested him and four other men, taking the other two into custody near the ground. An imitation gun was found during a search and the seven were charged with conspiracy to commit blackmail, and joint possession of a firearm with intent to commit GBH. David Williams QC, prosecuting at Blackfriars Crown Court, compared it to a scene from *The Sopranos*.

Ian Holloway, the QPR manager at the time, knew nothing of any of this until chairman Bill Power approached him after the Hoops' 2-1 victory. "I'm saying congratulations to my team, well done, lads," he said. "Then Bill Power gets hold of me. He's in a daze. He says: 'Er... something ... has ... ah ... happened. I don't know quite how to tell ...' So I'm like: 'Bill, do us a favour. Don't tell me.' That way, when I met the press after the match I didn't know what had – allegedly – gone on."

Holloway not knowing what was going on was not unknown at Loftus Road in those days. He learned that Paladini had sacked him before a match at Leeds, but the news came not from Paladini but opposition manager Kevin Blackwell. Paladini had told Leeds chairman Ken Bates in the boardroom and Bates had relayed the news to his manager, who played Holloway the voicemail message.

All those charged over the gun incident were later acquitted or had charges against them dropped, and Paladini did not emerge from the trial with his reputation enhanced. Morris's barrister, Jim Sturman QC, revealed over 60 inconsistencies in his evidence, and at one point asked him: "Did you ever say to manager Ian Holloway that you would kill him?" Paladini replied: "In a funny way, yes, but it didn't mean anything at all."

Yet Paladini survived and later became QPR chairman after putting together a consortium to buy Power out that included two Monaco-based companies and former Brazil captain Dunga. And he stayed on as chairman when Formula One moguls Flavio Briatore and Bernie Ecclestone and steel magnate Lakshmi Mittal became involved in 2007.

All were billionaires, and throwing that amount of money at a club should have been a sure-fire way of guaranteeing success, but an award-winning documentary, *The Four-Year Plan*, showed that rampant egos and impatience are not a combination that works in the uncertain world of football.

Briatore came across in the documentary as the loudest boardroom voice, threatening to sell the club unless he was given the names of fans who were booing him, and saying: "We've got to sell this fucking idiot," when Martin Rowlands missed a chance in a game at Birmingham. He said of the fans: "Why do I care about the opinions of someone who turns up on Saturday and pays £20?"

Paladini, filmed kicking the front of the directors' box and yelling: "Fucking coach!", was unhappy with his portrayal in the documentary. "If I wasn't saying yes to Flavio then I was running around screaming, shouting and swearing," he told the *Sun*. "It made me look like an inbetweener — the man who Flavio sent to sack the managers." Eleven managers in those four years, to be precise, before Neil Warnock finally delivered promotion.

One man who made his name as a potential owner rather than an actual one was Michael Knighton, who volleyed his way into the headlines in August 1989, when he announced himself as the prospective new owner of Manchester United. However, he chose not to do it in the conventional way, with an interview in the local paper or a wave from the touchline. Instead he ran out on the pitch at Old Trafford in front of 47,000 people in August 1989 in United kit and a club sweatshirt to perform a spot of keepy-uppy then smash the ball into the Stretford End goal.

One paper described him at the time as "a small tubby bloke with a moustache; the sort of chap you might mistake for a (door) commissionaire". But he was anything but your run-of-the-mill wannabe owner. For one thing, he had been an apprentice at Coventry City. His own website calls him 'a British businessman, artist, poet, and a political commentator.' Knighton, then 37, had hoped to buy United, including the shareholding of chairman Martin Edwards, for what would have been a bargain £20m. He correctly foresaw that proper commercial development of the club's brand would net profits way beyond that initial investment. In the end, although he later claimed that he had had the money to complete the takeover, he abandoned his bid in favour of a seat on the board.

That decision probably did not look too good when the club was sold to the Glazer family for £790 million in 2005. But at least Knighton's vision for the club, which it later exploited – making Edwards a very wealthy man in the process – was proved accurate. That tends to be forgotten these days, but Knighton's on-field antics before United's opening game of the season, at home to Arsenal, will never be.

Twenty-five years later, in 2014, Knighton contacted *FourFourTwo* magazine to put his side of the story. He admitted to 'wanton showmanship,' 'sheer self-indulgence' and a 'showy and … somewhat egocentric entrance', adding that 'my unannounced pitch invasion was rather a novel method of introducing myself as the club's new chairman-elect."

"I can forgive him [Martin Edwards] if he might have thought that he sold the club to some kind of fantasist maverick and that he had made a massive mistake," he said. "I'm sure that the near £100 million he clawed in for eventually selling his shares a few years later would rather sweeten any embarrassment that he may have suffered on that day that I wooed the fans of this great club back onside. For all of Martin's claims that he was cringing with embarrassment on that day, he still invited me onto the United board of directors a few weeks later. I was a director at Old Trafford for three years, 1989–1992."

Merely being a director was not enough for Knighton, though, and he took over Carlisle United in 1992, promising to take them to the Premier League. Perhaps this time he was lucky that his achievements at the club were again overshadowed by a headline-grabbing story – his claims in 1996 to have seen a UFO.

For Carlisle, as you may have noticed, never reached the Premier League. They gained promotion to the Second Division and won the Football League Trophy, but after Knighton sacked manager Mervyn Day and put himself in charge of the team, things went less well. Carlisle were relegated and Knighton the chairman was forced to sack Knighton the manager, who had won only 19 of 68 games in charge. Knighton the chairman wisely appointed Nigel Pearson instead, and United avoided the drop to non-league thanks to on-loan goalkeeper Jimmy Glass's injury-time goal.

Knighton left the board in 1999, and a court later banned him from any involvement in a company for five and a half years. The club – still 93 per cent owned by him – went into administration in 2002 and he eventually sold it.

What's that? You want to know more about the UFO? You were not supposed to know anything about it all. Knighton apparently told a reporter from the local paper, the *Evening News and Star*, that he and his wife Rosemary had seen an alien craft near their home in Yorkshire 20 years earlier, and that he had received a telepathic message: "Don't be afraid, Michael." The paper ran the story with the headline: "Knighton: Aliens Spoke To Me".

Knighton was furious – not because the story was untrue but because, he insisted, he had told the reporter that it was not for publication, and that his nine-year-old son would face ridicule. The *Evening News and Star* printed a front-page apology by Keith Sutton, the editor, that included the immortal insult: "Just because Michael Knighton has seen a UFO doesn't disqualify him from being a football club chairman."

Another would-be owner whose name has lodged in the public memory is Spencer Trethewy – so much so that he later changed it to Spencer Day. Under his original name, he achieved notoriety when he presented himself as the potential rescuer of Aldershot in August 1990. A 19-year-old self-styled property investor, he offered to save the financially embarrassed club with a £200,000 signed affidavit.

He was big news and even appeared on the Terry Wogan show. Unfortunately, he was proved to be a fantasist. There was no money, and when this became clear three months later he was thrown off the club's board. He had also run up some considerable hotel bills and was jailed for fraud in 1994. Aldershot went broke and were forced to work their way back up the football pyramid as Aldershot Town.

Trethewy/Day later emerged as owner and manager of Chertsey Town, then manager of Farnborough Town. But neither club had anything to fear, as Day had apparently finally succeeded in building a bona fide and successful property business. "To put it simply, he's saved this football club," Chertsey secretary Chris Gay told *The Non-League Paper* in 2007. "Spencer has always been up front in his dealings with us and we're very happy with everything he's done."

Less well remembered than Trethewy is John Gurney, who was the public face of a mysterious consortium that bought Luton Town for just £4 in 2003. He announced that he wanted Luton to become the largest club in Europe. Yes, you read that right: Luton Town.

Of course, no club could even plan to become the largest in the Home Counties playing in the restricted confines of Kenilworth Road, so a new stadium would have to be built, and what a stadium – sited on concrete rafters over Junction 10 of the M1, and big enough not only to hold 70,000 fans but also to stage Formula 1 races. Oh, and the name of the club would be changed to London Luton – like the airport.

The press conference called to announce all this was held in the club's Eric Morecambe Suite, which said it all.

What do you think of it so far? Rubbish? Well, there was more. The management team of Joe Kinnear and Mick Harford had been sacked, not by Gurney but by a man named Peter Miller, who worked for Northampton Town. How exactly this had happened was never explained, although it broke the League rule that no individual could have an interest in more than one club. But since the club was now without a manager, Gurney announced that there would be a phone poll to decide upon the new one, at 50p per call.

Five interested groups would get to pick from a shortlist of Kinnear, Steve Cotterill and former player Mike Newell. The board and shareholders voted for Newell, season-ticket holders and players for Kinnear. The fifth group were the general public, and although Gurney said that Kinnear was the front-runner a week before voting closed, Cotterill told Radio Five that he had turned the job down, and somehow Newell was announced as the winner, after a recount, by a reported four votes. It was suggested that a large number of Watford fans had voted.

The League was unimpressed, imposed a transfer embargo and demanded full details of the consortium. When they failed to get satisfactory answers, they withheld television and sponsorship funds and called on the FA to investigate. But within days, creditors put the club into administrative receivership anyway and Gurney was gone.

Luton fans were happy about it at the time, but of course the club's difficulties were far from over. Down the line there were points deductions and four seasons in non-league football before they regained their Football League place. The plans Gurney announced seemed far-fetched at the time, but what if they had ended up with a new ground, albeit scaled down a little and somewhere more sensible than over a motorway junction? Might it not be a better place to watch football than Kenilworth Road? And isn't introducing a democratic element to manager selection quite a good idea? Or only when fans suggest it?

Next time they chant "Sack the board" they should be careful what they wish for.

11.

Sex, Drugs and Rock and Roll

"Football is all very well as a game for rough girls, but it is hardly suitable for delicate boys."

Oscar Wilde

FOOTBALLERS are usually healthy, young(ish) people in the prime of life, so it is hardly surprising that they are as much prey to the same temptations of wine, women and song as anyone else in their teens, twenties and early thirties.

But while students can shrug off the occasional heavy night or three, players these days are expected to maintain a healthy lifestyle. Although a booze-fuelled team such as Arsenal's renowned bunch of drinkers of the 1980s would be unlikely to win two Premier League titles now, the occasional wild escapade does take place, usually while the club is looking the other way.

Tottenham Hotspur manager Harry Redknapp had had some bad experience of players' pre-Christmas celebrations, so told his squad not to indulge in December 2009. He might never have got to hear the truth about a 'golfing' trip to Ireland organised by captain Robbie Keane if pictures had not emerged of his players out drinking, and not at the 19th hole, unless that was the name of a hostelry in the Temple Bar area of Dublin.

The team lost their next match, at home to Wolves, and Keane was substituted after an hour, and on his way out of White Hart Lane and heading for Celtic on loan by the end of the January transfer window. Redknapp decided that the 16 players on the trip should be invited to donate to a charity. "It is widely known I do not approve of Christmas parties and I've always made it clear players should only drink in moderation," he said. "Wednesday was their day off and Robbie told me they were going to Dublin to play golf. I had no problem with that."

But that's footballers' Christmas parties for you. They have often been the excuse for players to, er, 'enjoy themselves' and too many have resulted in embarrassing headlines and even court appearances. Take Manchester United's 2007 outing, for example.

Like Redknapp, Sir Alex Ferguson disapproved of parties. He built a network of spies around Manchester to sniff out any untoward activities, and once, when he got wind of a party at Lee Sharpe's house, he turned up unannounced on the doorstep, much to the consternation of Sharpe and Ryan Giggs, who was also present. The notorious hairdryer treatment ensued.

So it was against his better judgement that he allowed his United players to hold this particular Christmas party, after which all such events were banned while he remained at Old Trafford. The squad had invited around 100 women to the Great John Street Hotel in the Castlefield area of the city for an evening from which wives and girlfriends were barred – so there might have been some clue as to what would be going on.

Defender John O'Shea, perhaps keen at that stage to downplay rumours that he was gay, was one of the unmarried players who had gone around town 'trawling' upmarket shops and modelling agencies for attractive potential guests. Unfortunately, one of the invitees, Sarah Tetter, turned out to be an undercover reporter, who later described all manner of goings-on, including her own experience of the suggestion of a threesome from Wayne Rooney.

Many of the players had begun drinking over a long lunch and they later attended the Old Grapes pub, owned by a member of the Coronation Street cast, before moving on to the Long Legs lap-dancing club, a visit that was cut short by the presence of a photographer.

So it was on to the main event, which lasted until around 4am, the invited guests supplemented by a bevy of hopeful young ladies who had got wind of the party and waited outside on spec. The evening was a riotous affair to judge only by the final bill, including damage, which added up to £41,000, and the fact that Jonny Evans was arrested on suspicion of rape, but cleared.

Perhaps the most surprising aspect was the shock that professional footballers had behaved in such an excessive way. "The players were treating girls like pieces of meat," one female guest told the reporter. "It was like a horrendous cattle market."

No doubt she had gone along to a no-WAGs players' party anticipating a discussion on philosophy, literature and politics. She had obviously got her Uniteds mixed up and expected Oxford or Cambridge instead.

Speaking of Uniteds and Christmas parties leads inevitably to West Ham, whose seasonal bashes have also ended embarrassingly on occasion. In 1998, defender Neil Ruddock and winger Trevor Sinclair finished up in court after the players' seventies fancy dress night out at Secrets nightclub in Romford. Ruddock was charged with affray and later cleared, but Sinclair was found guilty of criminal damage, fined £250 and ordered to pay £225 costs after a bottle was thrown at a Mini driven by a 19-year-old beauty therapist, Belinda Knowles.

The 2001 affair was perhaps less serious but much funnier unless you happened to be leaning against the bar in the VIP area of the Sugar Reef nightclub in Soho when Hayden Foxe made his only serious impression on the club's history. Although it was actually the mark he left on the bar that will live longest in the memory.

The Australian defender lived down to his countrymen's reputation for extreme informality when he relieved himself on the polished wooden surface. Which he was standing on at the time, by the way. "There were no fights or yelling of abuse or anything," he told the club's official website by way of mitigation. "What I did was wrong and got blown right out of proportion as if it was a huge, huge event.

"You do have a few drinks at your Christmas party – and I'm not saying that to promote drinking, but it was a case of the lads enjoying themselves." Well yes, sometimes you do. But does 'a few drinks' usually result in a reported bar bill of around £2,000? And do you take a leak over the bar? "Some people are taking it light-heartedly and some are taking it the other way," Foxe continued. "I can't turn back the clock even though it's something I'm definitely not proud of." Well, that's a relief. Although not on the scale of Foxe's.

Liverpool's Jamie Carragher has attempted to become a voice of reason and analysis on TV since retiring, but in 1998 he got involved with some strippers and a can of whipped cream while dressed as the Hunchback of Notre Dame at one of Liverpool's festive occasions. Paul Ince was DJing and said to be 'concerned' at the development and at one point was reported to have yelled "put her down" over the mic while the young Michael Owen stood well out of the way. The *News of the World* was so shocked at the manner in which Carra 'cavorted' with the women that it felt duty-bound to devote four pages to pictures of the goings-on, with certain anatomical features discreetly blacked-out, of course.

Newcastle upon Tyne is a renowned party city, but the Toon players would be far too well known locally to risk a night out in Bigg Market, the Diamond Strip or on the Quayside. That, though, did not stop the Celtic squad heading for Tyneside in

2002, where they would not be familiar faces. Anonymity was sought after an incident in Glasgow the previous year when Neil Lennon had passed out on the pavement outside Sizzlers steakhouse and smashed his head on the kerb.

But an incident as the players left Buffalo Joe's Bar led to Lennon, Dutch winger Bobby Petta, Swedish defender Johan Mjällby and Belgian fullback Joos Valgaeren being arrested. Lennon was released but the others spent a night in the police cells over the alleged theft of a press photographer's camera before being released without charge. "The players were in Newcastle for a night out," a club spokeswoman said. "It would be fair to say they were there in an effort to avoid attention." Nice try, lads.

In our smaller communities, more goes unnoticed. Lars Leese, a German goalkeeper playing for Barnsley, remonstrated with two teammates dressed as Adolf Hitler and Eva Braun at the Tykes' Christmas do, and tried to explain that they would be arrested for it in Germany, but was met with blank indifference.

But nightclubs can be dangerous places for footballers whatever the time of year. In June 2001, Northern Ireland played and lost a Euro 2002 qualifier against the Czech Republic in Teplice before returning to lick their wounds back in Prague at the team hotel, where the members of the media were also staying.

The next morning we were surprised to find the hotel surrounded by the proverbial ring of steel – well, several police vehicles – and a number of officers milling about in the hotel lobby. It transpired that some of the players had gone out to the Atlas Bar in central Prague to, er, 'relax' and had allegedly beaten up a bouncer.

The door official in question was also in the lobby, seeming none too much the worse for his traumatic experience bar an enormous cartoon-style bandage on his thumb. But he was a big man, who looked as if he could have been an NFL lineman, so we assumed that the police who had gone up in the lift to arrest those responsible – who had been identified from their passport photographs – would be coming back down with a couple of hulking defenders at least, maybe the entire back four.

But when the lift doors opened, it seemed the four officers had failed to make an arrest – until we spied the diminutive figure of Michael Hughes, all 5' 6" of him, dwarfed by the officers, who might have come up to the bouncer's stomach but not much further. A little later, goalkeeping coach Tommy Wright, winger Peter Kennedy and strikers Glenn Ferguson and David Healy were also taken into custody, but charges were eventually dropped.

* * * * *

But back to sex. Footballers are usually fit and energetic and some have large amounts of disposable income, which makes them mysteriously attractive to members of the opposite sex (yes, and the same sex). When training permits, they will often take advantage. They may even overdo it.

Frank Worthington was a unique talent. A skilful, imaginative player, he was described by Ian Greaves, his manager at Huddersfield Town, as the working man's George Best. – an entertainer and a showman who would often try the impossible on the field and sometimes pull it off. Playing for Bolton in a match at Burnden Park against Ipswich, he juggled the ball with his back to goal before flipping it over his head and the back four, turning, running between the defenders and volleying the dropping ball past goalkeeper Paul Cooper.

Off the field, Worthington, a great Elvis fan, was also, like Best, a great womaniser. His autobiography was entitled *One Hump or Two?* It was suspected that, when a potential move from Huddersfield Town to Liverpool in 1972 broke down when he failed a medical, it was because of a sexually transmitted disease. The cause was indeed to do with his sex life, but not disease. Instead it was high blood pressure caused by what he described as 'the fruits of being young'.

Liverpool manager Bill Shankly told him to take a break and return for a second medical. Worthington went on holiday to Majorca, but, although dating Miss Great Britain at the time, chatted up another woman on the plane, then had a threesome with a Swedish mother and daughter before seeing a Belgian lady. Not surprisingly, he failed the medical again when he got back.

Liverpool need not have worried that he was going to expire on the job. He went to Leicester instead of Anfield, then Bolton, Birmingham, Sunderland, Leeds, Southampton, Brighton and many other clubs, played over 800 games and scored more than 260 goals. He once said that the secret of prolonging his career was deciding to stop going out seven nights a week. He kept it down to six instead.

Dwight Yorke was another player who enjoyed the company of the ladies, for which there is video evidence. In 1998 he recorded a secret sex tape featuring himself, four girls, and Mark Bosnich, then the Aston Villa goalkeeper. Bosnich also knew the taping was happening, judging by his and Yorke's thumbs-ups to the hidden camera. Bosnich being spanked while wearing women's attire is an image we'd all like to get out of our minds, or never have had in there in the first place. But the tape came to light when Yorke threw it out but somehow a *Sun* reader found it and it was saved for posterity and the nation.

Sun readers also voted Arsenal's Freddie Ljungberg the sexiest player in the Premier League in 2007, although it was never revealed whether more votes came from women or men. The Sweden winger's decision to dye a red streak into his hair was a sign of dedication to the Gunners, but his taste for outrageous outfits and an appearance on the cover of *Attitude* magazine led to other assumptions. Plus he complained, after modelling underwear for Calvin Klein, about women being too forward towards him.

"It sounds so cocky and I will not whine, but if, for example, I'd go to a night club, girls would come up and grab my crotch," he told Swedish paper *Di*. "Just like that. It was happening everywhere. They came from behind, side, pulled and tugged at me. The worst part was that you could not do a damn thing about it. When I angrily removed my hands, people just laughed. Some people thought that I could blame myself, I had done Calvin Klein and played in a top team. But there was no limit to what others thought they were entitled to do."

A professed love of musicals seemed to be the clincher – after all, he couldn't have gone to see *Mamma Mia!* three times out of loyalty to his mother country, could he? Eventually he had to tell the *Daily Mail*: "I am not gay, but gay men can be very fashionable, so maybe it's a compliment." Even so, it was a major shock to many when he married long-term girlfriend Natalie Foster in 2014 – she is a Spurs fan.

England under-21 internationals Kieron Dyer, Frank Lampard and Rio Ferdinand were in Ayia Napa in June 2000 when England beat Germany in the European Championships in Belgium. To celebrate, they invited some female admirers back to their room. A camcorder was present and somehow the footage made its way into the hands of the *News of the World*. "I had sex with one girl, which was taped with her consent, and that was it," incurable romantic Ferdinand said in his autobiography *Rio: My Story*. "OK, I've played up to the camera a bit, but she knew it was on and it didn't bother her." Dyer's pregnant girlfriend did not appear to be on the trip.

Alcohol is a subject much discussed in the world of football and it was not too long ago that the alcoholic beverages were plastered across club shirts and even sponsored the Premier League and League Cup. Other drugs, though, are harder to speak about.

Arsenal, Villa and England star Paul Merson, though, has talked openly about his addiction. Actually, make that addictions. Alcohol and gambling have bedevilled footballers since the game was invented, but Merson was also addicted to hard drugs.

"Cocaine absolutely, 100 per cent, brought me to my knees," he wrote in his autobiography. "I'd already downed about

100,000 pints of lager top and spunked away millions of quid at the bookies, but that was nothing – it wasn't going to kill me.

"Coke took away my life for ten months and nearly finished me off. I could quite easily have snuffed it from a heart attack on the pitch, given the huge piles of stuff I was shovelling up my hooter. Once I'd started taking it, I couldn't get enough, and nothing was going to stop me from getting another line.

"My habit got so bad that I'd get home from training, draw the curtains and sit in the dark, a couple of piles of white powder chopped out on the table in front of me. Teletext's dog racing page was on hold and my bookie was on speed dial."

Merson was a quivering wreck and admitted that he was so paranoid that any knock on the door might have sent him over the edge.

"I don't know how much I spent on cocaine; I was so off my face when I bought it, I couldn't keep up with how much I was doing. What I do know was that I once owed a dealer £400 for a night's worth of gear. I was going out on benders three or four times a week, depending on how often Arsenal were playing. It didn't need Professor Stephen Hawking to work out a Theory of Misery to realise that I was spending shedloads of money on lorryloads of drugs and heading for the universe's biggest black hole."

Merson later sought treatment, but was not always as dedicated to recovery as he might have been. While with Portsmouth he was given time off during the season by manager Harry Redknapp to visit Tony Adams' Sporting Chance clinic in Hampshire, but was spotted in Barbados. "I was in the room when Harry took the phone call off his mate saying he'd seen him there," Portsmouth kit man Kev McCormack told *The News* in Portsmouth. "Harry told him that wasn't an issue if he was back the following Thursday. He turned up with a better tan than Phil Brown but Harry didn't say anything to him and he then turned in that performance in the 5-0 win at Millwall. The only thing the gaffer said afterwards was: 'Nice tan, Merse!'"

Mark Bosnich, who has already featured in this chapter, tested positive for cocaine while a Chelsea player in 2003. The club immediately terminated his contract, which was a problem as the Australian goalkeeper was spending an estimated £3,000 per week on the white powder. After retiring at 31 he cleaned up and went back down under.

Bosnich's fate did not prove enough of a warning to £15 million Romania forward Adrian Mutu when he also tested positive for cocaine in September 2004 and had his contract terminated the following month. Chelsea then took Mutu to court for compensation – for his transfer fee, the cost of replacing him and their legal costs. That would all have amounted to around £40 million, but the lawyers made it known that they would generously settle for "the replacement cost of £22,661,641." In the end, the FIFA Dispute Resolution Chamber ordered Mutu to pay Chelsea around £15m, the same as Chelsea had originally paid for him. Let's hope he'd never got around to cashing the cheque for his signing-on fee.

Michael Duberry, the former Chelsea, Leeds and Stoke defender, might also have failed a drugs test if an extraordinary plot to get his contract off Leeds' books had succeeded. According to a *Sunday Mirror* investigation, a Leeds director claimed that he had plotted with another club executive (who denied the allegations) to sprinkle cocaine disguised as parmesan cheese on Duberry's pre-match pasta. That would have been enough to make Duberry fail a drugs test so that his £24,000-per-week contract could have been cancelled, but there were other ideas of spiking his food with ecstasy and lacing a protein drink with banned steroids.

"I knew that Leeds were desperate to get me out of the club," Duberry told the paper. "What I didn't know at the time was that they were willing to use any means possible to get what they wanted. It is the kind of storyline that you normally get in an episode of *Footballers' Wives*."

In 1999, Robbie Fowler and his boyhood pal Stephen Calvey came up with the idea of answering suggestions from Everton fans that the Liverpool forward had a coke habit with a pre-planned goal celebration at the Merseyside derby at Anfield. And after Fowler scored from a penalty at the Anfield Road end where the visiting supporters were massed, he dropped to the turf in front of the Everton fans and pretended to snort the white line on the pitch.

"Not subtle, I know, but I wasn't auditioning for the Cambridge Footlights," he wrote in his autobiography, *Fowler*. "I'd show them who was a smackhead by scoring a goal against them and – if you'll forgive the crap pun – rubbing their noses in it."

Sadly, this piece of comedy gold drew a predictable reaction from the authorities. "Following a complaint from a member of the public the matter will be investigated and match officials will be spoken to by officers," said a spokesman for Merseyside Police. The media joined in the joyless and po-faced condemnation of Fowler's action, except for the great Simon Barnes of *The Times*.

"I am about to surrender all my credibility as a person of weight, of moral seriousness, as a person equipped to write with judgement on the follies of humankind," he wrote. "But I cannot deny it. I thought it was funny. I still do.

"I laughed at the picture, laughed at the grossness, the conceptual wit, the appositeness, the ludicrous exactness of the mime. The idea of turning a pitch marking into a monstrous line of cocaine had something almost Rabelaisian about it.

"I could see that it was going to make a lot of trouble, too. I felt, if anything, rather sad about that. Robbie Fowler could probably hear a still, small, John Le Mesurier voice deep inside him even as he dropped to his knees: 'You think that's quite wise, sir?' But there are some people who cannot resist a jest."

* * * * *

Sex, drugs, but what of the rock and roll, you ask? For a time, football *was* the new rock and roll and the links were everywhere. Half Man Half Biscuit's second album included a track called 'All I Want For Christmas Is A Dukla Prague Away Kit', St Etienne was suddenly a band as well as a French football club, and players like Chelsea and Everton winger Pat Nevin were listening to The Smiths and Crispy Ambulance instead of Frank Sinatra and Lionel Ritchie. And long before that, Elton John had bought his boyhood heroes, Watford, and made them into a top-flight club.

So David Beckham getting hitched to a Spice Girl and Ashley Cole marrying Cheryl Tweedy were nothing new. Football and music have gone together since England captain Billy Wright married Joy Beverley of the chart regulars the Beverley Sisters in 1958. Rod Stewart and The Faces got a ball out while performing 'Maggie May' on Top of the Pops in 1971, and Stewart was even sued by a fan hit by a ball kicked from the stage at a gig in the United States.

Rod the Mod is famously a huge fan of the game, especially Celtic and Scotland, despite being born in London after his father moved the family to London from Edinburgh. "Way back in the early 1970s I met Kenny Dalglish and he took me to meet the late Jock Stein. Once you met him, you were a Celtic supporter. He always made football sound like poetry." He was seen weeping tears of joy in the directors' box at Parkhead when The Bhoys beat Barcelona in a Champions League match.

But the other Rod Stewart football tale – that he was an apprentice with Brentford – is untrue, although he did attend a trial but was not invited back. "I didn't even get close," he says. "I was good but I wasn't good enough." He added: "It was exactly the same time as I got a start in music, and I was a lazy bugger and music gave me the chance to stay in bed another couple of hours."

But two members of a famous 1980s bands did get to play at the top level – sort of – when Steve Norman and Martin Kemp of Spandau Ballet were surprise signings for the 1985/86 season by Roy Race for Melchester Rovers, along with retired players-turned-pundits Bob Wilson and Emlyn Hughes, in the Roy of the Rovers comic strip.

The two Spands proved capable players, although neither made the starting team for the 3-0 Milk Cup final victory over Tynecaster United at Wembley. It was a move that was more unpopular and controversial with readers of the Roy of the Rovers strip than it was with fans of the fictional club. "I was a regular reader during this season and it certainly was ludicrous," 'Chris' told a Roy of the Rovers fan blog. "Of course the most ridiculous thing was that they portrayed Spandau Ballet as constantly pursued by hordes of screaming girls and able to sell out stadiums."

The Spandau Ballet hit 'Gold' has been adapted by plenty of fans, notably those of Watford for striker Odion Ighalo. The Nigerian forward heard that Martin Kemp lived nearby and invited him to lead the chanting at Vicarage Road. "It would be great for him to come to conduct a song. I don't know him but the first time I heard that I was so proud."

There was little chance of that. Kemp, his brother Gary and drummer John Keeble are lifelong Arsenal supporters, the Kemps naming their cat Bob after Bob Wilson. Sax player Norman and manager Steve Dagger were Spurs fans. When the band played Wembley Arena in 1986 they gave the teams complimentary tickets, but for different nights.

But Kemp and Norman playing proper football was just fantasy. No, really – Roy of the Rovers doesn't exist. Sorry. People in bands can play in testimonials and that's mostly that. And as for footballers trying their hand at singing, we would all like to forget Gazza's version of 'Fog on the Tyne' and Waddle and Hoddle's 'Diamond Lights', not to mention former Hull City manager Phil Brown serenading the crowd at the KC Stadium after delaying the Tigers' relegation for a year.

Christian Dailly, the Scotland defender, played lead guitar for a band named Hooligan that he described as "a cross between Coldplay and Queens of the Stone Age". Sadly they got no nearer the big time than Scotland did to the World Cup finals, and if you put 'Christian Dailly' into YouTube you will find a clip of him calling the Germany team 'cheats' after a match against Scotland while head coach Berti Vogts talks to the camera rather than anything musical.

The closest thing to a player/singer who was equally good in both areas was Paul McGregor of Nottingham Forest, Preston, Plymouth and Northampton, a striker and also the frontman of a band called Merc and, later, 'Goth-leaning' band Ulterior. He and midfielder Scot Gemmill would plan summer holidays around The Verve tours, but not all his teammates were as supportive. Midfield player Ian Woan told the *Nottingham Evening Post* after seeing Merc at the Rock City venue: "The way he plays on the pitch, he should pack the footy in and give music a go."

The pinnacle of McGregor's playing career was scoring Forest's only goal of a match against Lyon in the UEFA Cup in 1996, a rebound after a penalty by Stuart Pearce had been saved. He made all his seven Premier League starts the same season, appearing as a substitute on 23 more occasions and scoring three league goals. An overhead kick he scored against Sheffield Wednesday at Hillsborough was voted European Goal of the Month. But he knew his days at Forest were numbered after new manager Ron Atkinson pointed at him at the first team meeting and said, "I don't want any fucking rock stars in my team."

You might not think that a Britpop footballer, as the press dubbed him, with long blond hair would have lasted long in a Brian Clough Forest team either, but the great man was in charge when he was coming through the ranks. "Clough and [Archie] Gemmill had a presence and you wanted to please them so much," he said. "If you took a bollocking, you took a bollocking but you felt loved too," McGregor told the Forest fan site In The Top One. "Other clubs didn't have that, didn't have this icon." Clough once hugged and kissed him (and all his teammates) in the centre circle after the Forest youth team had won a League and Cup double.

In another match, with Forest's youth team on the attack against Derby, Clough suddenly yelled to him, "Blondie, stand still! Fucking stand still." He did as he was told – "because you did it" – and after play had surged to the other end and Derby had hit the post, Forest broke away again and the ball dropped right to McGregor's feet. "I struck it right in the top corner. Cloughie came running down the touchline, shouting: 'Archie, I fucking told him!' in joyous celebration. I'm not into any otherworldly superstitious bollocks but how do you logically explain that?"

It was Clough's successor Frank Clark, a renowned music lover, a fellow Doors fan and, by all accounts, a decent guitar player, who gave him his chance, and he rates David Moyes the best coach he played under while at Preston.

Wycombe Wanderers manager Gareth Ainsworth is also a decent singer and was in a band while playing for QPR prior to picking up the reins as caretaker on two occasions and taking over at Adams Park. And his repertoire was far from the stuff that most old-school bosses seemed to favour.

"Mum taught me to sing," Ainsworth told Henry Winter (then of the *Daily Telegraph*) in February 2015. "She was a professional singer in the Sixties, a big band singer, did Dusty Springfield and Brenda Lee numbers. It was a really musical household. Dad was a big Who fan. It was either the rock of The Who, Jimi Hendrix and the Kinks or Brenda Lee and the Everly Brothers on my mum's side."

Ainsworth is another Doors fan. "I loved The Doors, loved their sound. I know it's a bit depressive like Radiohead. I love Jim Morrison. I've been to Paris to his grave at Père Lachaise, an amazing place. I saw the graves of Oscar Wilde, Chopin, and Edith Piaf.

"At Wimbledon, I played in a band with Trond Andersen and Chris Perry called APA. At QPR, John Gregory played the guitar. We were going to cover a Bruce Springsteen song together but never got time with him being manager. I answered an ad in *Loot* magazine to become lead singer of a band. I went to the rehearsal, sang in front of these guys, didn't tell them who I was, they didn't know, and they said 'OK'. We wanted a cool name for the band so chose Dog Chewed The Handle after an old Terrorvision song.

"We were playing the Grand Junction Arms (in west London) one night, and had all the gear on the QPR team bus, drove the bus to the gig, unloaded, word got round and a lot of Rangers fans came. It was a great gig. We did a few. We had one shot at the big time, when we were asked if we could back Bad Manners on tour but one of their gigs was Boxing Day and I couldn't do it because of my career."

Dog Chewed The Handle split but Ainsworth and the lead guitarist, Lee Sargent, reformed as Road To Eden. "It's crazy to think you could make a living from music as well as be in football. Music's such a competitive industry. But there's an ember that's still burning. There are 20-30 tracks Lee and I wrote together which we could resurrect. We could get them professionally put on an album, pay for it ourselves, get it out on the Internet, use my name to lever a few doors open. We've got a solid following, and if we resurrect it, they would all come back. We won't be as big as Led Zeppelin but we'd give it a go."

It is not recorded whether QPR fan Pete Doherty, the Libertines and Babyshambles frontman, ever shared a stage with Ainsworth, but he would certainly have watched him play football. Doherty is a regular in the South Africa Road Stand at Loftus Road and one of those celebrity fans whose love of the game is genuine and not a fabrication aimed at giving him any sort of credibility.

Asked by the *Guardian Magazine* in 2007 where he would choose if he could go back to any moment in the past, Doherty answered: "Wembley 1967, QPR's finest hour", and two years earlier offered this pearl of fan wisdom: "If your woman sleeps with your best mate, it's over. If the Rs' manager Ian Holloway slept with my best mate, QPR would still be my team."

Brighton fan Norman Cook – alias super-star DJ Fatboy Slim – was never a director of the club, as was often misreported, but he was certainly an investor, and helped the Seagulls out a number of times when they struggled to pay bills while in their temporary accommodation at Withdean Stadium. He was, however, allowed a place in the directors' car park, which came in very handy in view of the extreme parking restrictions at Seagulls home games – "the most expensive parking place in history," as he called it.

He also helped ensure that the record label he recorded on, Brighton-based Skint Records, sponsored the club's shirts for almost a decade, which chairman Dick Knight called 'a delicious irony' even though to some it was simply telling it like it was.

Manchester City fan Noel Gallagher has always been up front about his footballing loyalties, and in 2015, before an appearance on BBC's *Match of the Day 2* , he picked a fantasy band of players he thought would make a decent band: George Best on vocals, Zinedine Zidane on guitar, Patrick Vieira on bass and Mario Balotelli on drums. That combination of characters might not make decent music, but the fly-on-the-wall documentary would be a killer. The only question is whether musical or footballing differences would cause them to split first.

"A lot of footballers these days are squares – to get in my band you need some charisma," Gallagher explained. "Zidane," he said, "might be my favourite ever player. All that and he smoked 20 cigs a day. He was rock 'n' roll to the core, man.

"The bass player has got to be solid and reliable – an immovable rock. I would have Patrick Vieira, because he would have the rhythm as well. You have got to have a headcase on the drums and Mario could also join in with a rap every now and again. He's like a modern-day rock star anyway. He's a little bit crazy, a little bit unreliable and a little bit flamboyant. You never know what his haircut is going to be doing from one day to the next. Plus he enjoys his social media and is clearly very bad at writing songs – put all of that together and he could be [Gallagher's brother] Liam's double.

"In any band, you want a good-looking lad as the singer. Georgie is my frontman because he was the greatest footballer of all time and he looked cool as well – he was football's first superstar. Yes, he played for Manchester United but I could never hate him. Everyone loved him.

"It was the same with Eric Cantona. All City fans loved him too, he was one of those you wished played for you. I loved Eric because he was psychedelic. If he was an album, he would be Sgt. Pepper. Personality matters as much as who they play for when it comes to the players I like – well, sort of. When I stood back and admired Cantona, I appreciated his greatness. But when he was on the pitch I loathed him. When he was scoring the winner against City I wanted to break both his legs."

That's showbiz …